STAGE 2

Mentals 3

Alan McSeveny Rachel McSeveny Diane McSeveny-Foster

Pearson Australia
(a division of Pearson Australia Group Pty Ltd)
459–471 Church St, Level 1, Building B, Richmond, Victoria, 3121
PO Box 23360, Melbourne, Victoria 8012
www.pearson.com.au

First published 2024 by Pearson Australia
2028 2027 2026 2025
10 9 8 7 6 5 4 3 2 1

Publishers: Sophie Matta and Kerry Nagle
Project Manager: Michelle Thomas
Production Editor: Laura Rentsch
Development Editor: Rachel Elliott
Designer: Anne Donald
Proofreader: Ann M. Philpott
Rights and Permissions Editor: Alice McBroom
Cover art: Michael Barter
Illustrator: Michael Barter
Publisher Services Analyst: Jit-Pin Chong
Printed in Australia by Pegasus Media and Logistics

ISBN 978 0 6557 0910 7
Pearson Australia Group Pty Ltd ABN 40 004 245 943

Acknowledgement of Country
Pearson respects and honours Aboriginal and Torres Strait Islander Elders past, present and future. We acknowledge the stories, traditions and living cultures of the Traditional Custodians of the lands on which our company is located and where we conduct our business. Pearson is committed to honouring Australian Aboriginal and Torres Strait Islander peoples' unique cultural and spiritual relationships to the land, waters and seas and their rich contribution to society.

Aboriginal and Torres Strait Islander peoples are advised that this text may contain images, voices and names of deceased persons.

Introduction

Using the Mentals Books

This book is used most effectively when it aligns with the suggested program in the Student Book contents.

Each unit of the Mentals Book is programmed to review Student Book content for the previous two weeks. For example, Unit 15 of the Mentals Book can be set as homework to review weeks 13 and 14 of the Student Book while week 15 of the Student Book is being taught.

Units 1 and 2 of this book revise work from the previous year and could be completed in weeks 1 and 2 of the school year.

Mixed-topic questions

The units present questions in a mixed-topic format to encourage thorough understanding and continuous review.

Presentation

- Number facts are reinforced to encourage instant recall.
- Essential skills are explained.
- The Arithmetic card (page 5) is a useful teaching tool for practising basic number skills.
- ID cards (pages 6 and 7) review the mathematical terms students need to learn.
- Measurement standards and examples (pages 8 and 9) are provided so that students can learn important facts and estimate measurements effectively.

Graded questions

- Column 1: easier
- Column 2 and 3: harder
- Column 4: Extension and Challenge

Motivation

- There are two lizards hidden on each page for students to find.
- The header allows students to record their score.

Extra activities

- Problem-solving **strategies** are introduced in a carefully planned sequence throughout the series.

- Important concepts from **Number and algebra** and **Measurement and space** are explored.

- **Measurement** concepts and activities are introduced and investigated.

- **Statistics and probability** concepts are presented for revision and extension.

- A **tables** program for each of addition, subtraction and multiplication is included. It is important for students to learn addition and multiplication tables by heart.

3 Contents

Activities at the bottom of each page

Unit	Content	Activity type
1:1/2 1:3/4	+ 2 Personal measures	+ tables Measure
2:1/2 2:3/4	+ 3, + 5 + 3, + 4	+ tables + tables
3:1/2 3:3/4	+ 4, + 6 + 6, + 7	+ tables + tables
4:1/2 4:3/4	Combinations to 10 and 13 + 7, + 9	Concept + tables
5:1/2 5:3/4	Skip counting Time	× tables Measure
6:1/2 6:3/4	Language Linking + and −	ID card B Concept
7:1/2 7:3/4	× 2, × 0 × 10	× tables × tables
8:1/2 8:3/4	× 5, × 2 × 5, × 10	× tables × tables
9:1/2 9:3/4	× 1, × 10 Subtracting 9	× tables Concept
10:1/2 10:3/4	Linking + and − + 8, + 9	Concept + tables
11:1/2 11:3/4	Rounding (nearest 10) Problem solving	Concept Strategy time
12:1/2 12:3/4	Rounding (nearest 100) Writing fractions	Concept Concept
13:1/2 13:3/4	Using number lines Addition grid	− tables + tables
14:1/2 14:3/4	× 5, × 10 − 10, − 10	× tables − tables
15:1/2 15:3/4	Chance + 10, + 10	Chance + tables
16:1/2 16:3/4	Time Time	Measure Concept
17:1/2 17:3/4	× 3 Skip counting	× tables × tables
18:1/2 18:3/4	Chance × 2, × 4	Chance × tables
19:1/2 19:3/4	− 2, − 4 + 3, + 4	− tables + tables

Unit	Content	Activity type
20:1/2 20:3/4	Language Number patterns, rules	ID card B Strategy time
21:1/2 21:3/4	× 5 × 4 7 −, 8 −	× tables − tables
22:1/2 22:3/4	11 −, 12 − 13 −, 14 −	− tables − tables
23:1/2 23:3/4	+ 5, + 5 + 3, − 3	+ tables + / − tables
24:1/2 24:3/4	rows of, groups of Multiplication fact families	Concept × tables
25:1/2 25:3/4	Linking × and ÷ + 4, + 3	Concept + tables
26:1/2 26:3/4	Language Multiplication fact families	ID card A Concept
27:1/2 27:3/4	Language Linking × and ÷	ID card B Concept
28:1/2 28:3/4	Language ÷ 2, ÷ 4	ID Card B ÷ tables
29:1/2 29:3/4	Place value + 5, + 6	Concept + tables
30:1/2 30:3/4	Chance Trading with blocks, +	Chance Concept
31:1/2 31:3/4	13 −, 14 − Chance	− tables Chance
32:1/2 32:3/4	Place value × 10, × 5, × 2	Concept × tables
33:1/2 33:3/4	× 2, × 4, × 5 24 +, 32 +	× tables + tables
34:1/2 34:3/4	Language Place value	ID card A Concept
35:1/2 35:3/4	Language Language	ID card A ID card B
36:1/2 36:3/4	15 −, 16 − Multiplication fact families	− tables Concept
37:1/2 37:3/4	÷ 5, ÷ 10 Personal measures	÷ tables Measure
Answers	These can be found in the middle of this book on pages A1 to A15.	

 • *AUSTRALIAN SIGNPOST MATHS NSW 3 MENTALS* • ISBN 978 0 6557 0910 7

Arithmetic card

	A	B	C	D	E	F	G	H	I	J
1	11	3	7	20	4	2	7	50	37	$6
2	17	7	4	16	25	10	11	80	93	$1
3	14	1	10	12	64	14	3	20	16	$7
4	19	5	3	17	16	4	15	70	55	$3
5	16	8	5	13	81	12	19	40	100	$8
6	12	6	8	18	1	16	1	60	71	$5
7	18	10	2	11	36	8	9	100	48	$9
8	15	4	6	14	9	20	17	30	82	$2
9	20	9	1	19	100	18	5	90	64	$10
10	13	2	9	15	49	6	13	10	29	$4

How to use this card

If students were told to 'subtract B from A', they would write:

1. 11 − 3 = 8
2. 17 − 7 = 10
3. 14 − 1 = 13
4. 19 − 5 = 14
5. 16 − 8 = 8
6. 12 − 6 = 6
7. 18 − 10 = 8
8. 15 − 4 = 11
9. 20 − 9 = 11
10. 13 − 2 = 11

Other instructions might be:

- **Multiply column B by 5.**
- **Subtract column F from column I.**
- **Halve column F.**
- **What multiplied by 10 gives column H?**
- **What is left from $30 if I spend the amount in column J?**
- **Double column C.**
- **Add column B and C.**
- **Subtract 10 from column I.**
- **Add 10 to column E.**
- **What must be added to column D to make 20?**

The applications of this card are endless.

ID card A

Do not write on this card.

ID Card A

1 **m** stands for m ________

2 **cm** stands for c ________

3 **mm** stands for m ________

4 **L** stands for l ________

5 **kg** stands for k ________

6 **min** stands for m ________

7 **Length = 1 cm**

square c ________

8 **Length = 1 cm**

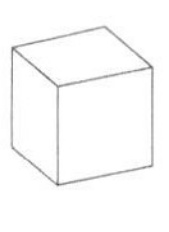

cubic c ________

9 **2, 4, 6, …** are the e ________ numbers

10 **1, 3, 5, …** are the o ________ numbers

11 **1st, 2nd, …** are the o ________ numbers

12 **816** has 3 d ________

13 **x** stands for t ________

14 **6 groups of 2 or 6 rows of 2** means 6 ____ 2

15 **÷** stands for d ________

16 **How many groups of…? or share between** means d ________

17 **=** means is e ________ to

18 0 1 2 3 4 is a n ________ l ________

19 **7 + 9 = 16** is a n ________ s ________

20 7 tens 2 ones is a n ________ expander

21

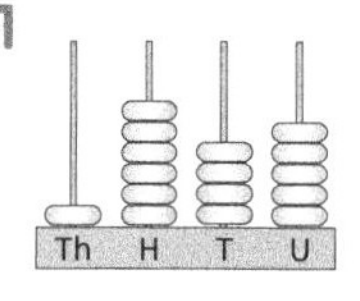

a ________

22

Animals	
birds	7
monkeys	5
lions	4

t ________

23

p ______ graph

24

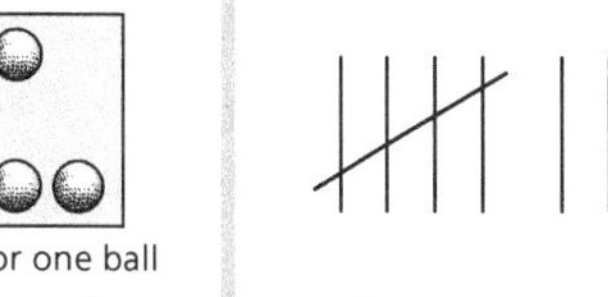

t ________

25

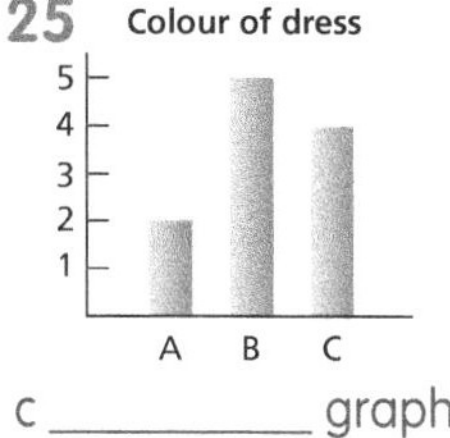

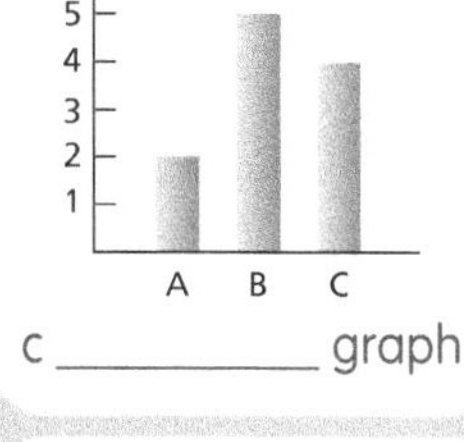

c ________ graph

26 Colour of balls: blue, green, yellow, red

s ________ graph

27 5:30 am

d ________ watch

28 a ________ clock

29 February

Sun	Mon	Tues	Wed	Thurs	Fri	Sat
1	2	3	4	5	6	7
8	9	10	11	12	13	14
15	16	17	18	19	20	21
22	23	24	25	26	27	28

c ________

30 b ________ scales

See page A1 for answers.

ID card B

Do not write on this card.

1 a ______	2 r ______ angle	3 p ______ lines	4 p ______ lines	5 t ______
6 s ______	7 r ______	8 r ______	9 t ______	10 p ______
11 q ______	12 p ______	13 h ______	14 c ______	15 o ______
16 r ______ shapes	17 i ______ shapes	18 s ______ c ______	19 line of s ______	20 net of a c ______
21 c ______	22 e ______	23 f ______	24 c ______	25 p ______
26 p ______	27 b ______	28 c ______	29 c ______	30 s ______

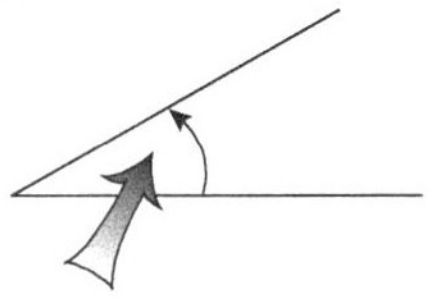

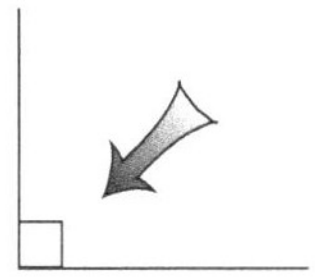

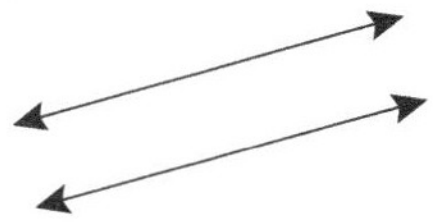

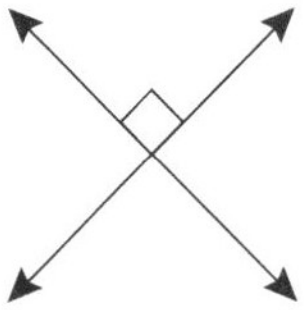

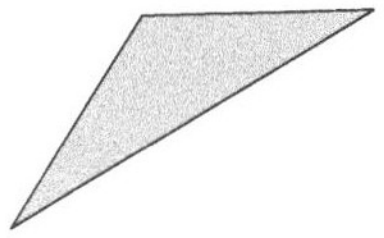

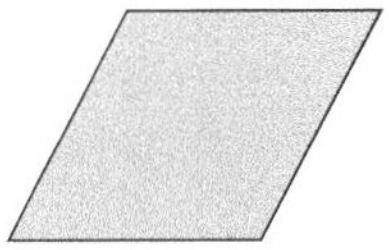

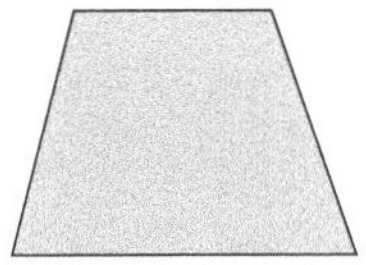

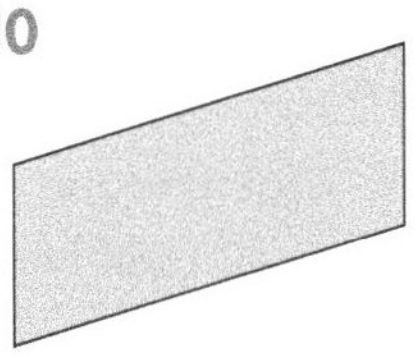

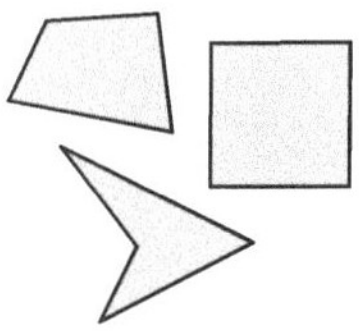

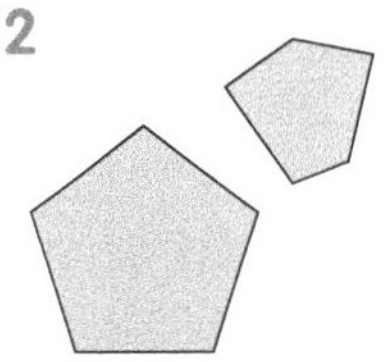

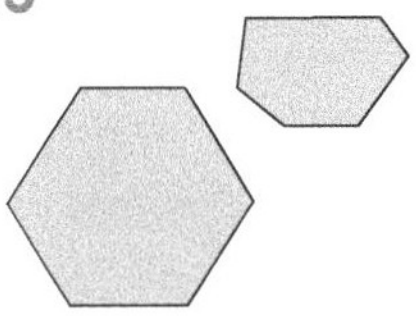

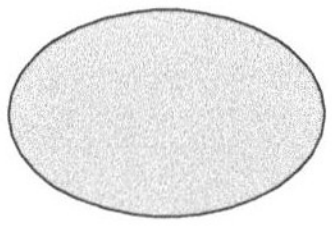

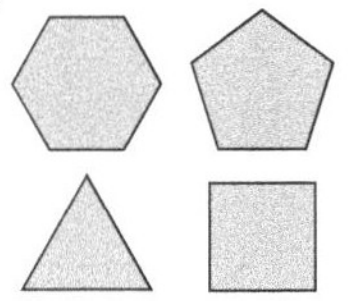

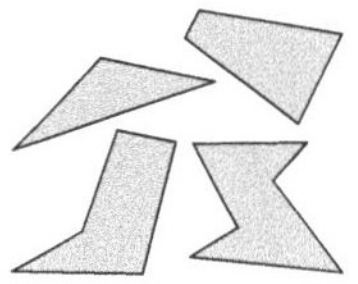

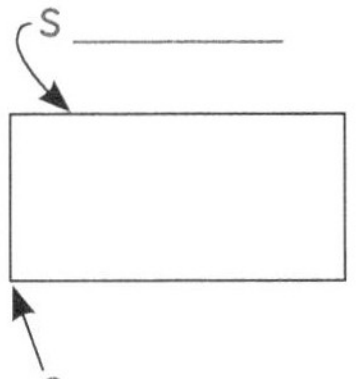

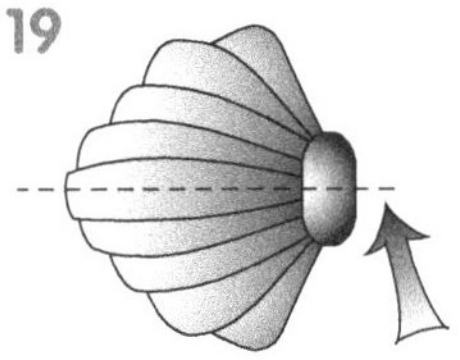

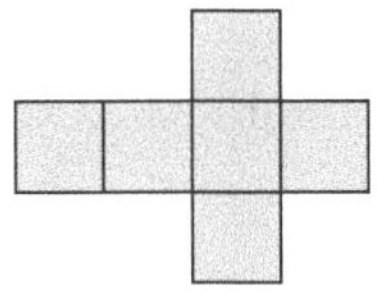

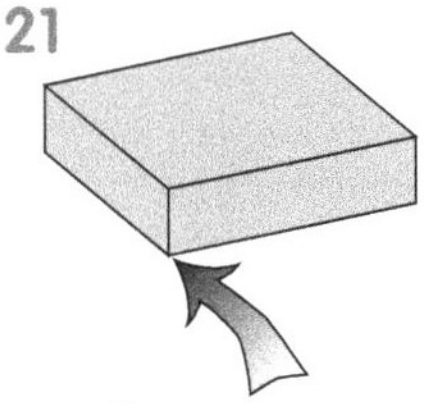

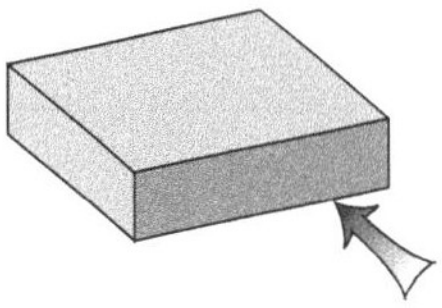

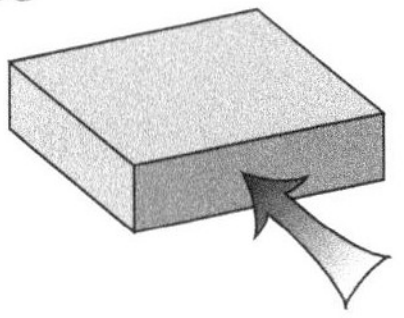

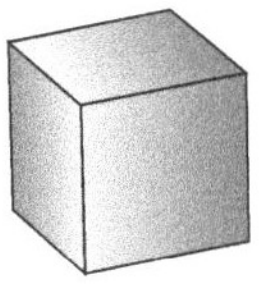

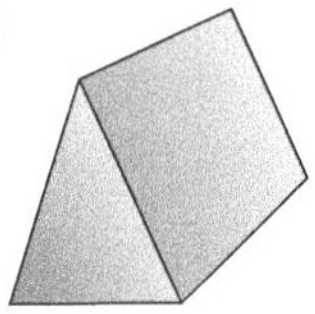

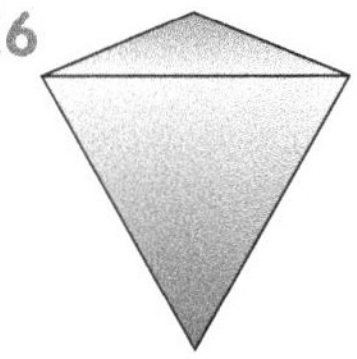

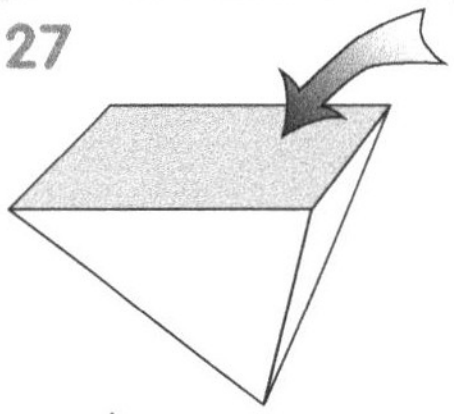

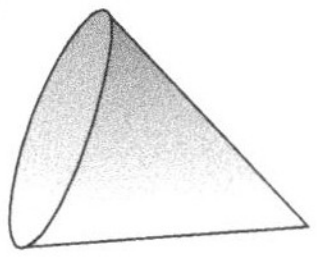

See page A1 for answers.

Tables of number and measurement

Length

1 centimetre = 10 millimetres
1 metre = 100 centimetres
1 metre = 1000 mm
1 kilometre = 1000 metres
metre = 1000 mm

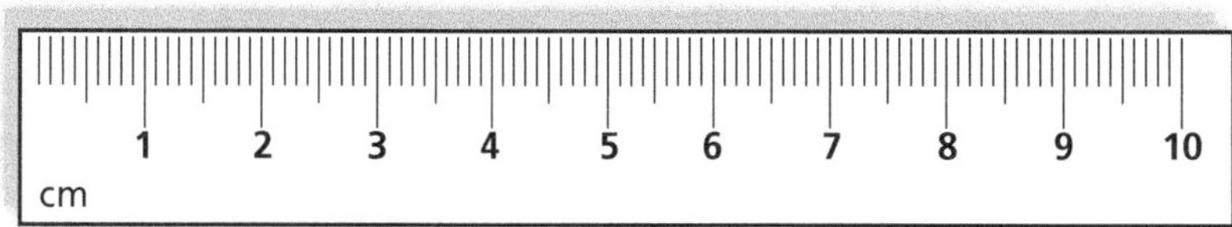

The **freezing point** of water is **0°C**.
The **boiling point** of water is **100°C**.

A temperature of **5°C** is **a cold day**.
A temperature of **35°C** is **a hot day**.

Mass

1 kilogram = 1000 grams

Capacity and volume

1 litre = 1000 millilitres

1 litre of water has a mass of 1 kg.
A carton of milk holds 1 L.

A teaspoon holds about 5 mL.

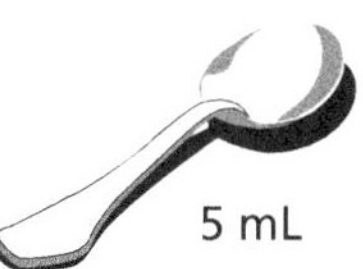

Roman numerals

1	= I	**6**	= VI	**20**	= XX	**90**	= XC
2	= II	**7**	= VII	**30**	= XXX	**100**	= C
3	= III	**8**	= VIII	**40**	= XL	**200**	= CC
4	= IV	**9**	= IX	**50**	= L	**500**	= D
5	= V	**10**	= X	**60**	= LX	**1000**	= M

Months of the year

Thirty days have September, April, June and November. All the rest have thirty-one, except February alone, which has twenty-eight days clear and twenty-nine days each leap year.

You can use the knuckles of your hands to find the number of days in each month.

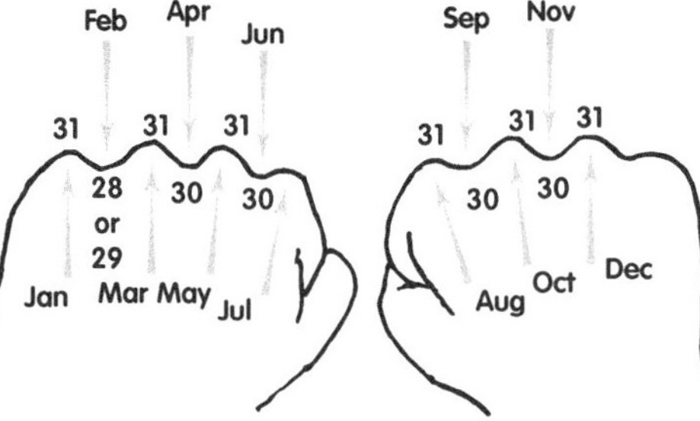

Time

1 minute = 60 seconds
1 hour = 60 minutes
1 day = 24 hours
1 week = 7 days
1 fortnight = 2 weeks
1 year = 52 weeks
1 year = 365 days
1 leap year = 366 days
1 decade = 10 years
1 century = 100 years

am stands for **ante meridiem**.
am means **before midday**.

pm stands for **post meridiem**.
pm means **after midday**.

Seasons

summer: December, January, February
autumn: March, April, May
winter: June, July, August
spring: September, October, November

Multiplication tables

1 × 2 = 2	1 × 3 = 3	1 × 4 = 4	1 × 5 = 5	1 × 6 = 6	1 × 7 = 7	1 × 8 = 8	1 × 9 = 9	1 × 10 = 10
2 × 2 = 4	2 × 3 = 6	2 × 4 = 8	2 × 5 = 10	2 × 6 = 12	2 × 7 = 14	2 × 8 = 16	2 × 9 = 18	2 × 10 = 20
3 × 2 = 6	3 × 3 = 9	3 × 4 = 12	3 × 5 = 15	3 × 6 = 18	3 × 7 = 21	3 × 8 = 24	3 × 9 = 27	3 × 10 = 30
4 × 2 = 8	4 × 3 = 12	4 × 4 = 16	4 × 5 = 20	4 × 6 = 24	4 × 7 = 28	4 × 8 = 32	4 × 9 = 36	4 × 10 = 40
5 × 2 = 10	5 × 3 = 15	5 × 4 = 20	5 × 5 = 25	5 × 6 = 30	5 × 7 = 35	5 × 8 = 40	5 × 9 = 45	5 × 10 = 50
6 × 2 = 12	6 × 3 = 18	6 × 4 = 24	6 × 5 = 30	6 × 6 = 36	6 × 7 = 42	6 × 8 = 48	6 × 9 = 54	6 × 10 = 60
7 × 2 = 14	7 × 3 = 21	7 × 4 = 28	7 × 5 = 35	7 × 6 = 42	7 × 7 = 49	7 × 8 = 56	7 × 9 = 63	7 × 10 = 70
8 × 2 = 16	8 × 3 = 24	8 × 4 = 32	8 × 5 = 40	8 × 6 = 48	8 × 7 = 56	8 × 8 = 64	8 × 9 = 72	8 × 10 = 80
9 × 2 = 18	9 × 3 = 27	9 × 4 = 36	9 × 5 = 45	9 × 6 = 54	9 × 7 = 63	9 × 8 = 72	9 × 9 = 81	9 × 10 = 90
10 × 2 = 20	10 × 3 = 30	10 × 4 = 40	10 × 5 = 50	10 × 6 = 60	10 × 7 = 70	10 × 8 = 80	10 × 9 = 90	10 × 10 = 100

Examples of measurements

1

2

3

4

5

6

1
- The width of your finger is about 1 cm.
- The length of a place-value tens block is 10 cm.

2
- The height of the girl is a little more than 1 m.

3
- The container of milk holds 2 L.
- The can of Fizz holds 375 mL.
- The teaspoon holds 5 mL.

4
- The boy has a mass of 40 kg.
- The margarine has a mass of 500 g.

5
- The area of the newspaper is about the same as the table.

6
- 30 degrees is a hot day.
- 3 degrees is a very cold day.

Use the pictures above to estimate the answers to these questions.

1 a How high is the glass?
b How wide is the table?

2 a How wide is the clothes line?
b How tall is the woman?

3 a How much will the bucket hold?
b How much will the cup hold?

4 a What is the mass of the dog?
b What is the mass of 2 L of milk?

5 a How many sheets of newspaper would cover the area of the window?
b How many place-value ones would cover the area of the top of the matchbox?

6 a What is the temperature on a very hot day?
b What is the temperature on a cool day?

1:1 out of 10

1. In **a** to **f**, write the number modelled.

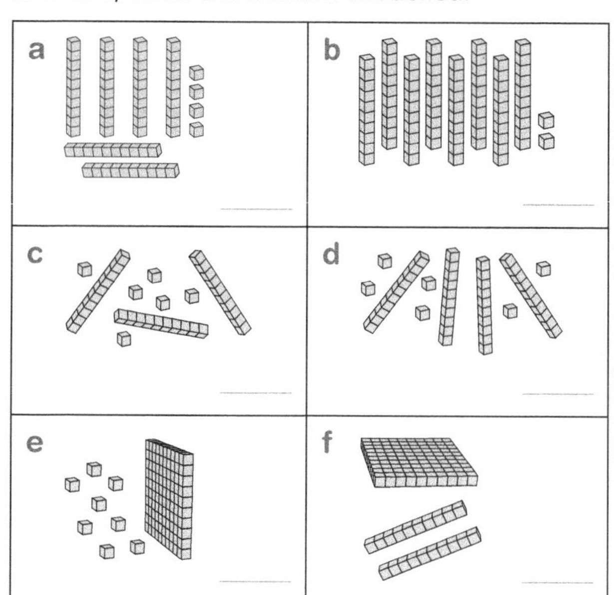

2. How many place-value ones blocks make one tens block? ______
3. The sign = means 'is e ______ to'.
4. Complete the pattern.

   2, 4, ______, ______, 10, 12
5. The tally  stands for: ______
6. 0 1 2 3 4 5

   This is a n______ l______.
7. How many digits in 13? ______
8. Josh had 5 toy trucks and was given 4 more by his Pa. How many has he now? ______
9. The numeral for twelve. ______
10. The number before 76 is ______.

1:2 out of 15

1. 2 + 8 ______
2. 17 + 3 ______
3. 20 − 5 ______
4. 20 − 7 ______
5. 13 + 34 ______
6. Digits in 184. ______
7. $7 + $7 ______
8. 7, 9, 11, ______, ______
9. Take 5 from 15. ______
10. 14 more than 35. ______
11. 

    The number sentence is:

    8 − ______ = ______
12. Colour one half of this rectangle.

    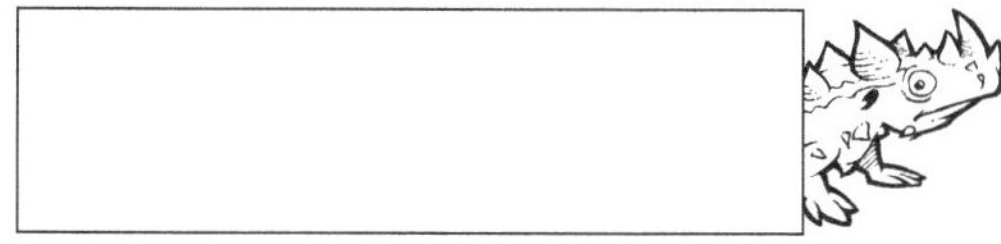
13. What time is shown?

    a 

    ______ past ______

    b 

    ______ past ______
14. Circle half of this group. 
15. How many in each box if we share the balls fairly? ______

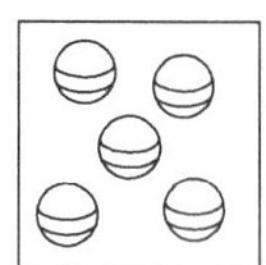 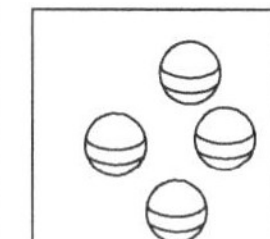 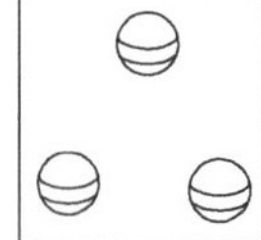 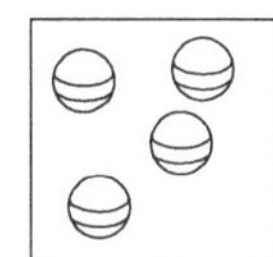

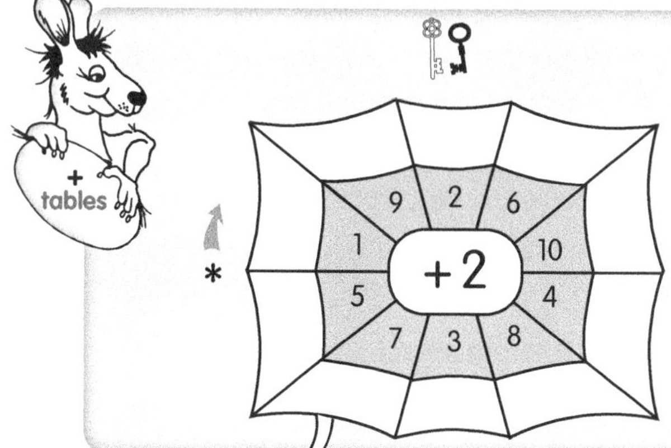

- Odd numbers end in 1, 3, 5, 7 or 9.
- Even numbers end in 2, 4, 6, 8 and 0.
- If you add an even number to an even number the answer is always even.

What happens when you add these types of numbers?

odd + odd = ______

even + odd = ______

1:3 ☐ out of 20

1. 24 − 10 ____
2. 13 + 4 ____
3. 25 − 6 ____
4. 27 + 6 ____
5. 18 + 4 ____
6. 2, 4, 6, ____, ____
7. Add 19 and 7. ____
8. 23 minus 4. ____
9. Write 19 in words. ____
10. 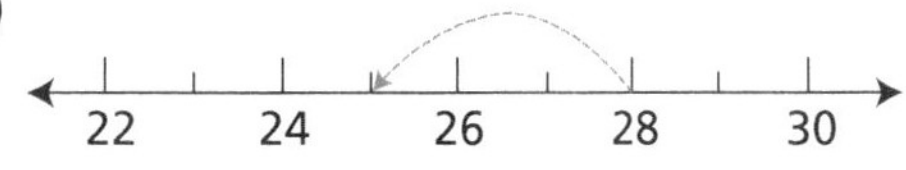

    a 28 – 3 ____ b 28 – 5 ____
11. 11 more than 17. ____
12. The numeral for fifty-two. ____
13. What month comes after December? ____
14. Use the split strategy to find:

    a 13 + 12 = ____ b 23 + 26 = ____

    c 45 + 51 = ____ d 33 + 42 = ____
15. Four equal q________ make 1 whole. Colour one quarter.

16. Wednesday is the ____ th day of the week.
17. Complete this pattern.

    42, 44, 46, ____, ____
18. Circle one quarter of this group. 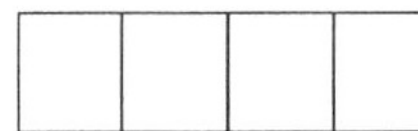
19. The value of these coins.     

    ____
20. How many days in one week? ____

1:4 Extension ☐ out of 10

1. 10 + ☐ = 16 ☐ = ____
2. 72, 62, 52, ____, ____, ____
3. 3, 6, 9 ____, ____, ____, ____
4. Use the split strategy. Show the working.

    15 + 38 = (10 + 30) + (5 + ____)

    = ____ + ____

    = ____
5. The difference between 20 and 17 = ____
6. If 8 + 12 = 20 then 12 + 8 = ____

8	12
20	

    20 − 8 = ____

    20 − 12 = ____
7. Three different counting numbers that add to give 7. ____
8. How many days altogether in summer? ____
9. Which season has the least days?

    ____
10. Two weeks is called a fortnight.

    Weeks in 4 fortnights? ____

Challenge

Write as many different number patterns as you can fit in this space.

Measure

Fill out this table about yourself, a relative or a friend.

Name: ____________ **Date:** ____________

Age: ____	Mass: ____ kg	Shoe size: ____
Height: ____ cm	Waist: ____ cm	Neck size: ____ cm

2:1 out of 7

1 In **a** to **f**, write the number modelled.

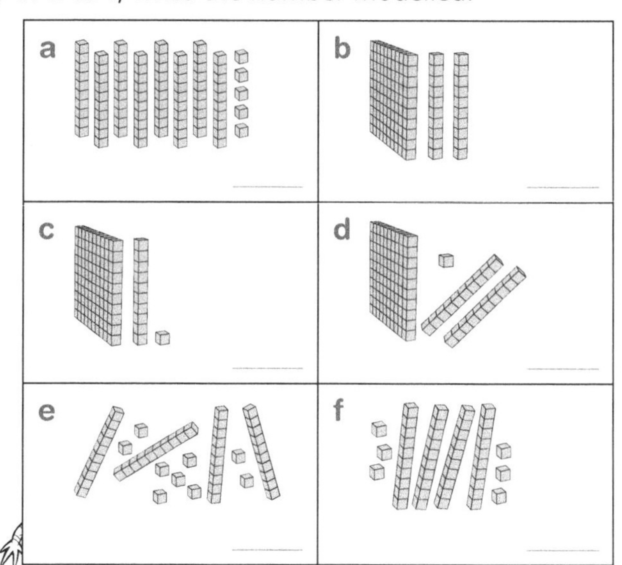

2 **a** 16 + 4 = ______ **b** 15 + 5 = ______

3 How many ones in 3 tens? ______

4 The numeral for eighteen. ______

5 Days in 1 week. ______

6

6 rabbits are shared by 2 families.

Each family has ______ rabbits.

7 How many minutes in half an hour? ______

2:2 out of 16

1 12 + 8 ______

2 20 − 6 ______

3 17 + ______ = 20

4 38 + ______ = 40

5 30 + 52 ______

6 4 × 2 ______

7 5 × 2 ______

8 10 shared by 2. ______

9 8 shared by 2. ______

10 16 less than 28. ______

11 **a** Colour one quarter.

b Colour one eighth.

12 Use the split strategy to find:

a 31 + 52 = ______ **b** 54 + 24 = ______

c 83 + 14 = ______ **d** 33 + 35 = ______

13 Use the jump strategy to find:

a 39 + 17 = ______

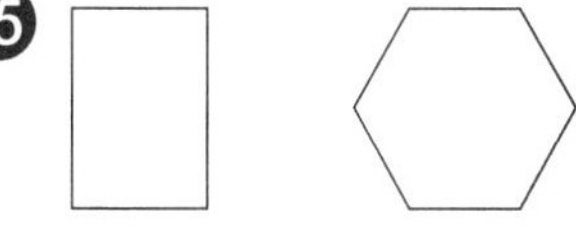

b 68 + 24 = ______

14 How many fingers on 3 hands? ______

3 groups of 5 = ______

15

A is a ______.

B is a ______.

C is a ______.

16 How many days in:

a March? ______ **b** September? ______

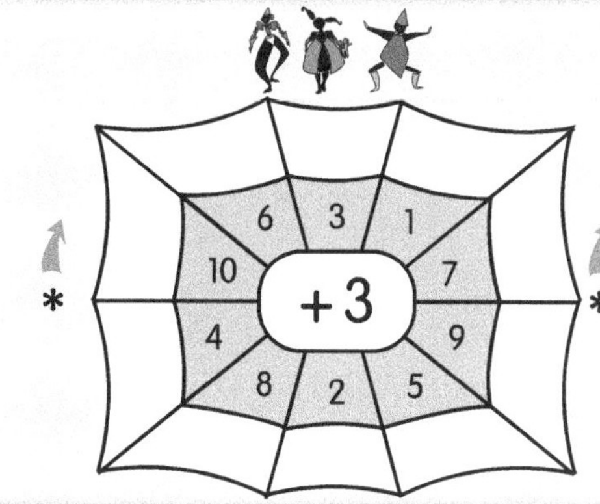

2:3 out of 13

1. 40 + 6 ____
2. 37 + 3 ____
3. 12 + 14 ____
4. 16 + 31 ____
5. Double 13. ____
6. Halve 22. ____
7. 56 + 10 ____
8. 28 + 12 ____
9. a 28 + 25 = ____

   b 39 + 34 = ____

10.      

   a 2 groups of 4 = ____ apples

   b 3 groups of ____ = ____ apples

11. 

   a The difference between 8 and 5. ____

   b The difference between 28 and 25. ____

12. Write two linking number sentences for

4 + 9 = ____

13. Circle the **heavier** object.

2:4 Extension out of 6

1. a 7 + ☐ = 15 ☐ = ____

   b ☐ + 16 = 24 ☐ = ____

2. In a race, I am 4th out of 5. How many are:

   a in front of me? ____

   b behind me? ____

3. Use the code to work out this message.

A	B	C	D	E	I	K	N	S
1	2	3	4	5	6	7	8	9

11 − 9	2 + 3

3 + 4	10 − 4	8 + 0	12 − 8

4. What is the time half an hour after quarter past three? ____

5. Colour one quarter of this shape.

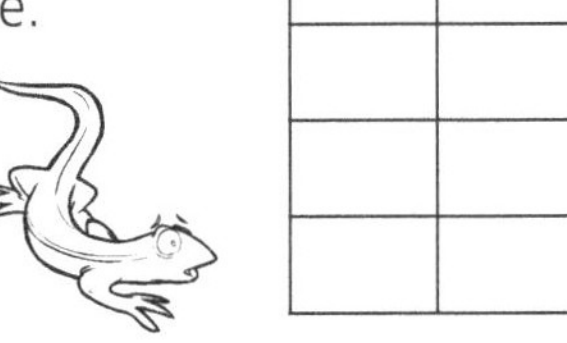

6. 2 + 8 + 3 + 7 + 1 + 9 ____

Challenge

Write different number sentences that equal 15.

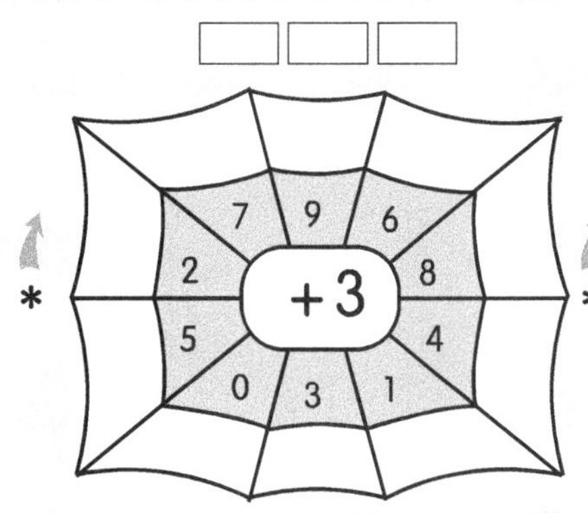

3:1 ☐ out of 7

1 a  b 

______ past ______ ______ to ______

2 a 3, 6, 9, ____, ____, ____, ____

b 2, 4, 6, ____, ____, ____, ____

c 10, 20, 30, ____, ____, ____, ____

3 a 4 shared by 2 = ____

b 6 shared by 2 = ____

4 Ryan had $20 and spent $10 to buy a toy bear. How much does he have left? ____

5 a 1 + 9 = ____ b 9 + 1 = ____

c 10 − 1 = ____ d 10 − 9 = ____

6 What is:

a behind the book? ____

b in front of the jug? ____

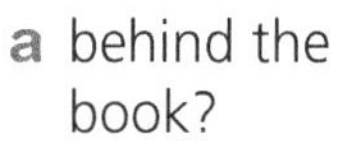

7 I had 10 toy dinosaurs. I sold 6. How many were left? ____

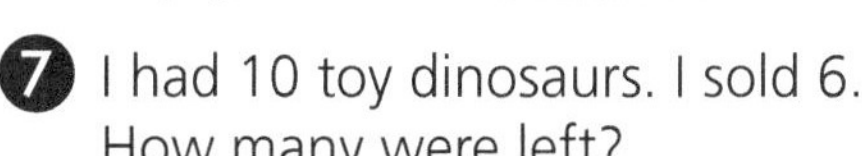

3:2 ☐ out of 17

1 14 + 6 ____

2 20 − 3 ____

3 15 + ____ = 20

4 48 + ____ = 50

5 $\begin{array}{r} 12 \\ +\ 7 \\ \hline \end{array}$

6 30 + 13 ____

7 50 + 17 ____

8 4 shared by 2. ____

9 12 shared by 2. ____

10 $\begin{array}{r} 28\text{c} \\ -\ 4\text{c} \\ \hline \end{array}$

11 Count on to the next 10 first, to find:

a 6 + ____ = 12 b 19 + ____ = 22

c 5 + ____ = 14 d 17 + ____ = 26

12 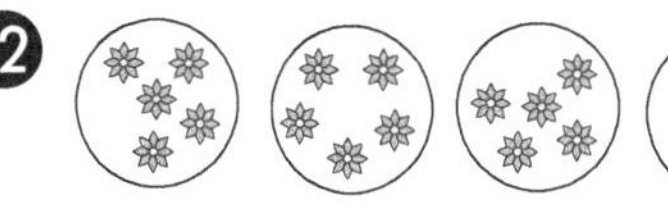

____ groups of ____ = ____

13 a 26 + 9 − 9 = ____ b 39 + 5 − 5 = ____

14 Complete these near doubles.

3 + 4 = ____ 7 + 8 = ____ 9 + 8 = ____

15 Use bridging to ten to find:

9 + 5 = ____ 8 + 6 = ____ 9 + 3 = ____

16 How many groups of 10 are there in:

a 46? ____ b 69? ____ c 37? ____

17 Circle the largest number. Underline the smallest number.

a 503 530 550 500

b 460 406 462 426

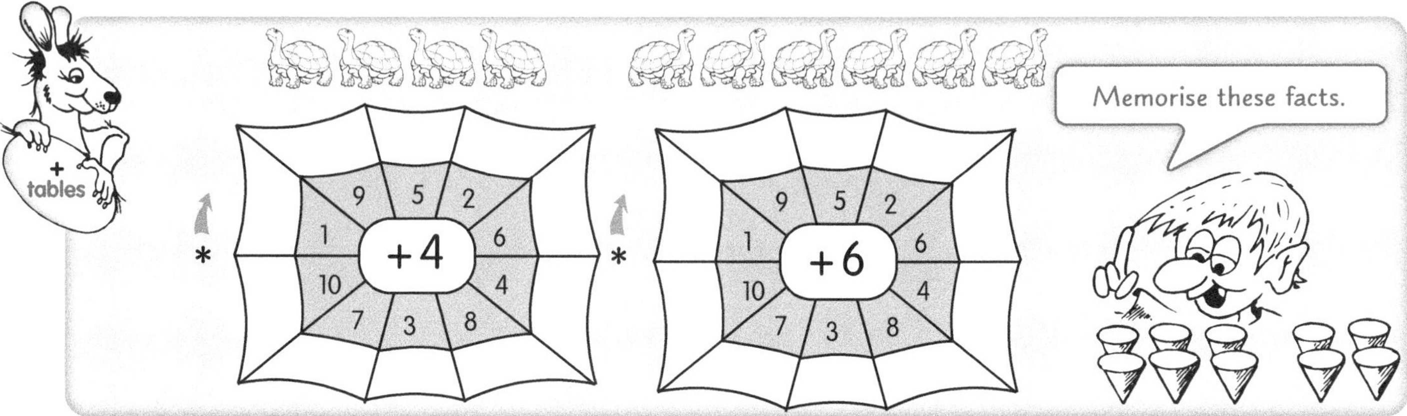

3:3 ☐ out of 10

❶ 4 ❷ 6 ❸ 8
6 3 4
+ 2 + 7 + 2

❹ Bridge to ten to find:

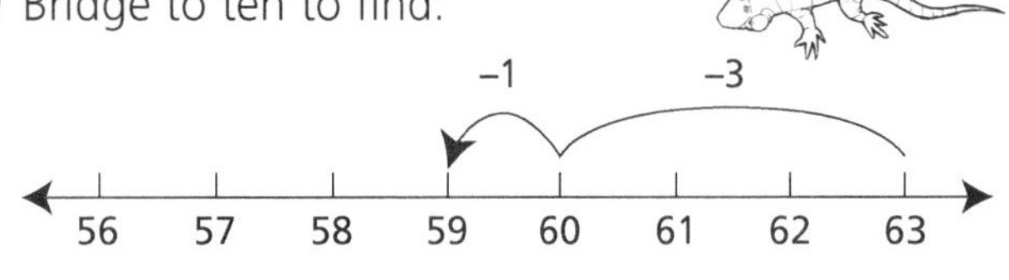

a 63 − 4 = ______ b 63 − 7 = ______

c 61 − 3 = ______ d 61 − 5 = ______

❺ Yoo-Jin had 5 pairs of shoes. How many shoes does he have altogether? ______

❻ ______ + 18 = 21 ______ + 15 = 23

❼ How many groups of 100 are in:

a 325? ______ b 729? ______

❽ Count on to the next 10 first to find:

a 9 + ______ = 15 b 18 + ______ = 26

c 16 + ______ = 21 d 15 + ______ = 23

❾ Write the total for each.

a

5	5
10	

b

5	5	5	5	5

c

4	4	4	4

d

4	4	4

❿ a How many days in 1 week? ______

b How many months in 1 year? ______

3:4 Extension ☐ out of 5

❶ Would a 4-digit number be bigger than a 3-digit number? ______

❷ a ☐ − 13 = 4 ☐ = ______

b 20 − ☐ = 6 ☐ = ______

❸

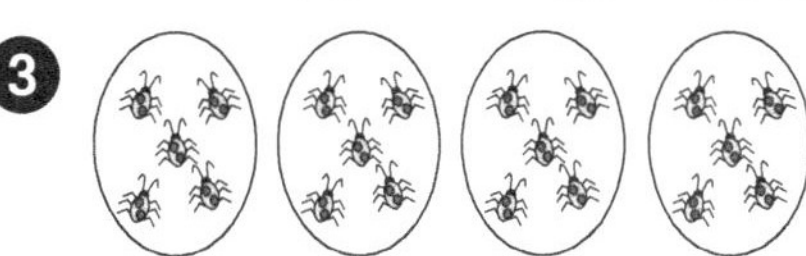

a How many bugs in 4 groups? ______

b How many bugs in 5 groups? ______

c How many bugs in 8 groups? ______

❹ a The smallest area below. ______

b The largest area below. ______

A B C

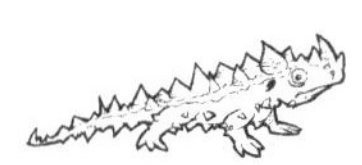

❺ Minutes in 3 hours? ______

Challenge

Show how you can make 50c in different ways.

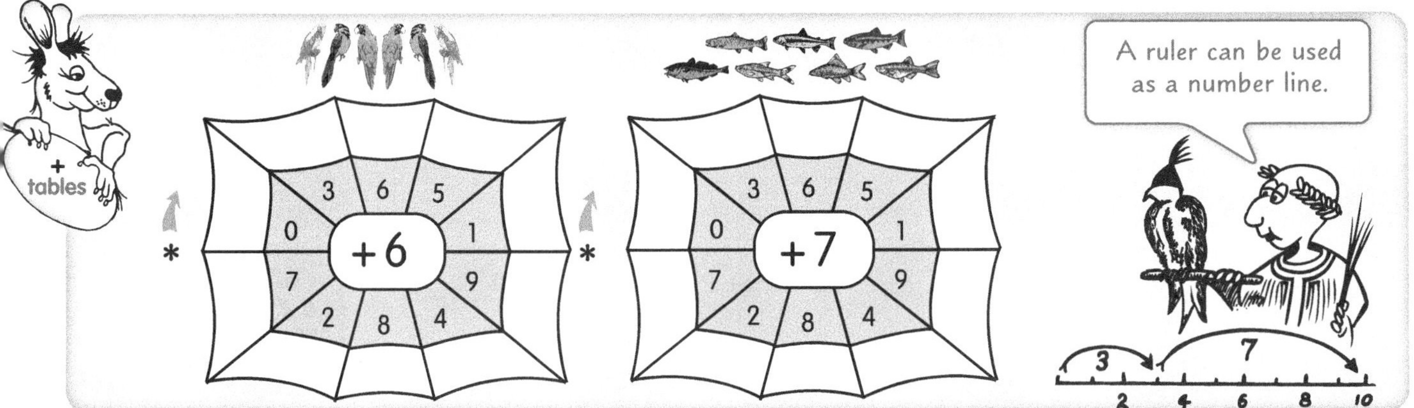

4:1 [ ] out of 14

1. 13 + 7 = ______
2. 20 − 9 = ______
3. 18 + ______ = 20
4. 28 + ______ = 30
5. 8 groups of 2. ______
6. 10 groups of 2. ______
7. 16 shared by 2. ______
8. 20 shared by 2. ______
9. **Favourite animal**

Bird	Dog	Cat	Mouse
7	13	4	1

   a The most popular animal was a ______.
   b The least popular animal was a ______.
   c How many people liked dogs? ______
   d How many people liked birds? ______

10. Count on to the next 10 first, to find:
   a 9 + ______ = 11   b 19 + ______ = 21
   c 8 + ______ = 13   d 18 + ______ = 23

11. Draw the line of symmetry.

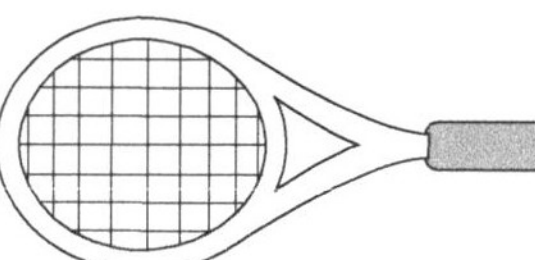

12. a 2, 4, 6, ______, ______, ______, ______
   b 100, 90, 80, ______, ______, ______, ______
   c 102, 104, 106, ______, ______, ______
   d 1000, 900, 800, ______, ______, ______
13. I have 6 pairs of socks.
   6 groups of 2 = ______
14. Show half past 3 on this clock.

4:2 [ ] out of 16

1. 27 − 5 = ______
2. 26 + 4 = ______
3. 12 × 2 ______
4. Halve 14. ______
5. 9 groups of 2. ______
6. 2 groups of 14. ______
7. 12 shared by 3. ______
8. 16 shared by 4. ______
9. Jasmine has 4 plates, 4 cups and 4 spoons. How many altogether? ______
10. Which is larger: 108 or 180? ______
11. Half of 16. ______
12. a 8, 10, 12, ______, ______, ______, ______
   b 5, 10, 15, ______, ______, ______, ______
   c 20, 18, 16, ______, ______, ______, ______
   d 134, 144, 154, ______, ______, ______
13. Luke is 9. How old will he be in:
   a 9 years? ______   b 10 years? ______
   c 16 years? ______   d 31 years? ______
14. **Favourite colours**

Red	Blue	Orange	Yellow
10	12	4	7

   a The most popular colour was ______.
   b The least popular colour was ______.
   c How many people liked blue? ______
   d How many people liked red? ______

15. Write tally marks for 12. ______
16. Show quarter past 8 on this clock.

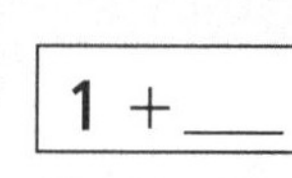

1 + ___
5 + ___
2 + ___
8 + ___
6 + ___
3 + ___
7 + ___
4 + ___

= 10 =

3 + ___
7 + ___
9 + ___
6 + ___
5 + ___
4 + ___
8 + ___
10+ ___

= 13 =

 • *AUSTRALIAN SIGNPOST MATHS NSW 3 MENTALS* • 978 0 6557 0910 7

4:3 ☐ out of 12

1

8
3
2
+ 7

2

5
1
9
+ 5

3

8
0
9
+ 2

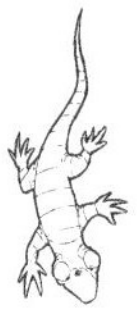

4 90, 80, 70, ______, ______, ______

5 6 hundreds 5 tens 3 ones = ______

6 What is one more than:

a 354 ____ **b** 746 ____ **c** 529 ____

7 **a** 93, 83, 73, ____, ____, ____, ____

b 695, 685, 675, ______, ______, ______

c 529, 629, 729, ______, ______, ______

8 When we count by 2s from zero, the numbers end in ______________.

9 Draw a line of symmetry on each picture.

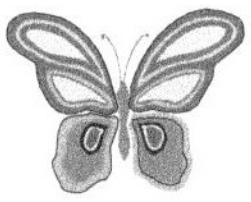

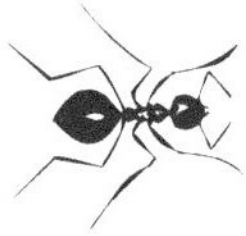

10 Use the split strategy to find:

a 16 + 13 = ______ **b** 41 + 53 = ______

c 52 + 46 = ______ **d** 58 + 21 = ______

11 Use the jump strategy to find:

a 29 + 8 = ______ **b** 48 + 23 = ______

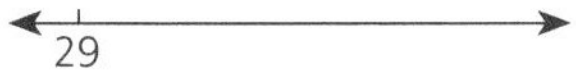

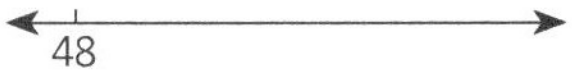

12 **a** 56 + ______ = 60 **b** 71 + ______ = 80

c 42 + ______ = 50 **d** 83 + ______ = 90

4:4 Extension ☐ out of 8

1 200, 250, 300, ______, ______, ______, ______

2 7 + 13 + 12 + 8 + 1 + 9 ______

3 28 − 4 − 4 − 4 − 4 − 4 ______

4 Weeks in 1 year. ______

5 Complete the pattern.

15, 12, 9, ____, ____

6 Can you work out the message?

Code

A	E	I	L	M	S	T
@	?	/	$	^	•	*

•	^	/	$	?	@	*	^	?

7 Complete:

a 20 + ____ = 100

b 100 − 20 = ____

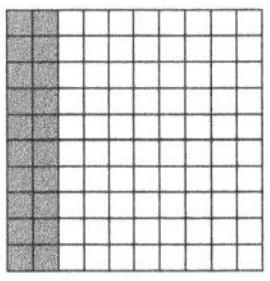

8 Days in 1 fortnight? ______

Challenge

The first dot plot shows goals scored in soccer. Draw a dot plot for the number of shapes below.

Goals scored	
Charlie	••
Lachlan	••••••
Harvey	••••
Leo	•

Shapes	
triangle	
square	
pentagons	
hexagons	

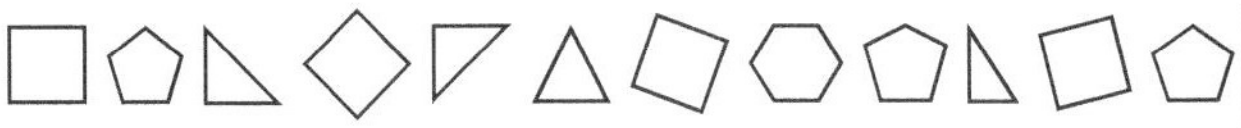

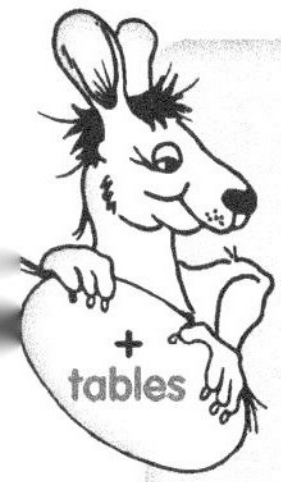

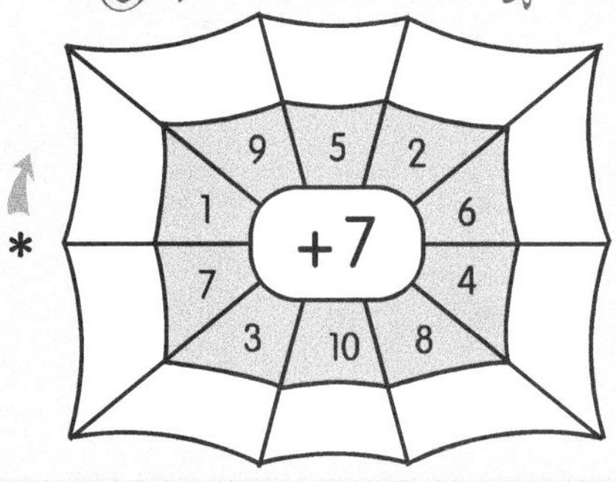

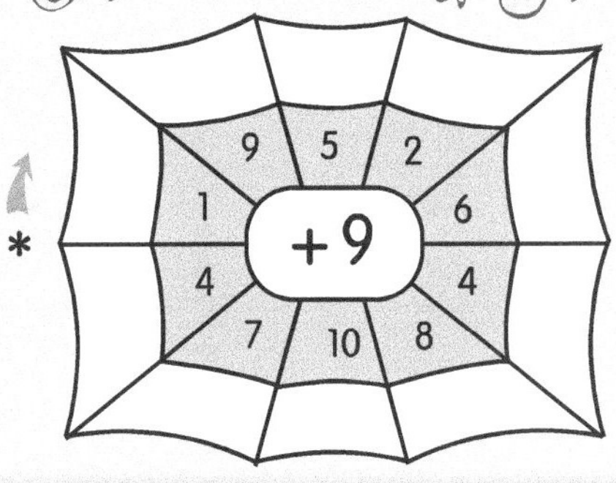

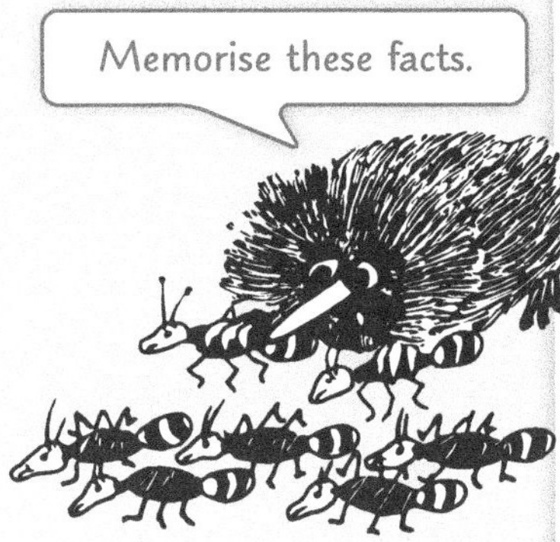

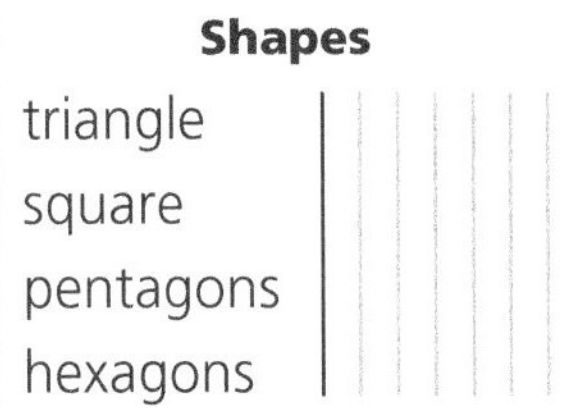

5:1 [ ] out of 14

1. 28 + 2 = ______
2. 20 − 5 = ______
3. 11 + ______ = 20
4. 25 + ______ = 30
5. 3 groups of 10. ______
6. Half of 12. ______
7. 12 shared by 2. ______
8. 4 shared by 2. ______
9. Draw a:

   a triangle **b** pentagon

    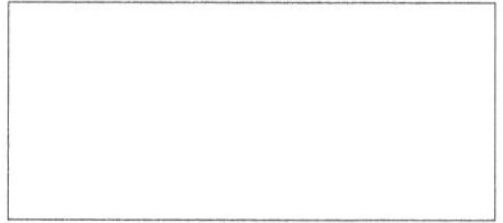

   c A triangle has ____ sides, ____ corners.

   d A pentagon has ____ sides, ____ corners.

10. Write the answer and fill in the numeral expander.

    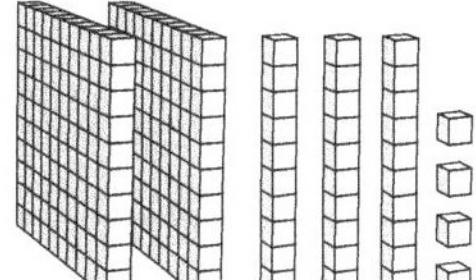

    ______

	hundreds		tens		ones

11. Write the above number in words.

    ____

    ____

12. Which is larger: 354 or 345? ______
13. Show how you jump to the next ten to find:

    7 + 5 = ______

    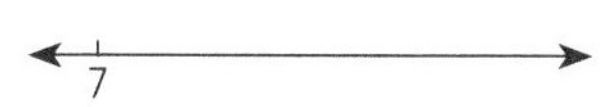

14. 33, 43, 53, ______, ______, ______, ______

5:2 [ ] out of 18

1. 23 + 20 = ______
2. 40 − 6 = ______
3. 34 + ______ = 40
4. 34 + ______ = 41
5. $\begin{array}{r} 62 \\ +\ 12 \\ \hline \end{array}$
6. 8 groups of 2. ______
7. Half of 18. ______
8. 16 shared by 2. ______
9. 14 shared by 2. ______
10. $\begin{array}{r} 38\text{c} \\ -\ 23\text{c} \\ \hline \end{array}$ ______

11. What shape is this? ______

    It has ____ sides and ____ corners.

    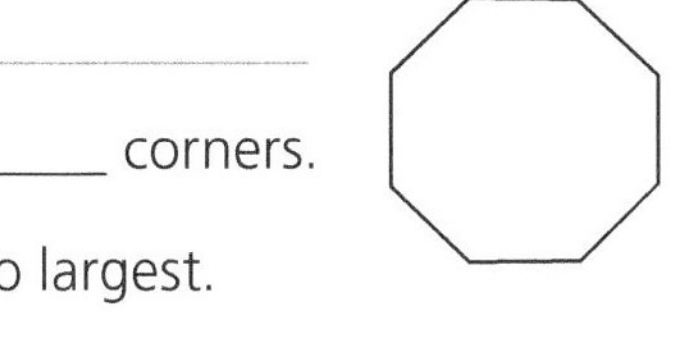

12. Order from smallest to largest.

    391, 902, 535 ______, ______, ______

13. Six hundred and four as a numeral. ______
14. Write the numeral for:

    ______

15. The season after summer? ______
16. **a** 3, 6, 9, ______, ______, ______, ______

    b 76, 66, 56, ______, ______, ______, ______

    c 172, 162, 152, ______, ______

    d 425, 435, 445, ______, ______

17. Draw the axis of symmetry.

    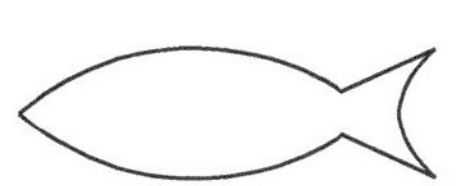

18. What is the time half an hour after:

    a quarter past 4? ______

    b quarter to 7? ______

0 5 10 15 20 25 30 35 40 45 50 55

In each case, skip count, writing in the numbers as you go. Use the number line to help you.

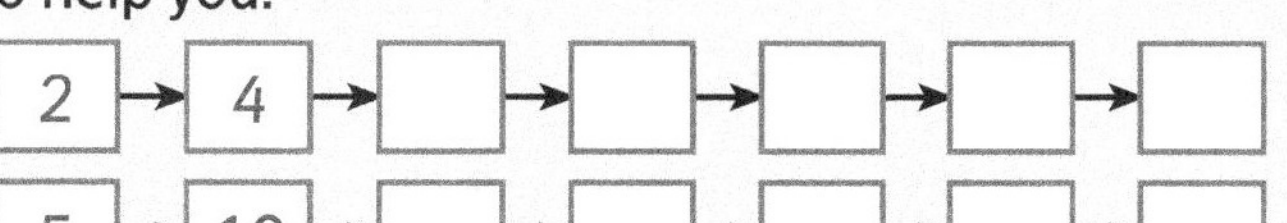

a Skip count by 2. 2 → 4 → [ ] → [ ] → [ ] → [ ] → [ ]

b Skip count by 5. 5 → 10 → [ ] → [ ] → [ ] → [ ] → [ ]

c Skip count by 10. 10 → [ ] → [ ] → [ ] → [ ] → [ ] → [ ] → [ ] → [ ]

5:3 out of 9

1. 35 + 21 = ______
2. 35 + 45 = ______
3. 43 + 62 = ______
4. 55 + 25 = ______
5. **Swimming attendance**

	Day 1	Day 2	Day 3	Day 4	Day 5	Day 6	Day 7	Day 8
Yuri		•		•	•	•		•
Sue	•	•	•		•			
Tan	•	•	•		•	•		•
Jess	•	•	•	•	•	•	•	
Greg	•	•	•	•	•	•	•	•
Mari	•		•	•	•	•	•	•

a Who was never away? ______
b Who was away the most? ______
c How many days was Jess present? ______

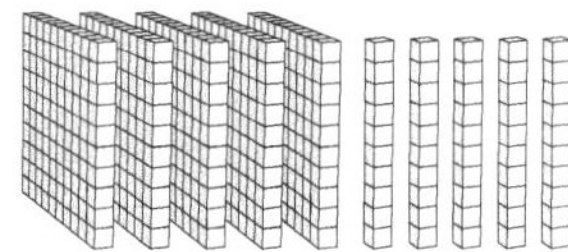

☐ hundreds ☐ tens ☐ ones

7. a 2, 4, 6, ______, ______, ______, ______
b 23, 33, 43, ______, ______, ______, ______
c 165, 155, 145, ______, ______, ______
8. Draw a line of symmetry on this dog.

9. A pentagon has ______ sides and ______ corners.

5:4 out of 7 — Extension

1. a 46 + 25 = ______ b 58 + 34 = ______
2. 30 + 3 − 3 + 5 − 5 + 1 − 1 ______
3. 100 − 2 − 2 − 2 − 2 − 2 − 2 − 2 ______
4. 57 + 3 + 3 + 3 + 3 + 3 + 3 + 3 ______
5. Complete this picture if the dotted line is a line of symmetry.

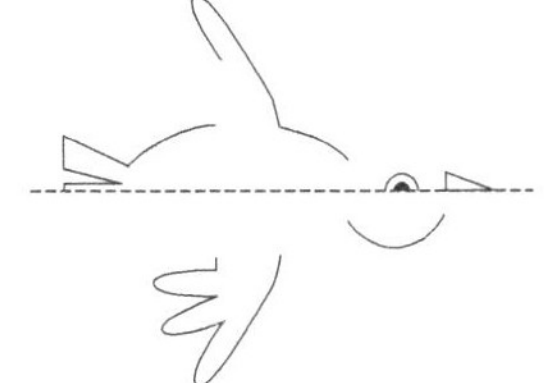

6. Write 342 in words. ______
7. Continue each pattern then write the rule.
a 8, 11, 14, ______, ______, ______ Rule: ______
b 7, 13, 19, ______, ______, ______ Rule: ______
c 4, 11, 18, ______, ______, ______ Rule: ______

Challenge

Draw a picture that has symmetry.

Measure

Time

60 minutes = 1 hour
30 minutes = half an hour
7 days = 1 week
14 days = 1 fortnight
52 weeks = 1 year
12 months = 1 year

Write the months of the year in order.

J ______ F ______ M ______
A ______ M ______ J ______
J ______ A ______ S ______
O ______ N ______ D ______

Underline the months that have 31 days.

6:1 ☐ out of 18

1. 47 + 3 ______
2. 19 − 3 ______
3. 16 + ______ = 20
4. 27 + ______ = 30
5. 3 groups of 10. ______
6. Digits in 451. ______
7. 12 shared by 2. ______
8. 4 shared by 2. ______
9. A hexagon has ____ sides, ____ corners.
   A square has ____ sides, ____ corners.
10. 493 = ______ hundreds, ______ tens, ______ ones
11. Write these numbers in order from smallest to largest. 212, 129, 76, 318, 236

    ____

12. How many flat surfaces has:
    a A? ______
    b B? ______

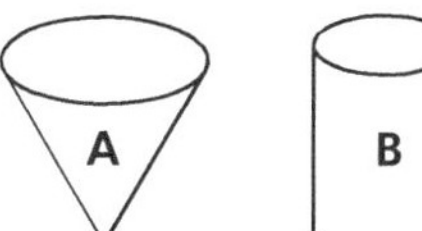

13. This is a quadrilateral.
    How many:
    a sides: ______ b corners: ______
14. Show 725 on this numeral expander.

	hundreds		tens		ones

15. The odd numbers between 10 and 20 are:
    ______, ______, ______, ______, ______
16. Which is larger, fifty or fifteen? ______
17. Write 903 in words.

    ____

    ____
18. The number after 168 is ______.

6:2 ☐ out of 16

1. 28 + 8 ______
2. 29 − 7 ______
3. 16 + 5 ______
4. 19 + 4 ______
5. 4 groups of 10. ______
6. Digits in 324. ______
7. Digits in 32. ______
8. Double 23. ______
9. a Describe this array.

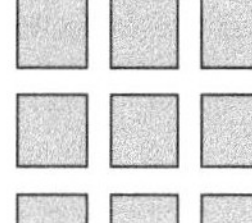

____

____

   b Is 9 a square number? ______
10. 942 = ______ hundreds, ______ tens, ______ ones
11. Which number is larger: 326 or 801? ______
12. Is 713 larger than 709? ______
13. Order from smallest to largest.
    857, 758, 875 ______, ______, ______
14. The number modelled. ______

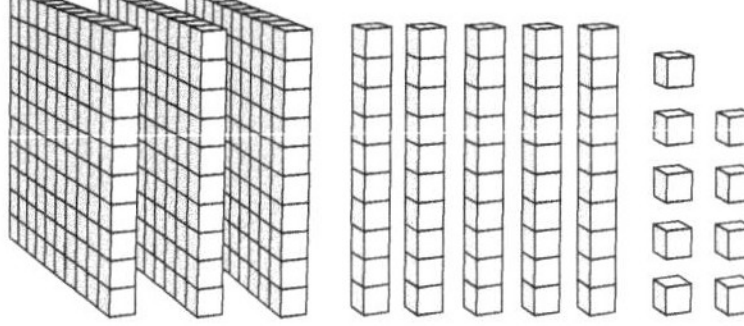

15. Finish these pictures using symmetry.

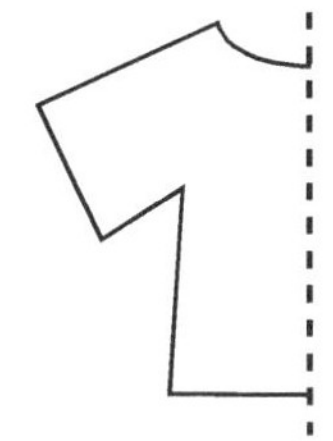

16. a Halve the answer to 8 + 10. ______
    b Double the answer to 14 + 6. ______

Turn to ID card B on page 7.
Give the answers for these numbers.

(5)	______	(6)	______
(7)	______	(11)	______
(12)	______	(13)	______
(14)	______	(15)	______
(18) s	______	c	______

6:3  out of 10

1
$$\begin{array}{r} 25 \\ +\ 23 \\ \hline \end{array}$$

2
$$\begin{array}{r} 47c \\ -\ 24c \\ \hline \end{array}$$

3
$$\begin{array}{r} 73 \\ +\ 15 \\ \hline \end{array}$$

4 452 = ______ hundreds, ______ tens, ______ ones

5 Which shapes have only flat surfaces?

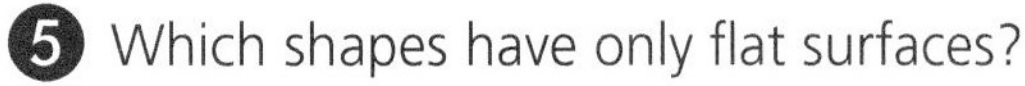

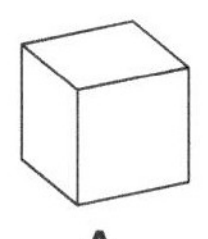   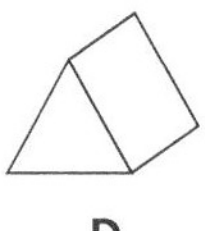

A B C D

____

6 What is the usual cross-section of a:

a cube? ______ b cone? ______

7 Use the jump strategy to find:

a 36 + 7 = ______

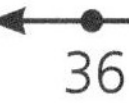

36

b 58 + 16 = ______

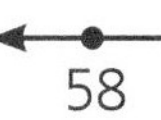

58

8 Draw the line of symmetry on this picture.

9

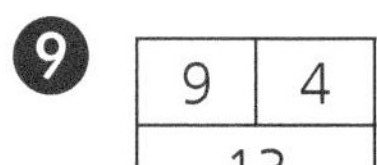

9	4
13	

a 9 + 4 = ____ b 13 − 9 = ____

c 4 + 9 = ____ d 13 − 4 = ____

10 How many days in January? ______

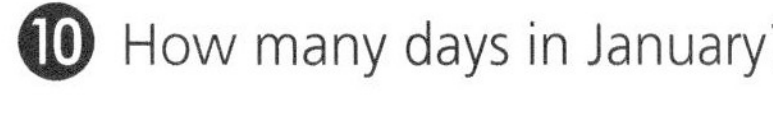

6:4  out of 7

Extension

1 Draw two lines of symmetry on this shape.

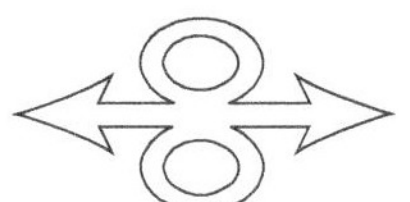

2 9 + 1 + 8 + 2 + 10 + 0 ______

3 40 − 4 − 4 − 4 − 4 − 4 ______

4 These ladybirds have the same number of dots on both sides. How many dots altogether? ______

5 If this wavy line were made 3 times as long, how many hills would be drawn? ______

6 Rachel saw the same number of koalas in 5 trees. There were 15 koalas. How many in each tree? ______

7 Show this number as tens and ones.

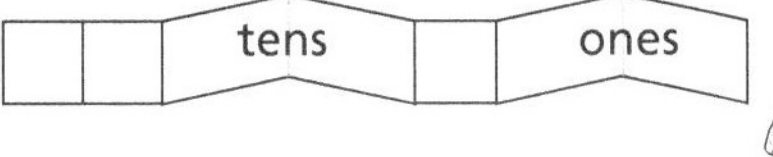

Challenge

Draw as many symmetrical letters, shapes and symbols as you can.

6 + 4 = 10, 4 + 6 = 10, 10 − 6 = 4, 10 − 4 = 6

Complete four number sentences for each picture.

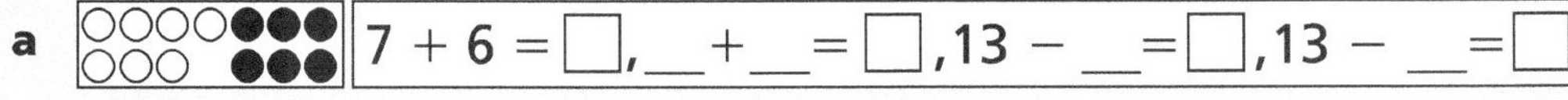

a 7 + 6 = ☐, ___ + ___ = ☐, 13 − ___ = ☐, 13 − ___ = ☐

b ___ + ___ = ☐, ___ + ___ = ☐, ___ − ___ = ☐, ___ − ___ = ☐

c ___ + ___ = ☐, ___ + ___ = ☐, ___ − ___ = ☐, ___ − ___ = ☐

7:1 ____ out of 16

1. 59 + 4 ____
2. 27 − 2 ____
3. 2 × 2 ____
4. 1 × 2 ____
5. $\begin{array}{r} 34 \\ +\,12 \\ \hline \end{array}$
6. 3 groups of 5. ____
7. 2 groups of 5. ____
8. 1 group of 10. ____
9. 3 groups of 10. ____
10. $\begin{array}{r} 34\text{c} \\ -\,22\text{c} \\ \hline \end{array}$
11. 635 = ____ hundreds, ____ tens, ____ ones
12. These are called t________ marks.

13. **Lollipops Eaten** 🍭 = one lollipop

Leah	🍭🍭🍭🍭🍭🍭🍭🍭🍭🍭🍭
Robert	🍭🍭🍭🍭🍭🍭
Chen	🍭🍭🍭🍭🍭🍭🍭
Anna	🍭🍭

a Who ate the most lollipops? ________
b Who ate the least lollipops? ________
c How many did Chen eat? ________
d How many lollipops were eaten altogether? ________

14. Complete the first 7 multiples of 2.
2, ____, ____, ____, ____, ____, ____

15. What shape is this cross-section of a cone? ________
16. a 2, 4, 6, ____, ____, ____, ____, ____
b 3, 6, 9, ____, ____, ____, ____, ____

7:2 ____ out of 16

1. 37 + 6 ____
2. 54 − 5 ____
3. 3 × 2 ____
4. 6 × 2 ____
5. 5 × 2 ____
6. 1 × 2 ____
7. 2 × 2 ____
8. 4 × 2 ____
9. What are the first 6 multiples of:
a 4? 4, ____, ____, ____, ____, ____
b 5? 5, ____, ____, ____, ____, ____
c 10? 10, ____, ____, ____, ____, ____
10. 586 = ____ hundreds, ____ tens, ____ ones
11. How many corners has
a A? ____
b B? ____

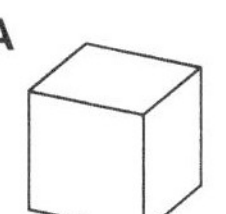

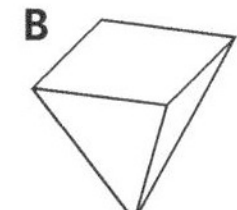

12. How many fingers on 8 girls? ________
13.

Sports team points			
Yellow	Blue	Green	Red
35	40	20	25

a Which team had the most points? ________
b Which team had 20 points? ________
c Red and Blue had ____ points.
d ________ had 15 more points than Green.

14.

7	8
15	

a 7 + 8 = ____
b 15 − 8 = ____
c 8 + 7 = ____
d 15 − 7 = ____

15. I have 2 bunches of 10 flowers.
How many flowers altogether? ________
16. Which is largest: 462, 264 or 459? ________

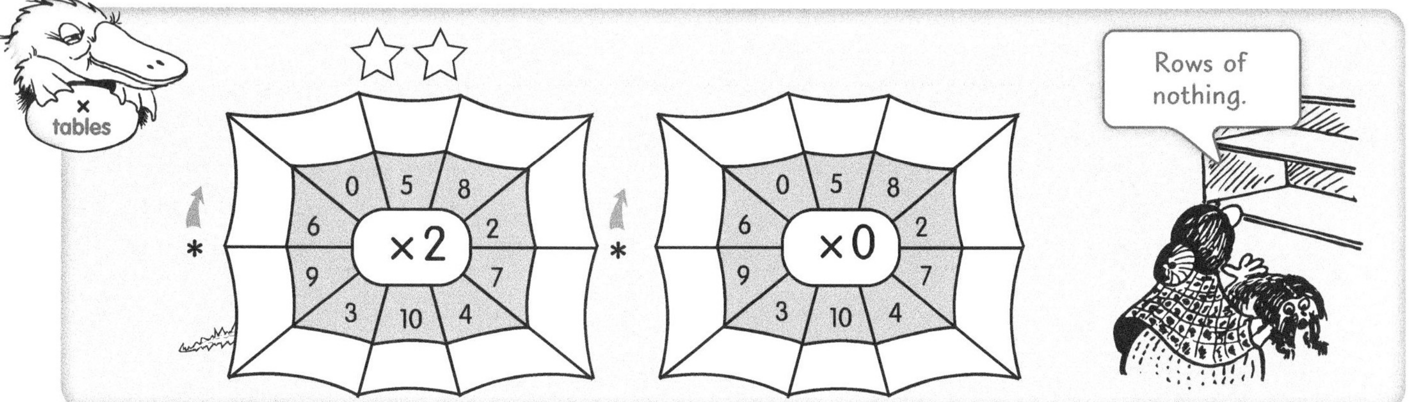

7:3 ☐ out of 10

❶
```
  37
+ 12
```

❷
```
  69c
− 27c
```

❸ a Name this shape. ______

How many: b faces? ______

c corners? ______ d edges? ______

e What would the cross-section of this object be? ______

❹ 5 + 9 = 14 and 9 + 5 = ______

Write the linking subtraction sentences.

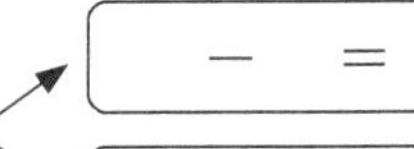

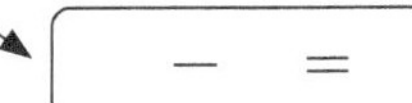

❺ a How many fingers on 4 hands? ______

b 4 × 5 = ______

c How many toes on 5 children? ______

d 5 × 10 = ______

❻ Which is largest, 707, 770 or 777? ______

❼ Complete the first 7 multiples of 10.

10, ______, ______, ______, ______, ______, ______

❽ Which is largest, 550, 555 or 505? ______

❾ December is the ______ month of the year.

❿ A triangle has ______ sides.

7:4 ☐ out of 5

Extension

❶ Complete this picture if the broken line is a line of symmetry.

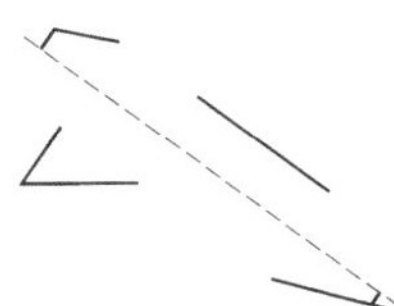

❷ | 5 | hundreds | 3 | tens | 1 | ones |

= ______ tens and ______ one

❸ Complete the first 7 multiples of 5.

5, ______, ______, ______, ______, ______, ______

❹ Write 3 square numbers. ______

❺ I played golf. What was my total score for these 4 holes? ______

Hole	Score
Hole 1	8
Hole 2	9
Hole 3	7
Hole 4	10

Challenge

What facts are shown in this graph?

Name	Trips to the shop
Greg	𝍸 𝍸 𝍸 |
Kate	𝍸 𝍸 ||||
Emily	𝍸 ||
Sophie	|||

______

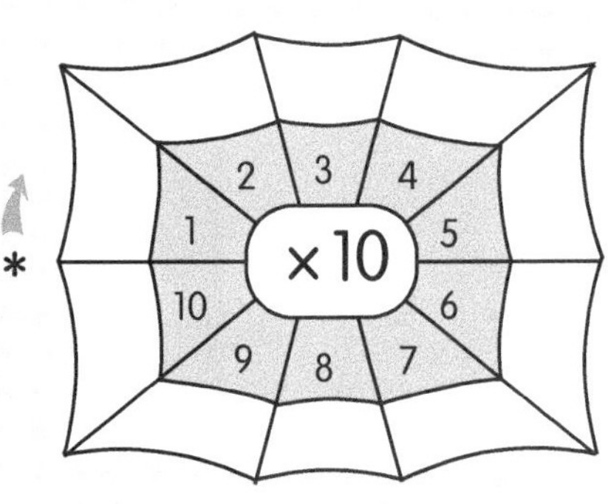

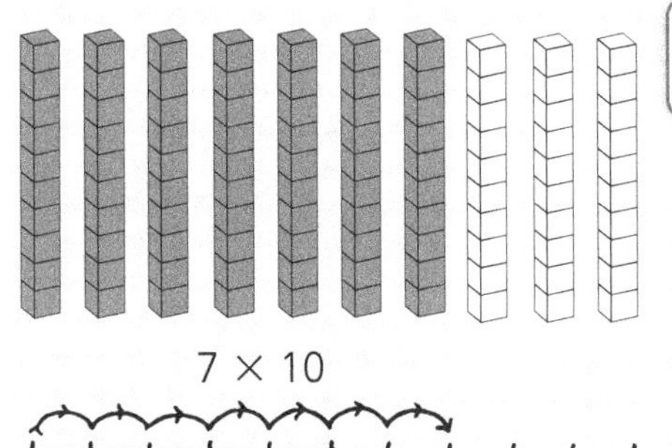

8:1   ☐ out of 16

1. 26 + 4 ______
2. 56 − 6 ______
3. 8 × 2 ______
4. 10 × 2 ______
5. $\begin{array}{r} 40 \\ +\ 11 \\ \hline \end{array}$
6. 10 × 5 ______
7. 2 × 5 ______
8. 6 × 10 ______
9. 7 × 10 ______
10. $\begin{array}{r} 42c \\ -\ 11c \\ \hline \end{array}$
11. 3 groups of 6. ______

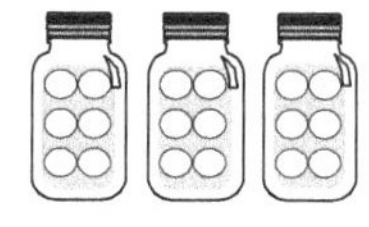

12.

	3	7	4	5	2	10	6	9
× 5								

13. Which is closer to 1 metre, the height of a cat, the width of a door or the length of a car? ______
14. ______ rows of ______ = ______
15. Two weeks is called a fortnight. How many days in 1 fortnight? ______
16. Use a ruler to measure the length and width of this rectangle.

____ cm

____ cm

8:2   ☐ out of 15

1. 47 + 23 ______
2. 67 − 17 ______
3. 4 × 2 ______
4. 8 × 2 ______
5. $\begin{array}{r} 66 \\ +\ 31 \\ \hline \end{array}$

6. 8 × 5 ______
7. 6 × 5 ______
8. 5 × 10 ______
9. 10 × 10 ______
10. $\begin{array}{r} 87c \\ -\ 16c \\ \hline \end{array}$
11. I swam 20 metres, then 30 metres and then 40 metres. How far did I swim altogether? ______
12. I have 63 birds.
    How many more do I need so I have 77?
    ______ + ______ = ______
13. Write 128 in words. ______
    ______
14. **a** Write the smallest 3-digit number possible using 0, 9 and 7. ______
    b Write the largest 3-digit number possible using 9, 9 and 8. ______
15. Use a ruler to measure the length and width of this rectangle.

____ cm

____ cm

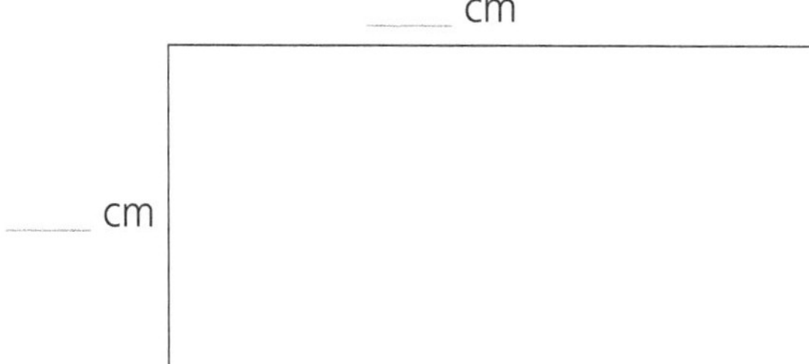

× tables

×5: 0, 5, 8, 2, 7, 4, 10, 3, 9, 6

×2: 0, 5, 8, 2, 7, 4, 10, 3, 9, 6

This is 6 groups of 2 or 6 x 2.

8:3 ☐ out of 5

1. Complete the first 6 multiples of:

   a 2. 2, ____, ____, ____, ____, ____

   b 4. 4, ____, ____, ____, ____, ____

2. Use the jump strategy to find:

   a 51 − 23 = ____

   b 39 + 24 = ____

3. a 14 − 5 = ____ b 24 − 5 = ____

   c 34 − 5 = ____ d 44 − 5 = ____

   e 36 + 7 = ____ f 46 + 7 = ____

   g 56 + 7 = ____ h 66 + 7 = ____

4. 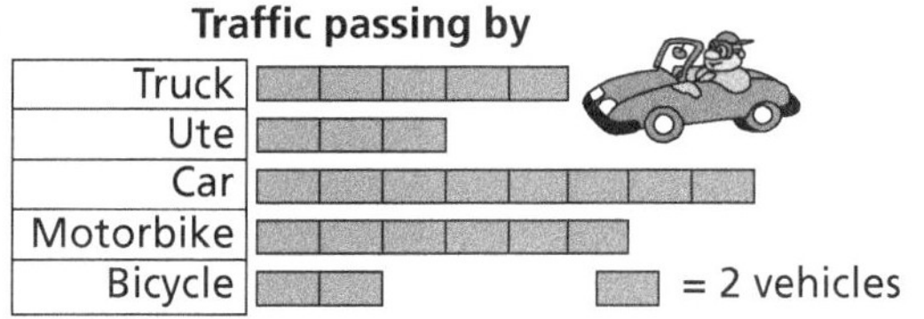

   a Which was the most popular? ____

   b Which was the least popular? ____

   c How many more cars were there than motorbikes? ____

   d How many trucks and utes were there altogether? ____

   e How many vehicles altogether? ____

5. Write the largest number possible using 1, 7 and 3. ____

8:4 ☐ out of 5 Extension

1. How many place-value tens blocks, placed end-to-end, would reach:

   a 1 metre? ____ b 2 metres? ____

2. a 17 + 9 = ____ b 35 + 9 = ____

   c 32 − 9 = ____ d 45 − 9 = ____

3. I came 1st in a race out of 8. How many came:

   a in front of me? ____

   b behind me? ____

4. I will give Li two of these toys. How many different groups of 2 could I give? ____

5. Estimate the number of stars, circle groups of 10, then count. ____

Challenge

42 + 35 = ____

Explain how you found your answer.

Two 5s can be traded for one 10.

rows of 5

groups of 5

	2	4	6	8	10
× 5					

	1	2	3	4	5
× 10					

9:1 out of 17

1. 32 + 6 ____
2. 42 + 6 ____
3. 52 + 6 ____
4. 62 + 6 ____
5. 5 × 2 ____
6. 6 × 2 ____
7. 8 × 10 ____
8. 4 × 10 ____
9. Write the value of each note.

____ ____ ____

10. 11 − 6 = ____ so 6 + ____ = 11

The difference between 6 and 11 is ____.

11. Fourteen fish are to be put into two equal groups. How many fish in each group?

12. How many pens would fit along the length of your ruler? ____
13. 12:15 can also be called ____ past ____.
14. Minutes in 1 hour. ____
15. What time is shown?

____

16. 5 + ____ = 11
17. Show quarter past 4 on the clock.

9:2 out of 16

1. 56 + 7 ____
2. 66 + 7 ____
3. 76 + 7 ____
4. 86 + 7 ____
5. 7 × 2 ____
6. 7 × 5 ____
7. 6 × 5 ____
8. 9 × 10 ____
9. 18 − 13 = ____ so 13 + ____ = 18

The difference between 13 and 18 is ____.

10. 32 metres take away 7 metres. ____
11. a Minutes in half an hour. ____

b Minutes in one hour. ____

12. Is the length of a car closer to 2 metres, 4 metres or 20 metres? ____
13. Use a ruler to measure the length and width of this rectangle.

____ cm

____ cm

14. The total value of these notes. ____

15. 647 = ____ hundreds, ____ tens, ____ ones
16. Use the jump strategy to find:

a 38 + 57 = ____

b 42 − 27 = ____

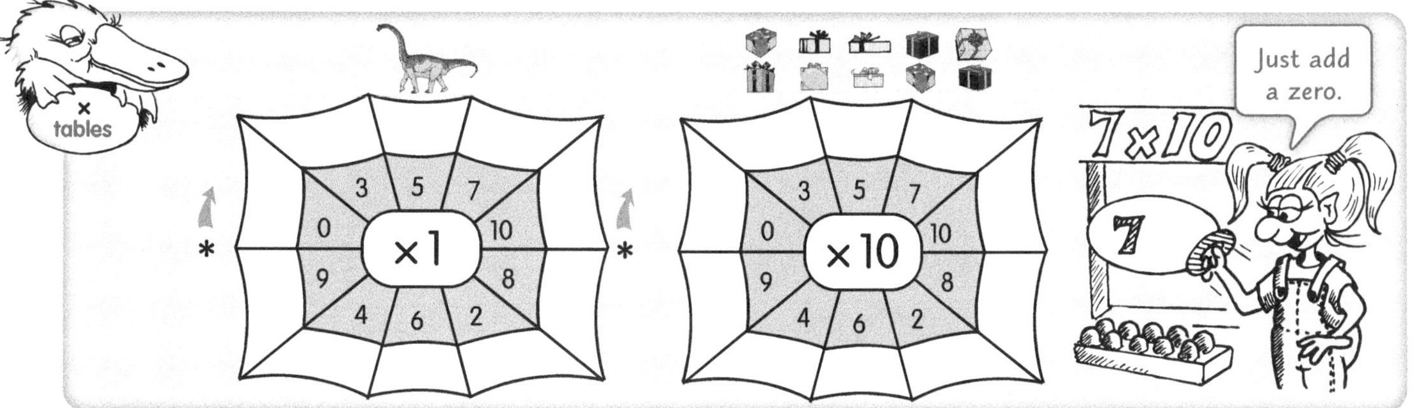

9:3

out of 10

❶ $\begin{array}{r} 75 \\ +\ 13 \\ \hline \end{array}$

❷ $\begin{array}{r} 54c \\ -\ 12c \\ \hline \end{array}$

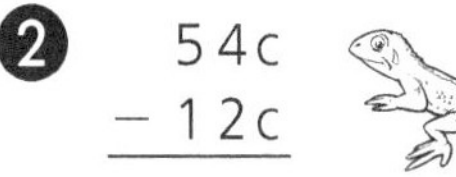

❸ Aziz saved his pocket money for five weeks. If he got $2 a week, how much did he save? ______

❹ Show 5 forty-five on this clock.
5 forty-five is the same as ______ to ____.

❺ 22 − 17 = ______ so 17 + ______ = 22

The difference between 17 and 22 is ______.

❻ Use the jump strategy to find:

a 46 + 39 = ______

b 51 − 36 = ______

❼ 5 fives take away 2 fives = ______

❽ How many wheels on 2 cars?

2 groups of ______ = ______ 2 × 4 = ______

❾ What is half of 16? ______

❿ Days in 5 weeks? ______

9:4

Extension

out of 7

❶ 76 − 27 = ______ so 27 + ______ = 76
The difference between 27 and 76 is ______.

❷

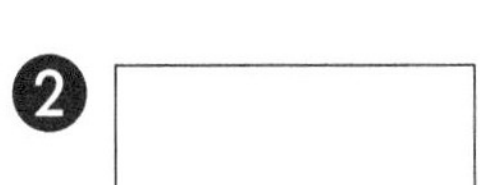

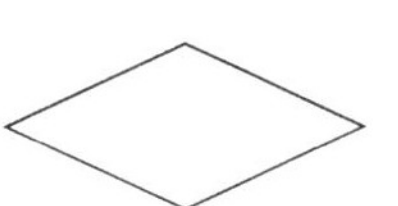

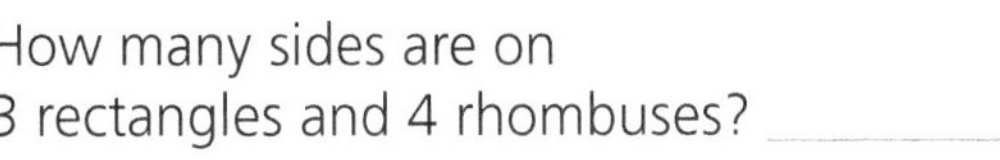

How many sides are on 3 rectangles and 4 rhombuses? ______

❸ Is the length of a 30 cm ruler closer to one quarter or one half of a metre? ______

❹ Which is larger, 3 × 5 or 8 + 8? ______

❺ How many lines of symmetry has a regular hexagon? ______

❻ **a** 3 rows of 5 plus 4 rows of 3. ______

b 2 rows of 5 plus 6 rows of 5 ______

c 2 rows of 7 plus 2 rows of 9 ______

❼ How many hexagons would be in row:

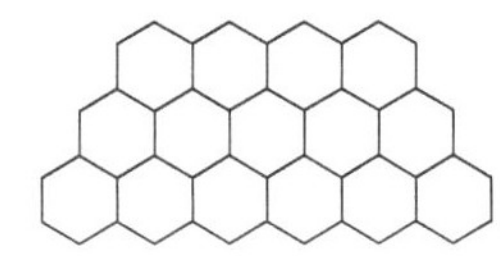

a 5? ______

b 10? ______

Challenge

Write as many number sentences as you can linking 40, 16 and 24.

______

______

______

Subtracting 9

Concept

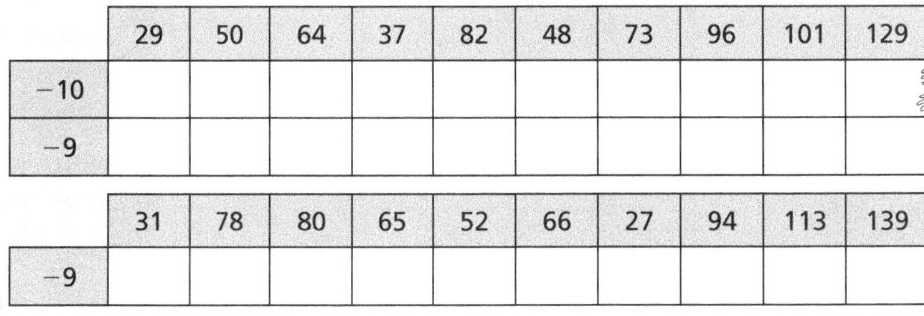

	29	50	64	37	82	48	73	96	101	129
−10										
−9										

	31	78	80	65	52	66	27	94	113	139
−9										

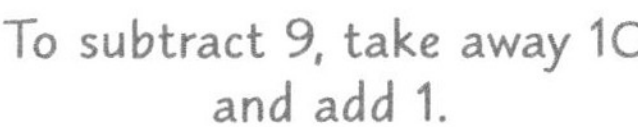

10:1 out of 18

1. 29 + 6 ____
2. 67 − 7 ____
3. 3 × 2 ____
4. 2 × 2 ____
5. $\begin{array}{r} 30 \\ +\ 12 \\ \hline \end{array}$
6. 3 × 5 ____
7. 1 × 5 ____
8. 2 × 10 ____
9. 4 × 10 ____
10. $\begin{array}{r} 53\text{c} \\ -\ 11\text{c} \\ \hline \end{array}$
11. 14 − 8 = ____ so 8 + ____ = 14

    The difference between 8 and 14 is ____.
12. Circle the abbreviation for metres.

    A M **B** ms **C** m **D** MS
13. What is the total of these coins? ____

14. I have 3 trays of cookies. There are 10 cookies on each tray.

    How many cookies altogether? ____
15. 50c + 20c + 10c ____
16. Which container would hold about 1 litre?

    A 

    B 

17. Use the jump strategy to find:

    26 + 8 = ____

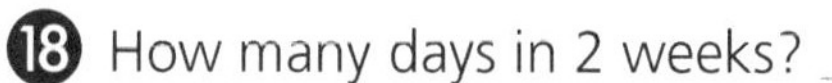

18. How many days in 2 weeks? ____

10:2 out of 18

1. 38 + 13 ____
2. 62 − 13 ____
3. 4 × 2 ____
4. 8 × 2 ____
5. 4 × 5 ____
6. 8 × 5 ____
7. 9 × 10 ____
8. 10 × 10 ____
9. The total value of these notes is ____.

10. Are you taller than 1 metre? ____.
11. 29 − 15 = ____ so 15 + ____ = 29

    The difference between 15 and 29 is ____.
12. Fingers on two hands. ____
13. **a** 12 − 6 = ____ **b** 22 − 6 = ____

    c 32 − 6 = ____ **d** 42 − 6 = ____

    e 34 + 9 = ____ **f** 44 + 9 = ____

    g 54 + 9 = ____ **h** 64 + 9 = ____
14. How many 5c coins make 50c? ____
15. I have 34 cards.

    How many more do I need so I have 42?

    ____ + ____ = ____
16. 2 thirty means ____ past ____.

    Show 2 thirty on this clock.

17. The abbreviation for 1 metre. ____
18. What holds more,

    a mug or a 1 litre bottle? ____

Addition linked with subtraction

a

7 − 4 = ____	4 + ____ = 7

The difference is ____.

b

10 − 8 = ____	8 + ____ = 10

The difference is ____.

c

13 − 5 = ____	____ + 5 = 13

The difference is ____.

d

28 − 12 = ____	12 + ____ = 28

The difference is ____.

e

34 − 12 = ____	12 + ____ = 34

The difference is ____.

f

44 − 36 = ____	36 + ____ = 44

The difference is ____.

10:3   ☐ out of 8

1. Complete the first 6 multiples of:

   a 10. 10, ____, ____, ____, ____, ____

   b 5. 5, ____, ____, ____, ____, ____

2. I have 6 rows of 10 trees.

   How many trees altogether? ____

3. Is the height of a door greater than 1 m? ____

4. What is the total of these coins? ____

5. Show 8 forty-five on this clock.

   We can also write this time as ________ to ____.

6. 32 – 23 = ____   so 23 + ____ = 32

   The difference between 23 and 32 is ____.

7. Use the jump strategy to find:

   a 47 + 35 = ____

   b 53 − 25 = ____

8. How many wheels on 5 cars? ____

   5 groups of ____ = ____
   5 × 4 = ____

10:4   Extension   ☐ out of 5

1. Chloe spent $2 each day for two fortnights.

   How much did she spend? ____

2. 5 sheep and 6 chickens.

   How many legs? ____

3. Colour the coins that are equal in value to twenty-two 10-cent coins.

4. What is the total value of three $2.00 coins and three 50c coins? ____

5. Find the difference between the total of the 2 smallest-value coins and the total of the 2 largest-value coins. ____

Challenge

Explain different ways you can make $3, e.g. $1 + $1 + 50c + 20c + 20c + 10c.

____

____

____

____

____

____

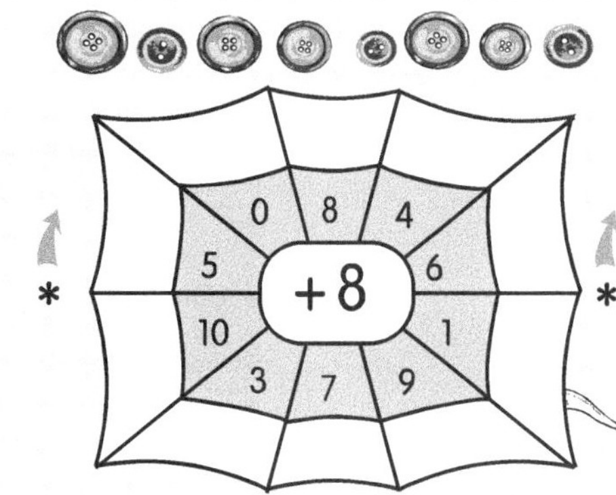

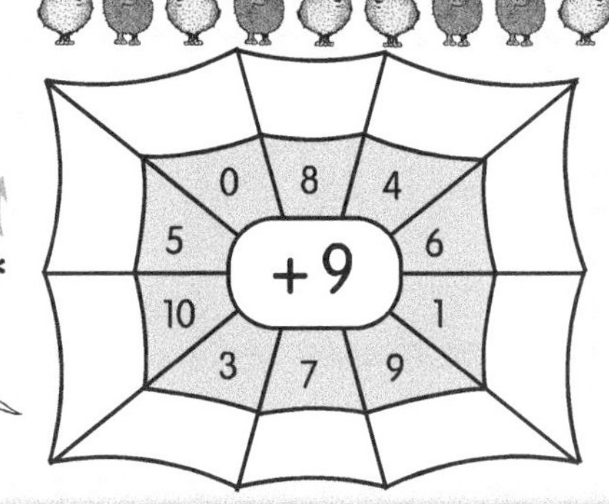

11:1 ☐ out of 18

1. 13 + 5 ______
2. 23 + 5 ______
3. 33 + 5 ______
4. 43 + 5 ______
5. $\begin{array}{r} 50 \\ +\ 30 \\ \hline \end{array}$
6. 10 × 2 ______
7. 5 × 2 ______
8. 2 × 10 ______
9. 5 × 10 ______
10. $\begin{array}{r} 70c \\ -\ 20c \\ \hline \end{array}$
11. 12 metres minus 6 metres. ______
12. Which coin is worth more than 20c, but less than $1? ______
13. I bought a cake for 10c and an iceblock for 50c. How much did I spend? ______
14.

Container	Estimate	Measure
Jug	8 cups	7 cups
Tub	28 cups	33 cups

How many cups does:

a the jug hold? ______

b the tub hold? ______

15. Circle the numbers that round off to 60.

54	61	67	69	51	56
55	59	64	58	65	

16. 563 = ______ hundreds, ______ tens, ______ ones
17. Double 6 then halve your answer. ______
18. a Share 10 between 2. ______ each

    b Share 10 between 5. ______ each

11:2 ☐ out of 18

1. 48 + 6 ______
2. 38 + 6 ______
3. 28 + 6 ______
4. 18 + 6 ______
5. 6 × 2 ______
6. 8 × 2 ______
7. 8 × 5 ______
8. 9 × 5 ______
9. 473 = ____ hundreds, ____ tens, ____ ones
10. 542 = ______ hundreds + ______ ones

    or ______ tens + ______ ones
11. Is the width of an elephant about 2 metres? ______
12. a How many 5 cent coins? ______

    b What is the total value? ______

13. 20c + 5c + 10c + 50c ______
14. Circle the numbers that round off to 400.

321	412	392	351
456	333	406	349

15. The total value of these notes.

______

16. 482 = ______ hundreds, ______ tens, ______ ones
17. 345, 355, 365, ______, ______, ______
18. a 265 + 17 − 17 = ______

    b 534 + 21 − 21 = ______

Rounding a number to the nearest ten

If it ends in 5, 6, 7, 8 or 9, round up.

If it ends in 1, 2, 3 or 4, round down.

a Is 36 closer to 30 or 40? ______

b is 33 closer to 30 or 40? ______

Round each of these to the nearest ten.

c 44 ______ **d** 17 ______ **e** 85 ______

11:3 ☐ out of 9

1. 9 is a square number. List other square numbers. ________

2. Is your teacher taller than 1 metre? ________

3. Circle the numbers that round off to 800.

851	809	751	793	783
824	750	850	849	

4. 904 = ____ hundreds, ____ tens, ____ ones

5. **a** Colour half. **b** Colour one quarter.

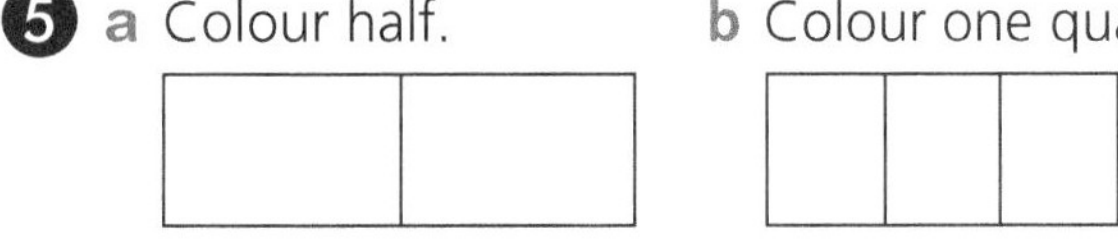

c Colour one eighth.

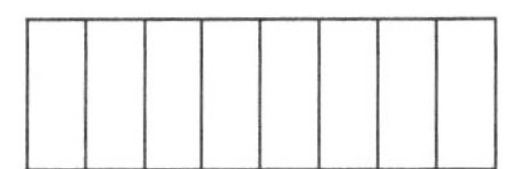

6. What is the total of these coins? ________

   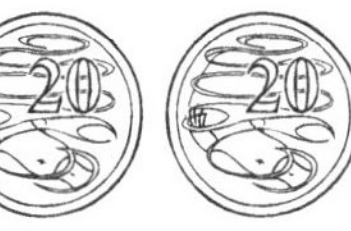

7. Write coins or notes that would make:

a $2.75 ________

b $5.25 ________

c $16.60 ________

8. Would it take 3 minutes or 3 hours to eat a sandwich? ________

9. **a** 10, 12, 14 ____, ____, ____, ____, ____

b 10, 20, 30 ____, ____, ____, ____, ____

c 23, 33, 43 ____, ____, ____, ____, ____

Extension

11:4 ☐ out of 6

1. How many 5c coins make $2? ________

2. How many 10c coins could I get from:

a $2.10? ________ **b** $4.20? ________

3. If this pattern were repeated, what would the 8th shape be? ________

 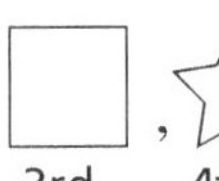

1st 2nd 3rd 4th

4. How many different ways can you order these pictures in a row? ________

5. Halve 84 then halve your answer. ________

6. 100 years = 1 c ________

Challenge

Draw and label containers that hold more than 1 litre.

When you play noughts and crosses, in how many different ways can you make:

a a line of three crosses? ________

b two noughts, side by side? ________

12:1   ☐ out of 14

1. 6 + _____ = 13
2. 8 + _____ = 14
3. 9 + _____ = 15
4. Digits in 354 _____
5. 5 × 5 _____
6. 5 × 2 _____
7. 5 × 10 _____
8. 3 × 5 _____
9. 935 = ____ hundreds + ____ tens + ____ ones

   or ____ tens + ____ ones

   or _____ ones
10. Circle the numbers that round off to 70.

    74   71   78   63   69   73
    68   65   66   75   67
11. cm stands for _________________.

    m stands for _________________.
12. 

    a Which is the longest path? ________

    b Which is the shortest path? ________
13. Colour:

    a $\frac{1}{3}$ b $\frac{1}{4}$

    c $\frac{1}{5}$ 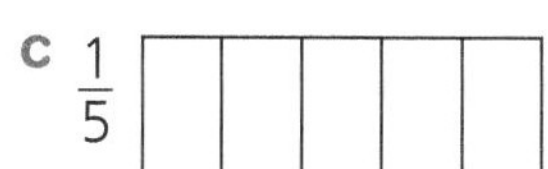   d $\frac{1}{10}$
14. a 349, 449, 549, _____, _____, _____

    b 418, 428, 438, _____, _____, _____

12:2   ☐ out of 20

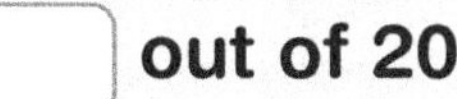

1. 16 + _____ = 25
2. 19 + _____ = 27
3. 35 + 15 _____
4. 25 + 65 _____
5. $\begin{array}{r} 40 \\ +\,30 \\ \hline \end{array}$
6. 8 × 2 _____
7. 8 × 5 _____
8. 8 × 10 _____
9. 6 × 5 _____
10. $\begin{array}{r} \$50 \\ -\,\$30 \\ \hline \end{array}$
11. Centimetres in 1 metre. ________
12. True or false? Your fingernail is about 1 cm long. ________
13. Write 3 metre 75 centimetres using short form. ________
14. 537 cm can be written as ____ m ____ cm.
15. 7 m 39 cm can be written as _____ cm.
16. The coloured part is _____ out of _____. $\frac{\square}{5}$ 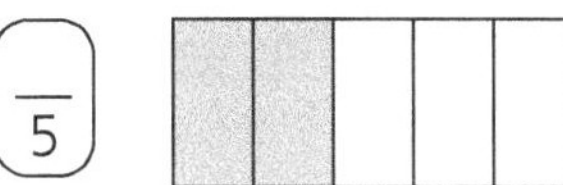
17. 91 tens and 5 ones = _____
18. Circle the numbers that round off to 300.

    328   349   250   241   249
    351   240   261   350
19. Circle 4 fifths. Write the fraction not circled.

     $\frac{\square}{\square}$
20. a 35 + 8 = 40 + _____

    b 67 + 9 = 70 + _____

Rounding to the nearest hundred

Look at the tens digit to see if you should round up or down.

Round up if the tens digit is 5, 6, 7, 8 or 9.
Round down if the digit is 1, 2, 3 or 4.

a Is 340 closer to 300 or 400? ________

b Is 653 closer to 600 or 700? ________

Round each of these to the nearest 100.

c 339 _____ **d** 814 _____ **e** 751 _____ **f** 490 _____ **g** 119 _____

12:3   ☐ out of 12

1.
$$\begin{array}{r} 34 \\ +\ 35 \\ \hline \end{array}$$

2.
$$\begin{array}{r} \$46 \\ -\ \$31 \\ \hline \end{array}$$

3.
$$\begin{array}{r} 53 \\ +\ 25 \\ \hline \end{array}$$

4. What part is shaded? $\frac{\square}{\square}$
   ______ out of ______ 
5. Is a giraffe taller than 1 metre? ______
6. Centimetres in 1 metre. ______
7. 629 cm can be written as ____ m ____ cm.
8. 9 m 21 cm can be written as ______ cm.
9. Circle the numbers that round off to 900.

937	949	950	957	849
851	840	961	850	

10. Colour:
    a $\frac{1}{5}$ ☐☐☐☐☐
    b $\frac{2}{5}$ ☐☐☐☐☐
    c $\frac{3}{5}$ ☐☐☐☐☐
11. a 2, 4, 6, ______, ______, ______, ______
    b 3, 6, 9, ______, ______, ______, ______
    c 5, 10, 15, ______, ______, ______, ______
    d 10, 20, 30, ______, ______, ______
12. a 28 + 7 = 30 + ____ b 48 + 9 = 50 + ____
    c 37 + 6 = 40 + ____ d 58 + 7 = 60 + ____

12:4   Extension   ☐ out of 8

1. 1 metre − 1 centimetre = ______
2. 50 cm is **half / a quarter / an eighth** of a metre.
3. Quarters in 6 apples. ______
4. a Half of 12 = ____ b A quarter of 12 = ____
5. How many 2 cm lengths could be cut from the ribbon below? ______
6. 
   What fraction is shaded?
   A $\frac{4}{20}$ B $\frac{5}{10}$ C $\frac{1}{4}$ ______
7. How many different ways can you order these pictures in a row? ______
8. a 5 pentagons have ______ sides.
   b 5 hexagons would have ______ sides.

Challenge

Write numbers that would round to 700.

______

______

______

______

Writing fractions

The part shaded is:

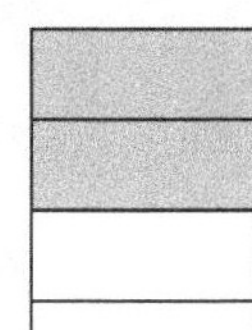

2 out of 4 or $\frac{2}{4}$

a 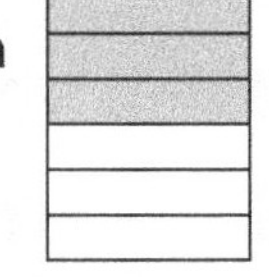 ____ out of ____ or $\frac{\square}{\square}$

b 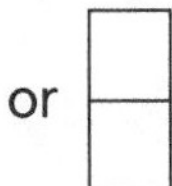 ____ out of ____ or $\frac{\square}{\square}$

c 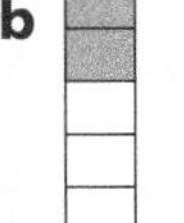 ____ out of ____ or $\frac{\square}{\square}$

d  ____ out of ____ or $\frac{\square}{\square}$

13:1 ☐ out of 16

1. 40 + 40 ____
2. 50 − 20 ____
3. 3 × 2 ____
4. 4 × 2 ____
5. 20 + 40 ____
6. 3 × 5 ____
7. 4 × 5 ____
8. 3 × 10 ____
9. 4 × 10 ____
10. 80c − 40c ____
11. Each half is: ☐☐
    ____ out of ____ equal parts.
12. Which line is:
    a 2 cm long? ____
    b 3 cm long? ____

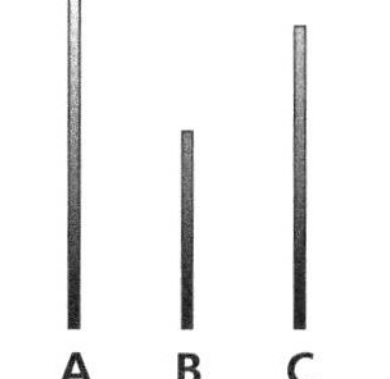

13. Would you use centimetres (cm) or metres (m) to measure the length of a rabbit? ____.
14. Is the width of your finger about 1 cm? ____
15. What part is shaded? ____ out of ____

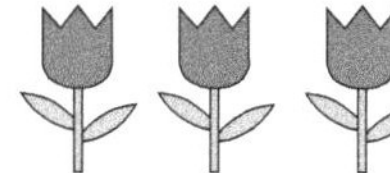

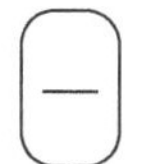

16. The part coloured is ____ out of ____.

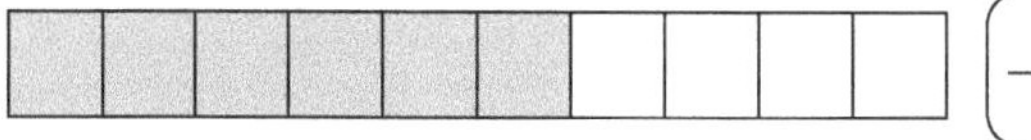

13:2 ☐ out of 18

1. 34 + 25 ____
2. 39 − 34 ____
3. 5 × 2 ____
4. 6 × 2 ____
5. 5 × 5 ____
6. 6 × 5 ____
7. 5 × 10 ____
8. 6 × 10 ____
9. Complete the first 7 multiples of:
   a 2. 2, ____, ____, ____, ____, ____, ____
   b 5. 5, ____, ____, ____, ____, ____, ____
10. Write 1 metre 65 centimetres using the short form. ____
11. 981 cm can be written as ____ m ____ cm.
12. 6 m 15 cm can be written as ____ cm.
13. The part coloured is ____ out of ____.

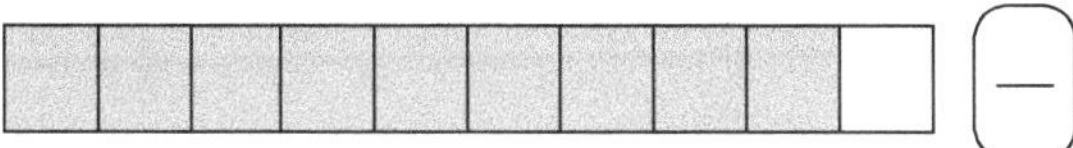

14. What part is shaded?
    ____ out of ____

15. An oven is less than 15 cm high. True or false? ____.

16. Measure each line in centimetres.
    A ____
    B ____
    C ____
17. Is 32 closer to 30 or 40? ____
18. Round 459 to the nearest hundred. ____

Using number lines

−4 −10 −2

19 20 21 22 23 24 25 26 27 28 29 30 31 32 33 34 35 36 37 38 39 40 41 42

We don't have to write all the numbers.

Jump to the nearest ten to add or subtract. These jumps show 42 – 16 = 26.

a 66 – 27 = ____ **b** 52 – 15 = ____ **c** 71 – 36 = ____

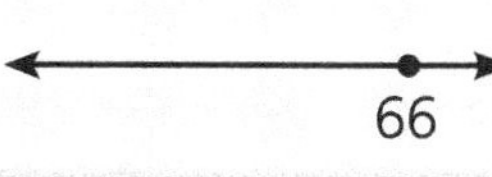

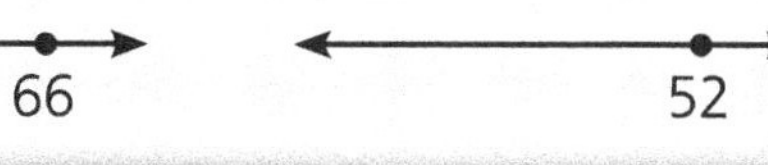

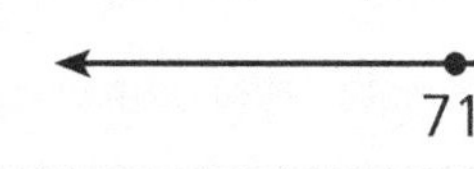

13:3 ☐ out of 11

1. The part coloured is ______ out of ______.

■	■								

$\frac{\square}{\square}$

2. Round 54 to the nearest 10. ______
3. Measure the height of this page to the nearest centimetre. ______
4. Write 4 metres 27 centimetres using the short form. ______
5. Which is bigger, one quarter or one half? ______
6. Is the length of this about 1 cm, 3 cm or 5 cm? ______

7. Would you use centimetres (cm) or metres (m) to measure the height of a cup? ______
8. 26 days and 22 days.

   How many days altogether?

   ______ + ______ = ______
9. Is the width of your finger about 1 cm? ______
10. Use the jump strategy to find:

    47 + 35 = ______

11. Which is larger, 492, 941 or 914? ______

13:4 ☐ out of 6

Extension

1. Centimetres in 3 metres. ______
2. a Draw a line to show the halfway point.

   b Draw 2 more lines to make quarters.

   c Colour one quarter of this group.
3. How many halves in 2 oranges? ______
4. a Colour half of this shape.

   b How many quarters in one half? ______

   c What is larger: $\frac{1}{2}$ or $\frac{1}{4}$? ______

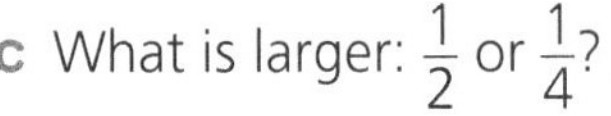

5. a What part is shaded?

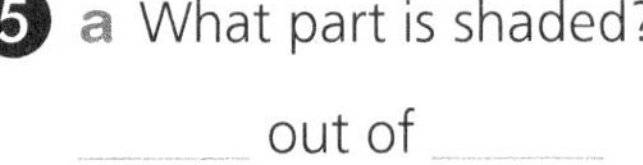

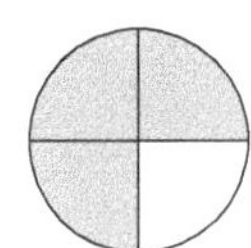

   ______ out of ______

   b 3 quarters plus 1 quarter. ______
6. Use this picture to fill in the boxes.

   a ☐ − 6 = ☐

   b ☐ − 9 = ☐

Challenge

Use the jump strategy to find 43 − 28.

+	5	10	4	0	2	6	1	3
2								
3								
4								
5								
10								

14:1 out of 16

1. 10 × 2 ______
2. 15 − 3 ______
3. 11 + 6 ______
4. 11 − 3 ______
5. 30 + 40
6. Add 4 and 7. ______
7. 6 minus 2. ______
8. Total 5 and 3. ______
9. 9 shared by 3. ______
10. 50c − 40c
11. Would you use centimetres (cm) or metres (m) to measure the length of a pool? ______
12. Circle the duck 2nd from the right.

13. Use the jump strategy to find:

    59 + 18 = ______

14. Use mental strategies to find:

    a 300 + 200 = ______ b 18 + 6 + 2 = ______

    c 32 + 21 = ______ d 19 + 9 = ______

15. Subtract 2 from each part on the left, to make these number sentences equal.

    a 19 − 12 = 17 − ______

    b 26 − 22 = 24 − ______

16. Write 6 metres 93 centimetres using the short form. ______

14:2 out of 15

1. 23 + 61 ______
2. 56 − 51 ______
3. 41 + 42 ______
4. 45 − 21 ______
5. 3 × 5 ______
6. 7 × 2 ______
7. 9 × 10 ______
8. 4 × 2 ______
9. Subtract 3 from each part on the left, to make these number sentences equal.

    a 22 – 13 = 19 – ______

    b 28 – 23 = 25 – ______

10. Going up from **A**, where do I finish if I turn 2nd on the left, then 1st right, then right then keep going?

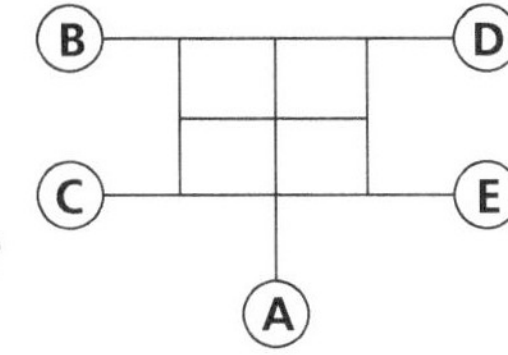

______

11. a Double the answer to 5 plus 16. ______

    b Halve the answer to 38 – 10. ______

12. Write 1 m 35 cm in centimetres. ______ cm
13. Follow the directions and colour the path of the counter.

    Move 2 down, then 4 right, then 3 up.

14. Use the jump strategy to find:
    34 − 16 = ______

15. Use the compensation strategy to find:

    a 38 + 19 = ______ b 27 + 19 = ______

rows of 5

groups of 5

	2	4	6	8	10
× 5					

	2	4	6	8	10
× 10					

14:3 ☐ out of 4

1. The part coloured is ______ out of ______.

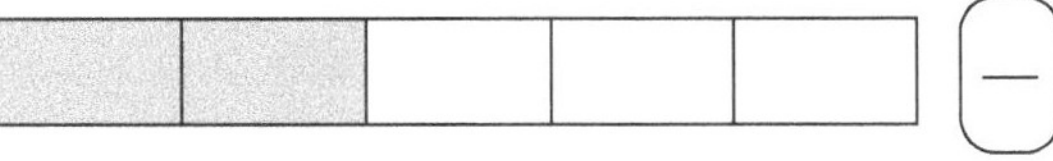

2. Use the compensation strategy to find:

   a $45 + 19 =$ ______ b $34 + 29 =$ ______

   c $68 + 26 =$ ______ d $83 - 19 =$ ______

   e $76 - 39 =$ ______ f $54 - 18 =$ ______

3. **Road map**

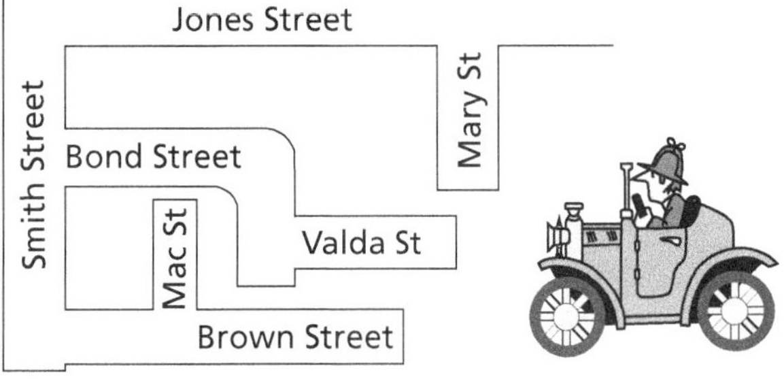

   a Mac Street joins ______

   b Mary Street joins ______

   c Valda Street joins ______

   d What Street joins Jones Street and Brown Street? ______

   e What other streets do you travel on to get from Valda Street to Mac Street?

   ______

   ______

4. Use the jump strategy to find:

   $61 - 24 =$ ______

14:4 ☐ out of 6

Extension

1. Centimetres in 7 metres. ______
2. 2 metres minus 50 cm. ______
3. Quarters in 5 pears. ______
4. Where does the ant stop if he goes: 2 up, 3 left, 1 down, 5 right and then 3 up? ______

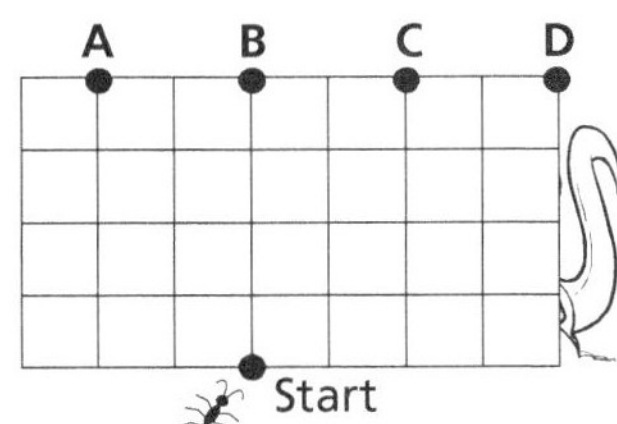

5. True or false?

   a $4 \times 5 = 2 \times 10$ ______

   b $8 \times 5 = 4 \times 10$ ______

6. Circle the correct number sentence for this picture.

   A $2 \times 5 = 10$ **C** $12 - 2 = 10$

   B $2 \times 7 = 14$ **D** $7 + 5 = 12$

Challenge

$39 + 25 =$ ☐

Explain how you found your answer.

______

______

______

tables

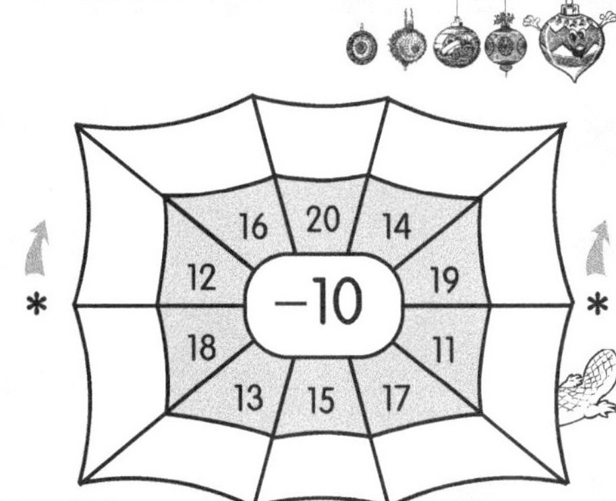

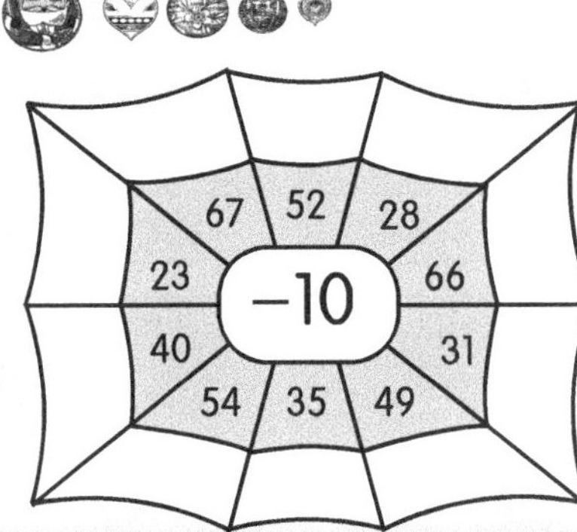

Take away one ten.

15:1 ☐ out of 17

1. 23 + 10 ____
2. 22 − 10 ____
3. 20 + 30 ____
4. 32 + 14 ____
5. $\begin{array}{r} 24 \\ +\ 24 \\ \hline \end{array}$
6. 8 × 2 ____
7. 5 × 5 ____
8. 7 × 10 ____
9. 9 × 10 ____
10. $\begin{array}{r} 35c \\ -\ 13c \\ \hline \end{array}$
11. The number modelled is ________.

12. Is the width of a door about 1 metre? ________
13. Can we measure height in metres, litres or grams? ________
14. Is it likely that you will go to school tomorrow? ________
15. Write a number sentence that has the same answer as 14 – 8, then write the answer.

____

16. a 546 = ____ tens + ____ ones

b 735 = ____ tens + ____ ones

c 937 = ____ tens + ____ ones

17. a 300 + 400 = ____ b 200 + 200 = ____

c 500 + 200 = ____ d 400 + 400 = ____

15:2 ☐ out of 15

1. 45 + 10 ____
2. 62 − 10 ____
3. 300 + 500 ____
4. 38 + 19 ____
5. 9 × 2 ____
6. 9 × 5 ____
7. 8 × 10 ____
8. 10 × 10 ____
9. Rewrite these by subtracting 20 or 30.

a 56 − 24 = ____ − ____ = ____
(–20) (–20)

b 69 − 28 = ____ − ____ = ____
(–20) (–20)

c 58 − 35 = ____ − ____ = ____
(–30) (–30)

10. Is the length of your foot longer than 40 cm? ________
11. Write the numeral shown on the abacus. ________

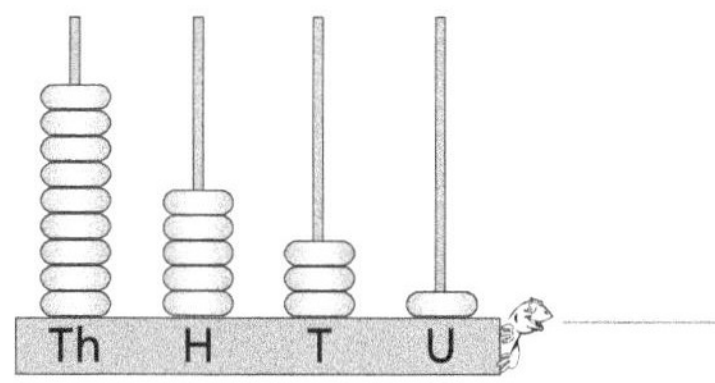

12. Write 4 m 72 cm in centimetres. ________ cm
13. What numbers could I roll on a standard 6-sided dice?

____

14. Write a number sentence that is equal to 24 – 13, then write the answer. ________
15. Colour 4 fifths of this shape.

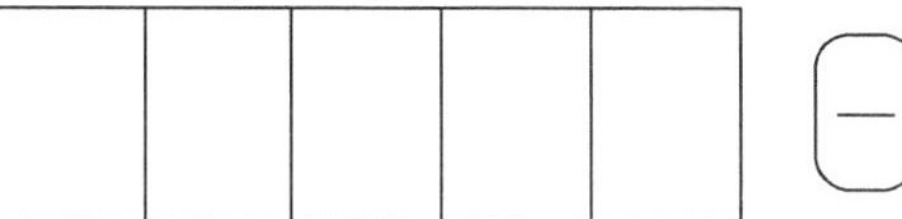

Place the letter from these boxes on the line below, in order, from *least likely* to *most likely*.

The next person to walk through the classroom door will be:

A a teacher	**B** the principal	**C** my mother
D a human	**E** a father	**F** a boy

least likely ________________ most likely

15:3 out of 10

1
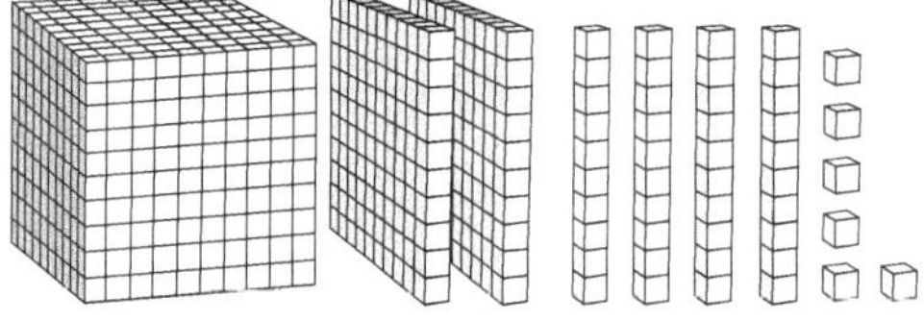

tens	ones
$4	4
+ $5	3

2

tens	ones
$6	3
+ $2	1

3 The number modelled is ______

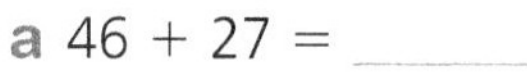

4 How many digits in 4302? ______

5 Write the numeral for five thousand, four hundred and twenty-three. ______

6 Bridge to the next 10 to find:

a 47 + 6 = ______ b 28 + 7 = ______

7 Use the jump strategy to find:

a 46 + 27 = ______

46

b 73 − 27 = ______

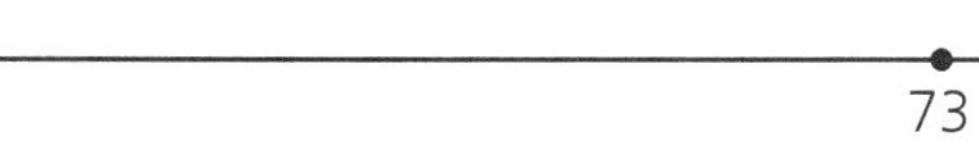

73

8 Use the compensation strategy to find:

a 46 + 19 = ______ b 38 + 29 = ______

9 Is 5192 odd or even? ______

10 a 5000 + 300 + 20 + 9 = ______

b 9000 + 500 + 10 + 7 = ______

15:4 out of 8

Extension

1 Quarters in 10 oranges. ______

2 Write 3 even numbers that are larger than 4203 and less than 4214.

______

3 How many faces are on 10 cubes? ______

4 In a race I am 7th out of 10. How many:

a are in front of me? ______

b are behind me? ______

5 How many cakes will be in the 16th row of this pattern?

______

6 Write three different 1-digit numbers that add to give 24. ______

7 Does 4 × 5 = 2 × 10? ______

8 Write the next odd number after 6029. ______

Challenge

84 − 29 = ☐

Explain how you found your answer.

______

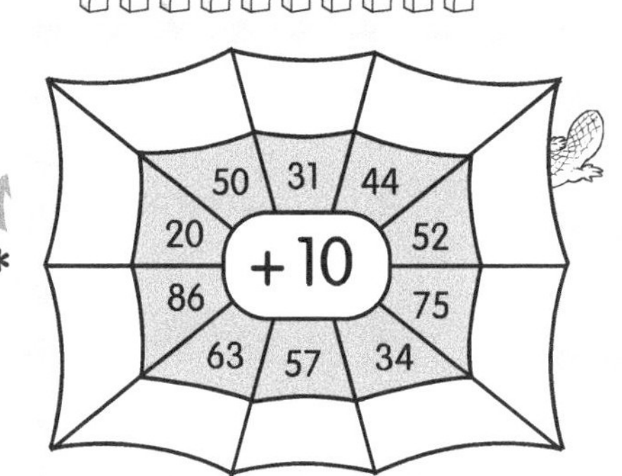

16:1 out of 18

1. 300 + 100 ____
2. 600 − 100 ____
3. 35 + 21 ____
4. 45 + 10 ____
5. 44 + 44
6. Digits in 193. ____
7. Half of 16. ____
8. Double 7. ____
9. 6 × 5 ____
10. 67c − 20c
11. Is it likely that the next school bus you see will have passengers on it? ____

12. When I toss a coin am I more likely to toss a head than a tail? ____
13. Write a number sentence that has the same answer as 15 – 12, then write the answer. ____
14. Write the numeral six thousand, five hundred and seventy-two. ____
15. Show the time twenty-two past 10.

16. Circle the largest number.

    5309, 5911, 5400
17. How many digits in 5299? ____
18. a September is the ____ month of the year.

    b July is the ____ month of the year.

16:2 out of 16

1. 400 + 500 ____
2. 800 − 500 ____
3. 67 + 24 ____
4. Half of 28. ____
5. Digits in 100. ____
6. Half of 18. ____
7. Double 9. ____
8. 8 groups of 5. ____
9. a 32 – 19 = ____ – ____ = ____ (+1) (+1)

   b 43 – 34 = ____ – ____ = ____ (+6) (+6)
10. Colour 3 fifths of this length.

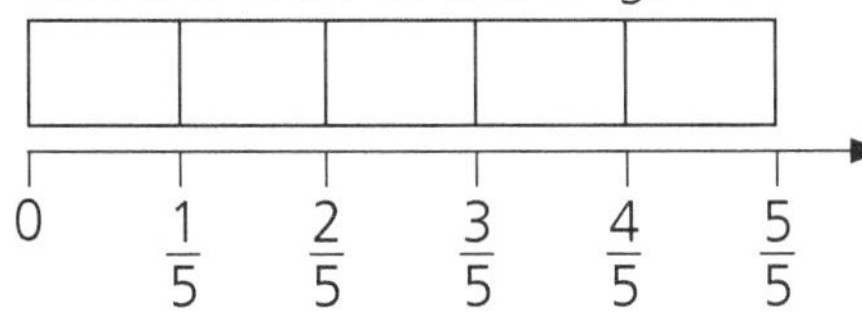

11. Write 4501 in words. ____
12. If I toss a coin 10 times, am I very unlikely to get 10 heads? ____
13. Is there an even chance that I will choose a white ball from the container if I choose without looking? ____

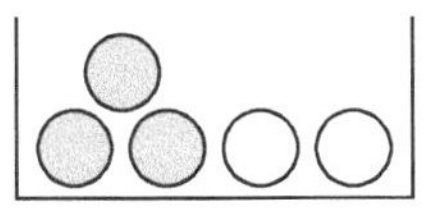

14. Is there an even chance of landing on **A**? ____

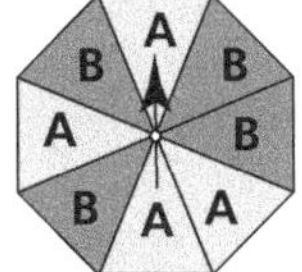

15. 3523 = ____ thousands, ____ hundreds, ____ tens, ____ ones
16. Is 5290 odd or even? ____

How many minutes are in:

a one hour? ____

b half an hour? ____

c a quarter of an hour? ____

d three quarters of an hour? ____

For this clock, how many minutes is it:

e after 6 o'clock? ____

f before 7 o'clock? ____

16:3 out of 9

1. a 200 + 500 = ______ b 600 + 300 = ______
   c 100 + 800 = ______ d 500 + 400 = ______
2. Show the time 11 minutes to 1.

3. What number is shown here? ______

4. Colour $\frac{3}{8}$ of this shape.

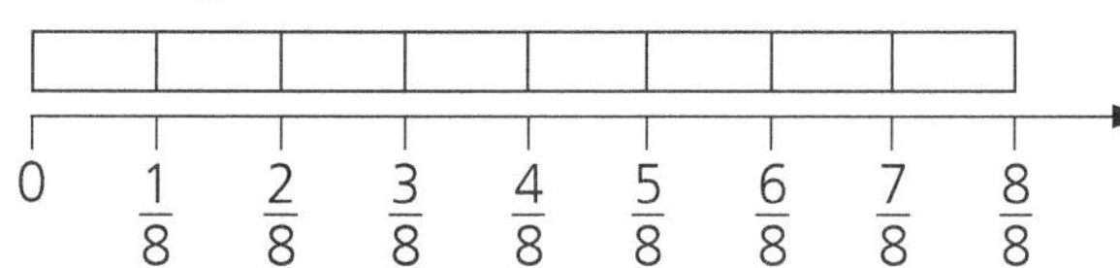

5. Circle the largest number.
   6999, 7020, 7011, 7001
6. If I toss 10 coins, will I always get the same number of heads and tails? ______
7. Am I more likely to pick out a white or grey ball when I take one without looking? ______

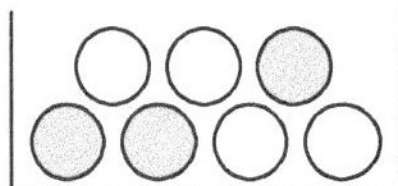

8. 38 – 27 = ______ – ______

   Each side is equal to ______.

Extension 16:4 out of 8

1. a 13 minutes after 20 to 4 is ______.
   b 18 minutes before two past 1 is ______.
2. How many blocks would be in the 6th row? ______

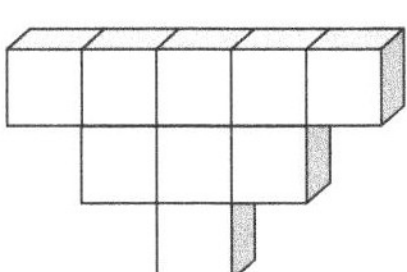

3. Circle $\frac{1}{3}$.
4. Wings on 14 owls. ______
5. 60 – 10 – 5 – 5 – 10 ______
6. How many eggs in 3 dozen? ______

7. 73 was doubled and that answer was halved. What was the result? ______
8. What fraction of an hour is.
   a 15 minutes? ______
   b 30 minutes? ______

Challenge

Write chance statements about this spinner.

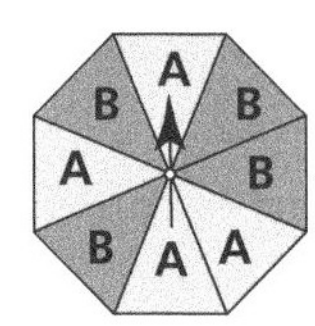

______
______
______
______
______

Concept

Use these clocks to give the Roman numeral for:

a 4 ______ b 5 ______ c 9 ______
d 10 ______ e 11 ______ f 12 ______

Write our numeral for:

g IX ______ h XI ______ i VI ______

17:1 out of 17

1. 3×2 ____
2. Double 7. ____
3. 2×5 ____
4. 6×5 ____
5. 62 + 23
6. Digits in 193. ____
7. 6 shared by 2. ____
8. Half of 16. ____
9. 10 shared by 2. ____
10. 83c − 31c
11. What is the abbreviation for kilogram? ____
12. Would your shoes weigh more or less than a kilogram? ____
13. How many sides on:
   a 2 triangles? ____
   b 3 triangles? ____

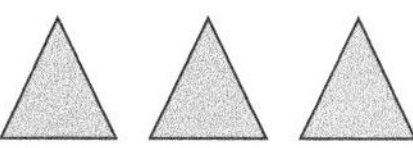

14. Colour one sixth of the fish.

15. The time shown is ____

16. Circle the correct abbreviation.

   4 KG, 4 kg, 4 Kg, 4 Kgs, 4 kgs

17. 345, 445, 545, ____, ____, ____

17:2 out of 16

1. 3×5 ____
2. 5×5 ____
3. 4×5 ____
4. 38 + 12 ____
5. 38 + 24 ____
6. 54 − 28 ____
7. 54 − 32 ____
8. 29 − 18 ____
9. a 3, 6, 9, ____, ____, ____, ____
   b 6, 12, 18, ____, ____, ____, ____
   c 7, 14, 21, ____, ____, ____, ____
10. True or false? 1 litre of water has a mass of 1 kilogram. ____
11. What is the time shown on this clock? ____ past ____

12. Use the short form to write 3 kilograms. ____
13. Write the numeral for the number shown on this abacus. ____

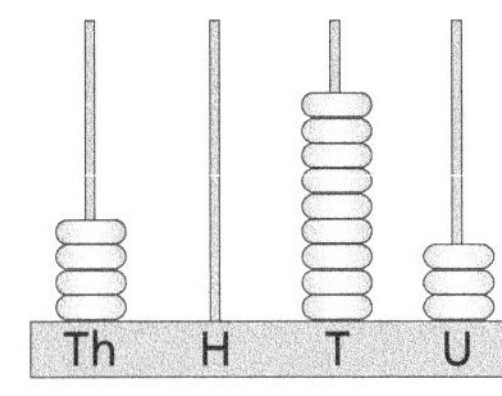

14. Write the time that is three minutes before:
   a 6 to 7 ____
   b 18 to 11 ____
15. What part is shaded? ____ out of ____
16. 18 more than 46. ____

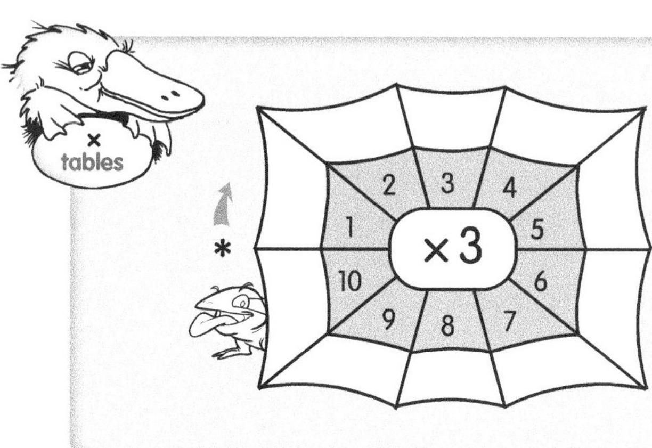

Can you memorise these x3 facts?

Answers

ID card answers

ID card A

1 metres 2 centimetres 3 millimetres 4 litres 5 kilograms 6 minutes 7 centimetre 8 centimetre 9 even numbers 10 odd numbers 11 ordinal numbers 12 digits 13 times (or multiply) 14 6 × 2 15 division or divide 16 division or divide 17 equal 18 number line 19 number sentence 20 numeral expander 21 abacus 22 table 23 picture graph 24 tally 25 column graph 26 sector graph 27 digital watch 28 analog clock 29 calendar 30 balance scales

ID card B

1 angle 2 right angle 3 parallel lines 4 perpendicular lines 5 triangle 6 square 7 rectangle 8 diamond or rhombus 9 trapezium 10 parallelogram 11 quadrilaterals 12 pentagons 13 hexagons 14 circle 15 oval 16 regular shapes 17 irregular shapes 18 side, corner 19 line of symmetry 20 net of a cube 21 corner 22 edge 23 face 24 cube 25 prism 26 pyramid 27 base 28 cylinder 29 cone 30 sphere

1:1

1 a 64 b 82 c 36 d 46 e 108 f 120 **2** 10 **3** equal

4 6, 8 **5** 7 **6** number line **7** 2 **8** 9 **9** 12 **10** 75

1:2

1 10 **2** 20 **3** 15 **4** 13 **5** 47 **6** 3 **7** $14 **8** 13, 15

9 10 **10** 49 **11** 8 – 4 = 4 **12** Half of the rectangle will be coloured.

13 a half past 8 (or 30 past 8) b quarter past 1 (or 15 past 1)

14 Four birds will be circled. **15** 4

Activity

3, 11, 4, 8, 12, 6, 10, 5, 9, 7

odd + odd = even

even + odd = odd

1:3

1 14 **2** 17 **3** 19 **4** 33 **5** 22 **6** 8, 10 **7** 26 **8** 19

9 nineteen **10** a 25 b 23 **11** 28 **12** 52 **13** January

14 a 25 b 49 c 96 d 75 **15** quarters, One quarter will be coloured. **16** 4th **17** 48, 50 **18** One pelican will be circled.

19 55c **20** 7

1:4

1 6 **2** 42, 32, 22 **3** 12, 15, 18, 21

4 (10 + 30) + (5 + 8) = 40 + 13 = 53 **5** 3 **6** 20, 12, 8

7 4, 2 and 1 **8** 90 days (91 days in a leap year)

9 summer (except in a leap year where summer and spring both have 91 days) **10** 8

Challenge

Answers will vary.

Activity

Answers will vary.

2:1

1 a 85 b 120 c 111 d 121 e 49 f 46 **2** a 20 b 20

3 30 **4** 18 **5** 7 **6** 3, Each family has 3 rabbits. **7** 30

2:2

1 20 **2** 14 **3** 3 **4** 2 **5** 82 **6** 8 **7** 10 **8** 5 **9** 4

10 12 **11** a One part of the rectangle will be coloured.
b One part of the rectangle will be coloured.

12 a 83 b 78 c 97 d 68

13 a 56 b 92

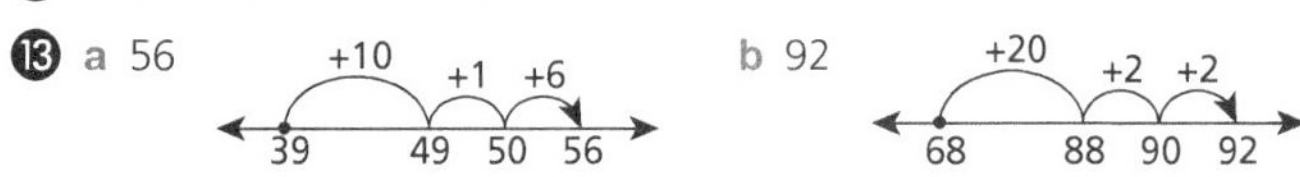

14 15, 15 **15** **A** rectangle **B** hexagon **C** trapezium

16 a 31 b 30

Activity

13, 9, 6, 4, 10, 12, 8, 5, 11, 7

15, 11, 8, 6, 12, 14, 10, 7, 13, 9

odd + odd = even

2:3

1 46 **2** 40 **3** 26 **4** 47 **5** 26 **6** 11 **7** 66 **8** 40

9 a 53 (number line: 28 +20 → 48 +2 → 50 +3 → 53) b 73 (number line: 39 +30 → 69 +1 → 70 +3 → 73)

10 a 8 apples b 3 groups of 4 = 12 apples **11** a 3 b 3

12 13, 13 – 4 = 9 13 – 9 = 4 **13** The fish will be circled.

2:4

1 a 8 b 8 **2** a 3 b 1 **3** BE KIND **4** quarter to 4 or 3:45

5 4 small rectangles will be coloured. **6** 30

Challenge

Answer will vary, e.g. 10 + 5, 3 × 5, 18 – 3

Activity

5, 10, 12, 9, 11, 7, 4, 6, 3, 8

12, 8, 7, 9, 6, 8, 13, 11, 10, 5

3:1

1 a quarter past 6 or 15 minutes past 6 b quarter to 11 or 15 minutes to 11 **2** a 12, 15, 18, 21 b 8, 10, 12, 14 c 40, 50, 60, 70

3 a 2 b 3 **4** $10 **5** a 10 b 10 c 9 d 1 **6** a jug b book **7** 4

3:2

1 20 **2** 17 **3** 5 **4** 2 **5** 19 **6** 43 **7** 67 **8** 2 **9** 6

10 24c **11** a 6 b 3 c 9 d 9 **12** 5 groups of 5 = 25

13 a 26 b 39 **14** 7, 15, 17 **15** 14, 14, 12 **16** a 4 b 6 c 3

17 a 550 will be circled. 500 will be underlined.
b 462 will be circled. 406 will be underlined.

Activity

5, 13, 9, 6, 10, 8, 12, 7, 11, 14

7, 15, 11, 8, 12, 10, 14, 9, 13, 16

3:3

1 12 **2** 16 **3** 14 **4** a 59 b 56 c 58 d 56 **5** 10 **6** 3, 8
7 a 3 b 7 **8** a 6 b 8 c 5 d 8 **9** a 10 b 25 c 16 d 12
10 a 7 b 12

3:4

1 yes **2** a 17 b 14 **3** a 20 b 25 c 40 **4** a A b B
5 180 minutes

Challenge

Answers will vary, e.g. 20c + 20c + 10c

Activity

6, 9, 12, 11, 7, 15, 10, 14, 8, 13
7, 10, 13, 12, 8, 16, 11, 15, 9, 14

4:1

1 20 **2** 11 **3** 2 **4** 2 **5** 16 **6** 20 **7** 8 **8** 10
9 a Dog b Mouse c 13 d 17 **10** a 2 b 2 c 5 d 5
11 **12** a 8, 10, 12, 14 b 70, 60, 50, 40
c 108, 110, 112 d 700, 600, 500
13 12 **14**

4:2

1 22 **2** 30 **3** 24 **4** 7 **5** 18 **6** 28 **7** 4 **8** 4 **9** 12
10 180 **11** 8 **12** a 14, 16, 18, 20 b 20, 25, 30, 35 c 14, 12, 10, 8
d 164, 174, 184 **13** a 18 b 19 c 25 d 40 **14** a blue
b orange c 12 d 10 **15** ~~||||~~ ~~||||~~ ||
16

Activity

5 + <u>5</u>, 1 + <u>9</u>, 8 + <u>2</u>, 3 + <u>7</u>, 7 + <u>3</u>, 4 + <u>6</u>, 6 + <u>4</u>, 2 + <u>8</u>
7 + <u>6</u>, 3 + <u>10</u>, 6 + <u>7</u>, 4 + <u>9</u>, 8 + <u>5</u>, 10 + <u>3</u>, 5 + <u>8</u>, 9 + <u>4</u>

4:3

1 20 **2** 20 **3** 19 **4** 60, 50, 40 **5** 653 **6** a 355 b 747
c 530 **7** a 63, 53, 43, 33 b 665, 655, 645 c 829, 929, 1029
8 2, 4, 6, 8 or 0 **9** **10** a 29 b 94 c 98 d 79
11 a 37 (+1, +7: 29, 30, 37) b 71 (+20, +2, +1: 48, 68, 70, 71)
12 a 4 b 9 c 8 d 7

4:4

1 350, 400, 450, 500 **2** 50 **3** 8 **4** 52 **5** 6, 3 **6** SMILE AT ME
7 a 80 b 80 **8** 14

Challenge

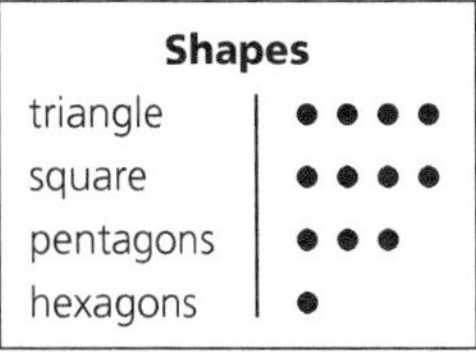

Shapes	
triangle	●●●●
square	●●●●
pentagons	●●●
hexagons	●

Activity

8, 16, 12, 9, 13, 11, 15, 17, 10, 14
10, 18, 14, 11, 15, 13, 17, 19, 16, 13

5:1

1 30 **2** 15 **3** 9 **4** 5 **5** 30 **6** 6 **7** 6 **8** 2
9 a △ b ⬠ c 3, 3 d 5, 5
10 234 | 2 hundreds | 3 tens | 4 ones |
11 two hundred and thirty-four **12** 354
13 12, (+3, +2: 7, 10, 12) **14** 63, 73, 83, 93

5:2

1 43 **2** 34 **3** 6 **4** 7 **5** 74 **6** 16 **7** 9 **8** 8
9 7 **10** 15c **11** octagon, 8, 8 **12** 391, 535, 902 **13** 604 **14** 518
15 autumn **16** a 12, 15, 18, 21 b 46, 36, 26, 16 c 142, 132
d 455, 465 **17** **18** a 4:45 or quarter to 5
b 7:15 or quarter past 7

Activity

a 6, 8, 10, 12, 14
b 15, 20, 25, 30, 35
c 20, 30, 40, 50, 60, 70, 80, 90

5:3

1 56 **2** 80 **3** 105 **4** 80
5 a Greg b Sue c 7 **6** | 5 hundreds | 5 tens | 0 ones |
7 a 8, 10, 12, 14 b 53, 63, 73, 83 c 135, 125, 115
8

9 5, 5

5:4

1 a 71 b 92 **2** 30 **3** 86 **4** 78 **5**
6 three hundred and forty-two
7 a 17, 20, 23 Rule: +3
b 25, 31, 37 Rule: +6
c 25, 32, 39 Rule: +7

Challenge

Answers will vary, e.g a face.

Activity

<u>January</u>, February, <u>March</u>, April, <u>May</u>, June, <u>July</u>, <u>August</u>, September, <u>October</u>, November, <u>December</u>

6:1

1 50 **2** 16 **3** 4 **4** 3 **5** 30 **6** 3 **7** 6 **8** 2 **9** A hexagon has 6 sides, 6 corners. A square has 4 sides, 4 corners.

10 4 hundreds, 9 tens, 3 ones

11 76, 129, 212, 236, 318

12 a 1 b 2 **13** a 4 b 4

14 7 hundreds 2 tens 5 ones

15 11, 13, 15, 17, 19 **16** fifty **17** nine hundred and three

18 169

6:2

1 36 **2** 22 **3** 21 **4** 23 **5** 40 **6** 3 **7** 2 **8** 46

9 a 3 squares × 3 squares b yes **10** 9 hundreds, 4 tens, 2 ones

11 801 **12** yes

13 758, 857, 875 **14** 359 **15**

16 a 9 b 40

Activity

(5) triangle (6) square (7) rectangle (11) quadrilaterals

(12) pentagons (13) hexagons (14) circle (15) oval

(18) side, corner

6:3

1 48 **2** 23c **3** 88 **4** 4 hundreds, 5 tens, 2 ones

5 **A** and **D** **6** a square b circle

7 a 43 b 74

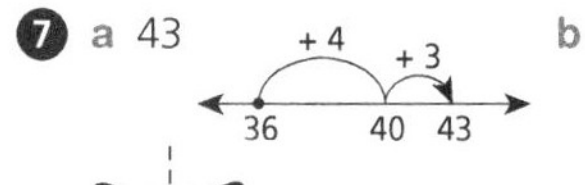

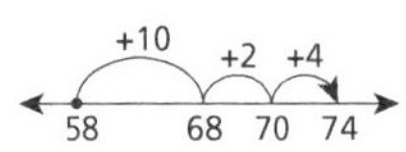

8 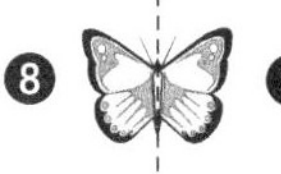 **9** a 13 b 4 c 13 d 9 **10** 31

6:4

1 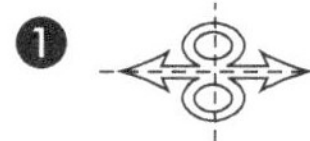 **2** 30 **3** 20 **4** 32 **5** 6 **6** 3

7 5 1 tens 8 ones

Challenge

Answers will vary, e.g. A or E

Activity

a 7 + 6 = 13, 6 + 7 = 13, 13 – 7 = 6, 13 – 6 = 7

b 8 + 5 = 13, 5 + 8 = 13, 13 – 8 = 5, 13 – 5 = 8

c 4 + 8 = 12, 8 + 4 = 12, 12 – 8 = 4, 12 – 4 = 8

7:1

1 63 **2** 25 **3** 4 **4** 2 **5** 46 **6** 15 **7** 10 **8** 10 **9** 30

10 12c **11** 6 hundreds, 3 tens, 5 ones **12** tally marks

13 a Leah b Anna c 7 d 26 **14** 4, 6, 8, 10, 12, 14

15 circle **16** a 8, 10, 12, 14, 16 b 12, 15, 18, 21, 24

7:2

1 43 **2** 49 **3** 6 **4** 12 **5** 10 **6** 2 **7** 4 **8** 8

9 a 8, 12, 16, 20, 24 b 10, 15, 20, 25, 30 c 20, 30, 40, 50, 60

10 5 hundreds, 8 tens, 6 ones **11** a 8 b 5 **12** 80

13 a Blue b Green c 65 d Yellow **14** a 15 b 7 c 15 d 8

15 20 **16** 462

Activity

12, 0, 10, 16, 4, 14, 8, 20, 6, 18

0, 0, 0, 0, 0, 0, 0, 0, 0, 0

7:3

1 49 **2** 42c **3** a rectangular prism b 6 c 8 d 12 e a rectangle **4** 14, 14 – 5 = 9, 14 – 9 = 5 **5** a 20 b 20 c 50 d 50 **6** 777 **7** 20, 30, 40, 50, 60, 70 **8** 555 **9** 12th **10** 3

7:4

1 **2** 53 tens and 1 one **3** 10, 15, 20, 25, 30, 35

4 Answers will vary, e.g. 0, 1, 4, 9, 16 **5** 34

Challenge

Answers will vary. For example, Greg made 16 trips to the store, Emily made 7 trips to the store, Kate made 7 more trips to the store than Emily.

Activity

10, 20, 30, 40, 50, 60, 70, 80, 90, 100

8:1

1 30 **2** 50 **3** 16 **4** 20 **5** 51 **6** 50 **7** 10 **8** 60

9 70 **10** 31c **11** 18

12

	3	7	4	5	2	10	6	9
× 5	15	35	20	25	10	50	30	45

13 the width of a door **14** 2 rows of 5 = 10 **15** 14

16 5 cm × 1 cm

8:2

1 70 **2** 50 **3** 8 **4** 16 **5** 97 **6** 40 **7** 30 **8** 50

9 100 **10** 71c **11** 90 metres **12** 63 + 14 = 77

13 one hundred and twenty-eight

14 a 709 b 998 **15** 5 cm × 3 cm

Activity

30, 0, 25, 40, 10, 35, 20, 50, 15, 45

12, 0, 10, 16, 4, 14, 8, 20, 6, 18

8:3

1 a 4, 6, 8, 10, 12 b 8, 12, 16, 20, 24

2 a 28 (–2, –1, –20: 28, 30, 31, 51) b 63 (+20, +1, +3: 39, 59, 60, 63)

3 a 9 b 19 c 29 d 39 e 43 f 53 g 63 h 73
4 a car b bicycle c 4 d 16 e 48 **5** 731

8:4

1 a 10 b 20 **2** a 26 b 44 c 23 d 36 **3** a 0 b 7
4 3 **5** Estimates will vary. 8 groups of 10 will be circled. 80

Challenge

77. Answers will vary, e.g. I used the split strategy. I added the tens first. 4 tens and 3 tens makes 7 tens. Then I added the ones. 2 and 5 makes 7. 7 tens and 7 ones makes 77.

Activity

5, 10, 15, 20, 25, 30, 35, 40, 45, 50

	2	4	6	8	10
× 5	10	20	30	40	50

	1	2	3	4	5
× 10	10	20	30	40	50

9:1

1 38 **2** 48 **3** 58 **4** 68 **5** 10 **6** 12 **7** 80
8 40 **9** $100, $20, $5 **10** 5, 5, 5 **11** 7 **12** Answers will vary.
13 15 past 12, or quarter past 12 **14** 60 **15** nine thirty or half past 9
16 5 + 6 = 11 **17**

9:2

1 63 **2** 73 **3** 83 **4** 93 **5** 14 **6** 35 **7** 30
8 90 **9** 18 – 13 = 5 so 13 + 5 = 18 The difference between 13 and 18 is 5. **10** 25 metres
11 a 30 minutes b 60 minutes **12** 4 metres **13** 7cm × 1 cm
14 $140 **15** 6 hundreds, 4 tens, 7 ones
16 a 95 (+50, +2, +5: 38, 88, 90, 95) b 15 (–5, –2, –20: 15, 20, 22, 42)

Activity

0, 3, 5, 7, 10, 8, 2, 6, 4, 9
0, 30, 50, 70, 100, 80, 20, 60, 40, 90

9:3

1 88 **2** 42c **3** $10 **4** 45 past 5 or quarter to 6
5 5, 5, 5
6 a 85 b 15

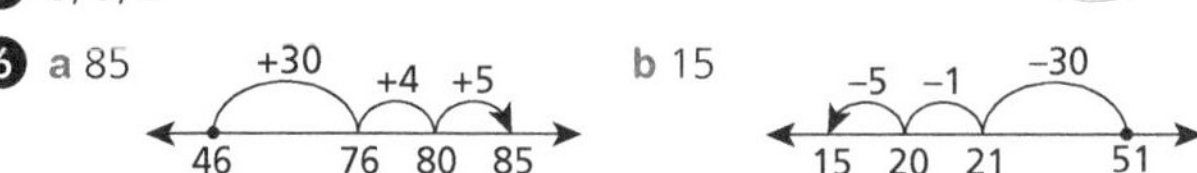

7 3 fives or 15 **8** 2 groups of 4 = 8, 8 **9** 8 **10** 35

9:4

1 76 – 27 = 49 so 27 + 49 = 76 The difference between 27 and 76 is 49. **2** 28 **3** one quarter **4** 8 + 8 **5** 6 **6** a 27 b 40 c 32
7 a 8 b 13

Challenge

16 + 24 = 40, 24 + 16 = 40, 40 – 16 = 24, 40 – 24 = 16

Activity

	29	50	64	37	82	48	73	96	101	129
–10	19	40	54	27	72	38	63	86	91	119
–9	20	41	55	28	73	39	64	87	92	120

	31	78	80	65	52	66	27	94	113	139
–9	22	69	71	56	43	57	18	85	104	130

10:1

1 35 **2** 60 **3** 6 **4** 4 **5** 42 **6** 15 **7** 5 **8** 20 **9** 40
10 42c **11** 6, 6, 6 **12** C (m) **13** $1.70 **14** 30
15 80c **16** B **17** 34 (+4, +4: 26, 30, 34) **18** 14

10:2

1 51 **2** 49 **3** 8 **4** 16 **5** 20 **6** 40 **7** 90
8 100 **9** $180 **10** Most Year 3 students are taller than 1 metre. **11** 14, 14, 14 **12** 10 **13** a 6 b 16 c 26 d 36 e 43 f 53 g 63 h 73 **14** 10
15 34 + 8 = 42 **16** half past 2 **17** 1 m
18 1 litre bottle

Activity

a 7 – 4 = 3, 4 + 3 = 7 The difference is 3.
b 10 – 8 = 2, 8 + 2 = 10 The difference is 2.
c 13 – 5 = 8, 8 + 5 = 13 The difference is 8.
d 28 – 12 = 16, 12 + 16 = 28 The difference is 16.
e 34 – 12 = 22, 12 + 22 = 34 The difference is 22.
f 44 – 36 = 8, 36 + 8 = 44 The difference is 8

10:3

1 a 20, 30, 40, 50, 60 b 10, 15, 20, 25, 30 **2** 60 **3** yes
4 $1.80 **5** 45 past 8 or a quarter to 9 **6** 9, 9, 9
7 a 82 b 28

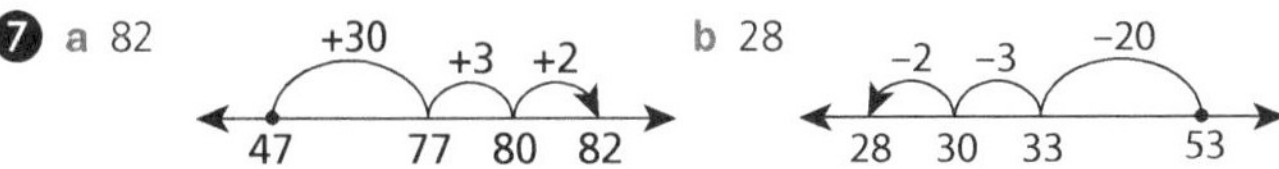

8 20

10:4

1 $56 **2** 32 **3** The $2 and 20-cent coins will be coloured.
4 $7.50
5 $2.85

Challenge
Answers will vary. Some examples are \$1 + \$1 + \$1, \$1 + \$1 + 50c + 50c, \$2 + 50c + 20c + 20c + 10c \$1 + \$1 + 50c + 20c + 20c + 10c, \$2 + \$1, \$1 + \$1 + 50c + 20c + 10c + 10c + 10c.

Activity
13, 8, 16, 12, 14, 9, 17, 15, 11, 18
14, 9, 17, 13, 15, 10, 18, 16, 12, 19

11:1

1 18 **2** 28 **3** 38 **4** 48 **5** 80 **6** 20 **7** 10 **8** 20
9 50 **10** 50c **11** 6 metres **12** 50c coin **13** 60c
14 a 7 b 33 **15** 55, 61, 59, 64, 58 and 56 will be circled.
16 5 hundreds, 6 tens, 3 ones **17** 6 **18** a 5 b 2

11:2

1 54 **2** 44 **3** 34 **4** 24 **5** 12 **6** 16 **7** 40
8 45 **9** 4 hundreds, 7 tens, 3 ones **10** 5 hundreds + 42 ones, or 54 tens + 2 ones **11** yes **12** a 30 b \$1.50 **13** 85c
14 412, 392, 406, 351 **15** \$110
16 4 hundreds, 8 tens, 2 ones **17** 375, 385, 395 **18** a 265 b 534

Activity
a 40 **b** 30 **c** 40 **d** 20 **e** 90

11:3

1 Answers will vary, e.g. 1, 4, 16, 25, 36.
2 Most likely yes **3** 824, 809, 750, 751, 793, 783 and 849 will be circled. **4** 9 hundreds, 0 tens, 4 ones
5 a One rectangle will be coloured out of 2.
b One rectangle will be coloured out of 4.
c One rectangle will be coloured out of 8.
6 \$6.40
7 Answers may vary, e.g.
a \$2 note + 50c + 20c + 5c
b \$5 note + 20c + 5c
c \$10 note + \$5 note + \$1 + 50c + 10c
8 3 minutes
9 a 16, 18, 20, 22, 24 b 40, 50, 60, 70, 80 c 53, 63, 73, 83, 93

11:4

1 40 **2** a 21 b 42 **3** a star **4** 3 **5** 21 **6** century

Challenge
Answers will vary, e.g. a bath, swimming pool or sink.

Activity
a 8 b 20

12:1

1 7 **2** 6 **3** 6 **4** 3 **5** 25 **6** 10 **7** 50 **8** 15
9 9 hundred, 3 tens, 5 ones, or 93 tens + 5 ones, or 935 ones
10 74, 68, 71, 65, 66, 69, 67 and 73 will be circled.
11 centimetres, metres **12** a A b C **13** a One rectangle will be coloured. b One rectangle will be coloured.
c One rectangle will be coloured. d One rectangle will be coloured.
14 a 649, 749, 849 b 448, 458, 468

12:2

1 9 **2** 8 **3** 50 **4** 90 **5** 70 **6** 16 **7** 40 **8** 80 **9** 30
10 \$20 **11** 100 **12** true, Answers will vary. **13** 3 m 75 cm
14 5 m 37 cm **15** 739 cm **16** 2 out of 5, $\frac{2}{5}$ **17** 915
18 328, 349, 250, 261 will be circled.
19 4 teddy bears will be circled. $\frac{1}{5}$
20 a 3 b 6

Activity
a 300 b 700 c 300 d 800 e 800 f 500 g 100

12:3

1 69 **2** \$15 **3** 78 **4** 3 out of 5, $\frac{3}{5}$ **5** yes **6** 100
7 6 m 29 cm **8** 921 cm **9** 937, 851, 949, 850
10 a One square will be coloured. b Two squares will be coloured.
c Three squares will be coloured.
11 a 8, 10, 12, 14 b 12, 15, 18, 21 c 20, 25, 30, 35 d 40, 50, 60
12 a 5 b 7 c 3 d 5

12:4

1 99 cm **2** half **3** 24 **4** a 6 b 3 **5** 3 **6** C
7 4 **8** a 25 b 30

Challenge
Any number from 650 to 749 could be written.

Activity
a 3 out of 6 or $\frac{3}{6}$ b 2 out of 5 or $\frac{2}{5}$ c 4 out of 5 or $\frac{4}{5}$ d 4 out of 5 or $\frac{4}{5}$

13:1

1 80 **2** 30 **3** 6 **4** 8 **5** 60 **6** 15 **7** 20 **8** 30 **9** 40
10 40c **11** 1 out of 2 equal parts **12** a C b A
13 cm **14** yes **15** 4 out of 6, $\frac{4}{6}$ **16** 6 out of 10, $\frac{6}{10}$

13:2

1 59 **2** 5 **3** 10 **4** 12 **5** 25 **6** 30 **7** 50 **8** 60
9 a 4, 6, 8, 10, 12, 14 b 10, 15, 20, 25, 30, 35
10 1 m 65 cm **11** 9 m 81 cm **12** 615 cm **13** 9 out of 10, $\frac{9}{10}$
14 4 out of 6 **15** false **16** A 4 cm B 3 cm C 5 cm **17** 30
18 500

Activity
a 39 b 37

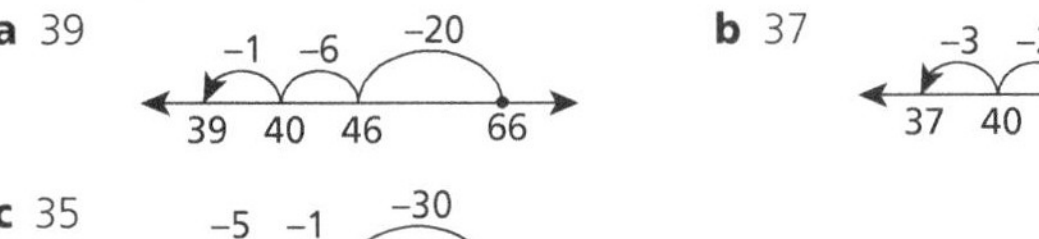

c 35

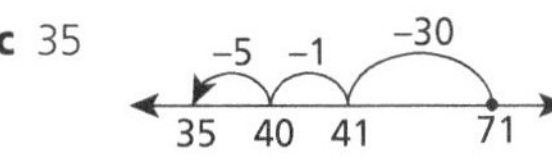

 • *AUSTRALIAN SIGNPOST MATHS NSW 3 MENTALS* • ISBN 978 0 6557 0910 7

13:3

1 2 out of 10, $\frac{2}{10}$
2 50 **3** 28 cm **4** 4 m 27 cm **5** one half
6 5 cm **7** cm **8** 26 + 22 = 48 **9** yes
10 82 **11** 941

+30 +3 +2
47 77 80 82

13:4

1 300
2 a b
c 2 seals will be coloured.
3 4 **4** a b 2 c $\frac{1}{2}$
5 a 3 out of 4 b 4 quarters or 1 **6** a 15 − 6 = 9 b 15 − 9 = 6

Challenge

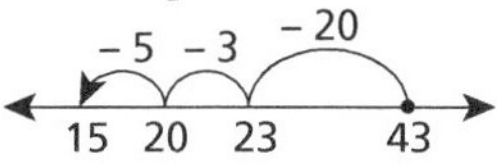

43 − 28 = 15

Activity

+	5	10	4	0	2	6	1	3
2	7	12	6	2	4	8	3	5
3	8	13	7	3	5	9	4	6
4	9	14	8	4	6	10	5	7
5	10	15	9	5	7	11	6	8
10	15	20	14	10	12	16	11	13

14:1

1 20 **2** 12 **3** 17 **4** 8 **5** 70 **6** 11 **7** 4 **8** 8 **9** 3
10 10c **11** m **12**
13 77

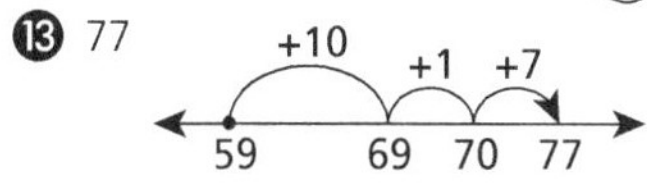

14 a 500 b 26 c 53 d 28 **15** a 10 b 20 **16** 6 m 93 cm.

14:2

1 84 **2** 5 **3** 83 **4** 24 **5** 15 **6** 14 **7** 90 **8** 8
9 a 10 b 20 **10** D **11** a 42 b 14 **12** 135 cm **13**

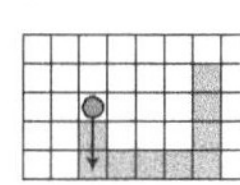

14 18

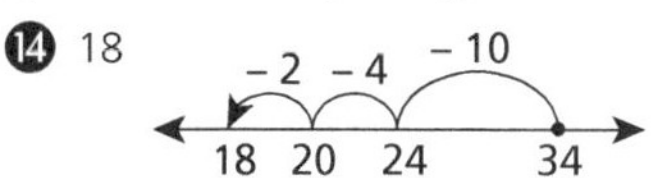

15 a 57 b 46

Activity

5, 10, 15, 20, 25, 30, 35, 40, 45, 50

	2	4	6	8	10
× 5	10	20	30	40	50

	2	4	6	8	10
× 10	20	40	60	80	100

14:3

1 2 out of 5, $\frac{2}{5}$ **2** a 64 b 63 c 94 d 64 e 37 f 36
3 a Brown St b Jones St c Bond St d Smith St
e Bond St, Smith St and Brown St **4** 37

− 3 − 1 − 20
37 40 41 61

14:4

1 700 **2** 1 m 50 cm **3** 20 **4** C **5** a True b True
6 D

Challenge

64, Answers will vary, e.g. I used the compensation strategy. I know that 40 + 25 = 40 + 20 + 5 which equals 65. 39 is one less than 40 so the answer is one less than 65. The answer is 64.

Activity

2, 6, 10, 4, 9, 1, 7, 5, 3, 8
13, 57, 42, 18, 56, 21, 39, 25, 44, 30

15:1

1 33 **2** 12 **3** 50 **4** 46 **5** 48 **6** 16 **7** 25 **8** 70
9 90 **10** 22c **11** 1357 **12** yes **13** metres
14 Answers will vary. **15** Answers will vary, e.g. 14 − 8 = 6, 12 − 6 = 6.
16 a 54 tens + 6 ones b 73 tens + 5 ones c 93 tens + 7 ones
17 a 700 b 400 c 700 d 800

15:2

1 55 **2** 52 **3** 800 **4** 57 **5** 18 **6** 45 **7** 80
8 100 **9** a 56 − 24 = 36 − 4 = 32 b 69 − 28 = 49 − 8 = 41
c 58 − 35 = 28 − 5 = 23 **10** no (although the largest recorded foot length for a person is about 47 cm) **11** 9531 **12** 472 cm
13 1, 2, 3, 4, 5, 6 **14** Answers will vary, e.g. 20 − 9 = 11, 11
15 4 of the rectangles will be shaded. $\frac{4}{5}$

Activity

Answers may vary. Least likely to most likely: C my mother, E a father, B the principal, A a teacher, F a boy, D a human

15:3

1 \$97 **2** \$84 **3** 1246 **4** 4 **5** 5423 **6** a 53 b 35
7 a 73 b 46

+20 +4 +3
46 66 70 73

−4 −3 −20
46 50 53 73

8 a 65 b 67 **9** even **10** a 5329 b 9517

15:4

1 40 **2** Possible answers are 4204, 4206, 4208, 4210 or 4212.
3 60 **4** a 6 b 3 **5** 32 **6** 9, 8 and 7 **7** yes **8** 6031

Challenge

55, Answers will vary, e.g. I used the compensation strategy. I know that 84 − 30 = 54 because 8 tens minus 3 tens is 5 tens. 29 is one less than 30 so I need to add one more so the answer is 55.

Activity

14, 17, 11, 19, 12, 15, 18, 20, 10, 16

30, 60, 41, 54, 62, 85, 44, 67, 73, 96

16:1

1 400 **2** 500 **3** 56 **4** 55 **5** 88 **6** 3 **7** 8 **8** 14

9 30 **10** 47c **11** Yes **12** No **13** Answers will vary, e.g. <u>14</u> – <u>11</u> = <u>3</u>, 3

14 6572

15 10 : 22

16 5911 **17** 4 **18** a 9th b 7th

16:2

1 900 **2** 300 **3** 91 **4** 14 **5** 3 **6** 9 **7** 18

8 40 **9** a 32 – 19 = <u>33</u> – <u>20</u> = <u>13</u> b 43 – 34 = <u>49</u> – <u>40</u> = <u>9</u>

10 3 rectangles will be coloured.

11 four thousand, five hundred and one

12 Yes **13** No **14** Yes

15 3 thousands, 5 hundreds, 2 tens, 3 ones **16** even

Activity

a 60 **b** 30 **c** 15 **d** 45 **e** 50 **f** 10

16:3

1 a 700 b 900 c 900 d 900 **2**

3 1354

4 3 out of 8 rectangles will be coloured. **5** 7020 will be circled.

6 no **7** white **8** Answers will vary, e.g. 31 – 20, 11

16:4

1 a 3:53 or 7 to 4 b 12:44 or 16 to 1 **2** 11 **3** 4 blocks will be circled. **4** 28 **5** 30 **6** 36 **7** 73 **8** a one quarter b one half

Challenge

Answers will vary. There is an equal chance of getting an A or B. It is impossible to spin a C. It is possible to get an A or a B.

Activity

a IV **b** V **c** IX **d** X **e** XI **f** XII **g** 9 **h** 11 **i** 6

17:1

1 6 **2** 14 **3** 10 **4** 30 **5** 85 **6** 3 **7** 3 **8** 8 **9** 5

10 52c **11** kg **12** less **13** a 6 b 9 **14** One fish will be coloured. **15** 6:53 or 7 to 7 **16** 4 kg will be circled.

17 645, 745, 845

17:2

1 15 **2** 25 **3** 20 **4** 50 **5** 62 **6** 26 **7** 22 **8** 11

9 a 12, 15, 18, 21 b 24, 30, 36, 42 c 28, 35, 42, 49 **10** true

11 3 past 9 **12** 3 kg **13** 4093 **14** a 9 to 7 b 21 to 11

15 <u>2</u> out of <u>4</u>, $\frac{2}{4}$ **16** 64

Activity

3, 6, 9, 12, 15, 18, 21, 24, 27, 30

17:3

1 Rectangle will be coloured up to $\frac{4}{6}$ mark. $\frac{4}{6}$ **2** grams **3** No

4 4:02 or 2 past 4 **5** 4:57 or 3 to 5 **6** 1537 **7** m **8** 3 m 35 cm

9 fourteen, forty, forty-four

17:4

1 3 **2** 4 blocks will be circled. **3** true **4** a 5 squares will be coloured red and 1 square will be coloured blue. b 6 sixths, 1 whole or $\frac{6}{6}$

5 24 **6** 3:32 **7** + **8** no

Challenge

Answers will vary, e.g a pencil case, pair of shoes or hat.

Activity

9, 12, 15, 18, 21

12, 16, 20, 24, 28

10, 15, 20, 25, 30, 35, 40, 45

18:1

1 4 **2** 8 **3** 6 **4** 30 **5** 35 **6** 10 **7** 4 **8** 12 **9** 78

10 99 **11** yes **12** pentagon **13** kilograms **14** 20, 20

15 C **16** <u>5</u> groups of <u>3</u> **17** 2 × 3 = <u>6</u>, 3 × 3 = <u>9</u>, 4 × 3 = <u>12</u>

18 Answers will vary, e.g. 20 – 11, 9

18:2

1 80 **2** 30 **3** 16 **4** 60 **5** 77 **6** 12 **7** 16 **8** 40 **9** 15

10 21c **11** 8 kg **12** 16 **13** a D b B

14 a 64 b 92 c 168 **15** square, rhombus **16** hexagon

Activity

a 5 b Answers will vary.

18:3

1 24 **2** yes **3** 3 rows of 3 = <u>9</u>, 3 × 3 = <u>9</u>, yes

4 a yes b yes c yes

5 <u>4</u> rows of <u>6</u> = <u>24</u>, <u>4</u> × <u>6</u> = <u>24</u> **6** yes

7

Kangaroos							
Emus							
Rabbits							

8 a 20, 25, 30 b 18, 16, 14 c 14, 24, 34 d 50, 40, 30

18:4

1 a 60c b 280c or $2.80 **2** 5 **3** 25 **4** a 1, 9, 7 b 3, 9, 7

5 +

Challenge

Answers will vary e.g. 20 – 3 =17; 35 – 18 = 17.

Activity

0, 10, 16, 4, 12, 18, 8, 20, 6, 8
4, 8, 12, 16, 20
4, 8, 12, 16, 20

19:1

1 8 **2** 12 **3** 40 **4** 20 **5** 39 **6** 18 **7** 9 **8** 55 **9** 55
10 $45 **11** 44, 48, 52, 56, 60 **12** 24 **13** **a** Jill **b** Kira **c** 7
d 5 **e** 27 **14** kite, quadrilateral

19:2

1 24 **2** 32 **3** 36 **4** 24 **5** 94 **6** 27 **7** 59 **8** 13
9 89 **10** $10 **11** **a** true **b** true **12** 20 **13** **a** 16, 12, 8, 4
b 46, 36, 26, 16 **c** 34, 24, 14, 4 **14** A
15 parallelogram **16** regular

Activity

even, odd
0, 3, 5, 8, 4, 6, 2, 7, 3, 9
7, 3, 10, 2, 6, 8, 4, 9, 5, 1

19:3

1 30 **2** 19 **3** 21 **4** **a** 6, 9, 12 **b** 17, 15, 13
c 33, 43, 53 **d** 86, 76, 66

5

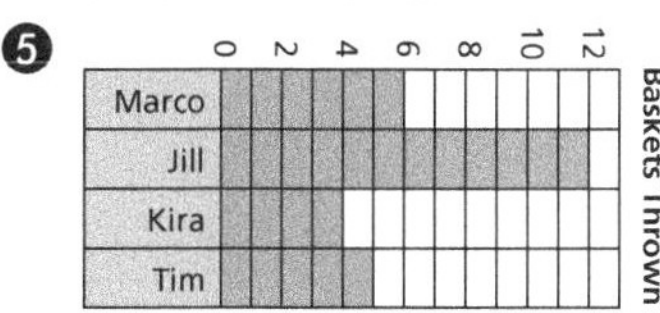

6 45, 50, 55, 60 **7** yes **8** **a** 40 **b** 20 **c** 28 **d** yes

19:4

1 **a** triangle **b** rectangle **2** circle **3** **a** 20 **b** $1\frac{2}{4}$
c Answers may vary, e.g. $2\frac{2}{4}$, $2\frac{1}{2}$ or 10 quarters **4** 26

Challenge

Answers will vary.

Activity

68, 61, 42, 57, 75, 21, 26, 55, 78, 72
69, 62, 43, 58, 76, 22, 27, 56, 79, 73

20:1

1 12 **2** 16 **3** 6 **4** 15 **5** 43 **6** 8 **7** 12 **8** 9 **9** 6
10 $10 **11** **a** cube, 12 **b** cylinder, 2 **12** **a** 50 **b** 30
13 yes **14** 12 **15** 12, 15, 18, 21
16 9 **17** **a** **b** 4 **c** 4 **18** $25

20:2

1 28 **2** 36 **3** 18 **4** 21 **5** 97 **6** 48 **7** 39 **8** 18
9 29 **10** $20 **11** Answers will vary. It has 6 faces, 12 edges and 8 corners. Its cross-section is a square (or a rectangle). It can stack and slide.
12 **a** 556, 566, 576, 586 **b** 799, 809, 819, 829 **c** 2470, 2480, 2490
13 **a** 5 **b** 5 **14** **a** 6 **b** 26

Activity

(3) parallel lines, (4) perpendicular lines, (8) rhombus, (11) quadrilaterals, (12) pentagons, (13) hexagons, (16) regular shapes, (17) irregular shapes

20:3

1 25 **2** 21 **3** 28 **4** yes **5** **a** 86, 76, 66 **b** 12, 15, 18, 21
c 145, 245, 345 **d** 17, 22, 27, 32 **6** <u>32</u> – <u>16</u> = <u>16</u>, 16
7 triangular rectangular pyramid, rectangular prism **8** parallel **9** 35
10 4 **11** 5

20:4

1 7 **2** **a** 12 **b** 14 **3** **a** **F** **b** **B** and **D** **4** square pyramid
5 <u>52</u> + <u>39</u> = <u>91</u>

Challenge

a 47 – 29 = <u>27</u> – <u>9</u> = <u>18</u> **b** 56 – 38 = <u>26</u> – <u>8</u> = <u>18</u>
c 53 – 36 = <u>23</u> – <u>6</u> = <u>17</u> **d** 65 – 27 = <u>45</u> – <u>7</u> = <u>38</u>

Activity

a 43, 46, 49, 52, 55, 58, 61, 64, Rule: + 3
b 41, 39, 37, 35, 33, 31, 29, 27, Rule – 2
c 568, 578, 588, 598, 608, 618, Rule: + 10
d 589, 489, 389, 289, 189, 89, Rule: – 100
e 1530, 1630, 1730, 1830, Rule: + 100

21:1

1 0 **2** 40 **3** 10 **4** 16 **5** 77 **6** 3 **7** 0 **8** 11 **9** 44
10 $33 **11** C and B **12** 20 **13** 45 **14** angle
15 rectangular prism (or square prism), 6, 12, 8, rectangle (or square)
16 15 **17** A, C, B, D

21:2

1 15 **2** 30 **3** 6 **4** 12 **5** 89 **6** 36 **7** 27 **8** 4 **9** 12
10 $50 **11** **a** 18 **b** 16 **12** C, A, B **13** 40
14 500 **15** yes **16** 2 **17** 44 and 46
18 28 (– 2, – 4, – 30; 28, 30, 34, 64) **19** 382

Activity

40, 5, 25, 30, 10, 45, 35, 15, 50, 20
32, 4, 20, 24, 8, 36, 28, 12, 40, 16

21:3

1 Answers will vary, e.g. 18 – 1 = 25 – 9 **2** a 8 b 6
c triangular prism d B, C and F e D, E and H
3 a A b C **4** 29 + 15 = 44 **5** cube, 6, 12, 8, square

21:4

1 18, 36, 24 **2** 3 **3** 61
4 46 **5** 35 + 18 = 53
6 68 b 98

+20 +2 +1
38 58 60 61

Challenge
Answers will vary.

Activity
4, 7, 1, 3, 6, 2, 5, 0
5, 8, 2, 4, 7, 3, 6, 1

22:1

1 30 **2** 24 **3** 4 **4** 20 **5** 6 **6** 12 **7** 10 **8** 22
9 a pyramid b prism **10** angle **11** 20 **12** yes
13 5006 **14** no **15** 3 kg **16** 4 thousands + 5 hundreds
17 **18** 7450, 7460, 7470

22:2

1 40 **2** 36 **3** 32 **4** 28 **5** 64 **6** 49 **7** 43
8 54 **9** square and rectangle
10 Any two angles of 90° can be drawn. Examples:

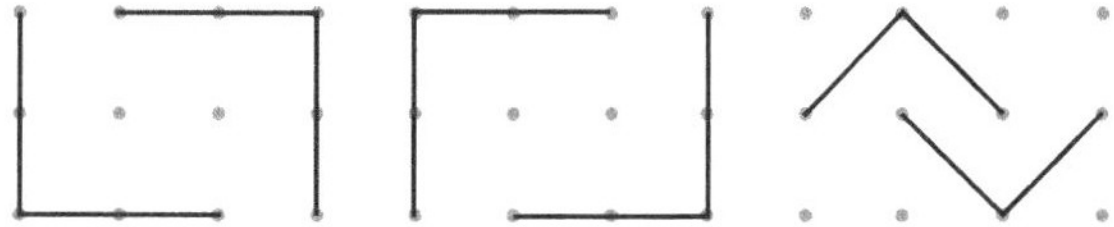

11 a 57 kg b 11 kg **12** ,9 **13** 4

14 The angle will be copied.

A

Activity
7, 11, 2, 5, 10, 8, 6, 4, 9, 3
8, 12, 3, 6, 11, 9, 7, 5, 10, 4,

22:3

1 30 **2** 19 **3** 21
4 5 thousands + 7 hundreds + 3 tens + 5 ones **5** 6031
6 yes **7** 3505, 3605, 3705 **8** 7 kg **9** a 4637, 4638, 4639
b 9203, 9204, 9205 **10** C **11** a 7483 b 8

22:4

1 a \$3 b 85c **2** a 5 b 11 **3** 6 rectangles will be coloured.
4 3200 **5** \$120 **6** $\frac{2}{3}$ **7** 16 **8** 5288

Challenge
Answers will vary.

Activity
3, 8, 4, 9, 6, 2, 10, 5, 11, 7
4, 9, 5, 10, 7, 3, 11, 6, 12, 8

23:1

1 20 **2** 6 **3** 18 **4** 15 **5** 12 **6** 9 **7** \$15
8 \$12 **9** one row of 2 or 2 square centimetres **10** 9
11 7 thousands + 2 hundreds + 9 tens + 4 ones **12** C
13 $\frac{5}{8}$ **14** 30 **15** 7 **16** 20, 25, 30, 35, 40

23:2

1 34 **2** 42 **3** 67 **4** 83 **5** 7 **6** 55 **7** 27
8 38 **9** 85 kg **10** $\frac{3}{4}$
11 9 thousands + 7 hundreds + 2 tens + 9 ones
12 62 **13** March, April, May **14** 60 **15** 28 kg **16** 13.4.26
17 3278 **18** yes **19** a 1 4 hundreds 7 tens 9 ones
b 1 4 7 tens 9 ones
20 68, 58, 48, 38, 28

Activity
10, 15, 20, 25, 30, 35, 40, 45, 50, 55
11, 16, 21, 26, 31, 36, 41, 46, 51, 56

23:3

1 a $\frac{3}{8}, \frac{6}{8}$ b 7 pieces will be coloured. $\frac{7}{8}$
c $\frac{7}{8}$ will be ticked. **2** a October b 5 c Friday d 31
e 7th October or October 7 f 27th of October or October 27
3 3 rows of 3, area = 9 square centimetres **4** a 31 b 30

23:4

1 a 8 b 10 **2** a 120c or \$1.20 b 300c or \$3 **3** 3390
4 Answers will vary, e.g. $\frac{9}{10}$ or $\frac{99}{100}$. The higher the number at the base of the fraction, the smaller the parts of a whole will be. The higher the number at the top, the larger the fraction will be. **5** 9

Challenge
Answers will vary.
a Number sentences will equal 15.
b Number sentences will equal 36.

Activity
14, 22, 26, 19, 37, 57, 15, 29, 32, 43
8, 16, 20, 13, 31, 51, 9, 23, 26, 37

24:1

❶ 15 ❷ 0 ❸ 25 ❹ 50 ❺ 10 ❻ 15c ❼ $6 ❽ 10

❾ a $\frac{3}{4}$ b Answers may vary, e.g. $\frac{2}{4}$ or $\frac{1}{2}$.

❿ 8002 = 8 thousands + 2 ones

⓫ a R b J c D d L e B ⓬ 4931

⓭

	3	7	4	5	2	10	6	9
× 2	6	14	8	10	4	20	12	18

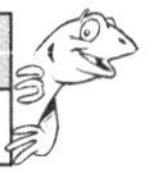

⓮ $8

24:2

❶ 12 ❷ 0 ❸ 6 ❹ 12 ❺ 10 ❻ 15c ❼ $2 ❽ 6

❾ December ❿ a 5 b Tuesday c Sunday (7th of June)

⓫ a 8, 8, 4, 2 b 10, 10, 5, 2 ⓬ 3, 3 ⓭ 3207

⓮ a 59 b 74 c 88 d 65

Activity

a 3, 30, 30, 10, 3 **b** 4, 20, 20, 5, 4

24:3

❶ a b c $\frac{3}{4}$

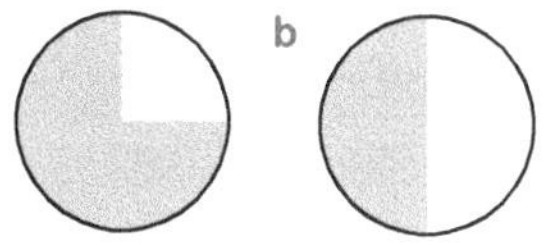

❷

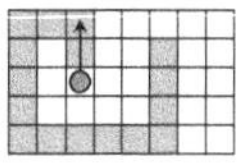

❸ 2 rows of 3, 6 ❹ a 12 b February c January d 11th e 5.5.2026 or 5.5.26

❺

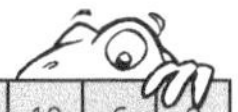

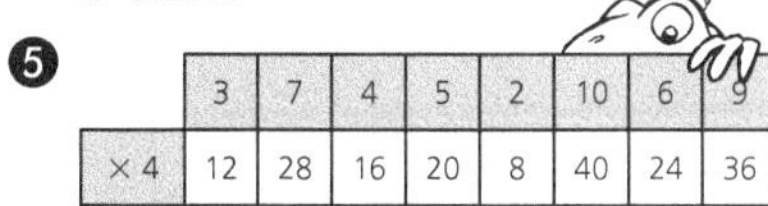

	3	7	4	5	2	10	6	9
× 4	12	28	16	20	8	40	24	36

❻ a 3 b 2

24:4

❶ 2 bells will be coloured red. 4 bells will be coloured blue. $\frac{6}{8}$ or $\frac{3}{4}$

❷ a one fifth b one twentieth ❸ 9089 ❹ 72 ❺ 60

❻ a Sunday b Tuesday ❼ a 35 b 70 ❽ a $16 b $127

Challenge

Answers will vary.

Activity

a 14, 14, 7, 2

b 32, 32, 4, 8

c 45, 45, 5, 9

d 70, 70, 10, 7

25:1

❶ 20 ❷ 20 ❸ 20 ❹ 20 ❺ 36 ❻ 12 ❼ 15 ❽ 13

❾ a 30 b 30 c 31 d 31 ❿ a 4 b 20 c 20 d 4 e 5

⓫ a 8 b 4 c 4 d 2 ⓬ Area = 14 square centimetres

⓭ 9, 12, 15, 18, 21 ⓮ a 35 b 27 c 44 d 45

25:2

❶ 13 ❷ 56 ❸ 30 ❹ 38 ❺ 58 ❻ 34 ❼ 23 ❽ 70

❾ 3, 2 ❿ 7, 7 ⓫ a Row 2 b Fruit c Soap d Row 1 e Lollies

⓬ 97, 107, 117, 127

Activity

a 2 rows of 4 = 8, How many 2s in 8? 4, 2 × 4 = 8 so 8 ÷ 4 = 2

b 3 rows of 5 = 15, How many 5s in 15? 3, 3 × 5 = 15 so 15 ÷ 3 = 5

c 3 groups of 2 = 6, How many 2s in 6? 3, 3 × 2 = 6 so 6 ÷ 3 = 2

25:3

❶ 8,8 ❷ 20, 20, 10 ❸ a 40 b 4 c 10 d 10

❹ Area = 6 square centimetres
Area = 12 square centimetres

❺ 5634 ❻ a 6 b 3 c 2

❼

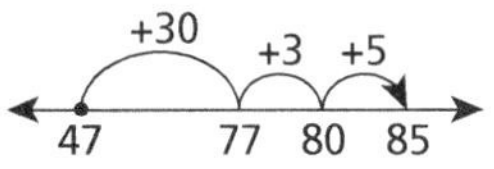

25:4

❶ a 4 b 3 ❷ 8 ❸ 23 ❹ 1872 ❺ 9 ❻ a yes b 3

❼ a 599 b 296

Challenge

Answers will vary.

Activity

20, 31, 26, 19, 15, 40, 49, 64, 25, 23

21, 25, 44, 15, 37, 42, 50, 53, 28, 39

26:1

❶ 12 ❷ 6 ❸ 18 ❹ 9 ❺ 50 ❻ 5 ❼ 15 ❽ 3

❾

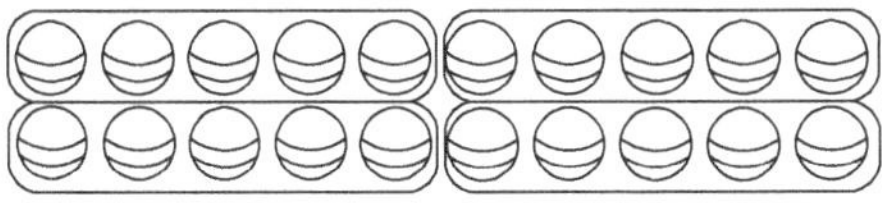

20, 20, 4, 4, 5, 5 ❿ 18 L ⓫ yes ⓬ 2

⓭ 27 ⓮ 6, 6 ⓯ 3 ⓰ a 200 (or 2 hundreds) b 20 (or 2 tens)

⓱ yes ⓲ a 3 b 5

26:2

❶ 20 ❷ 4 ❸ 16 ❹ 4 ❺ 90 ❻ 9 ❼ 14 ❽ 7

❾

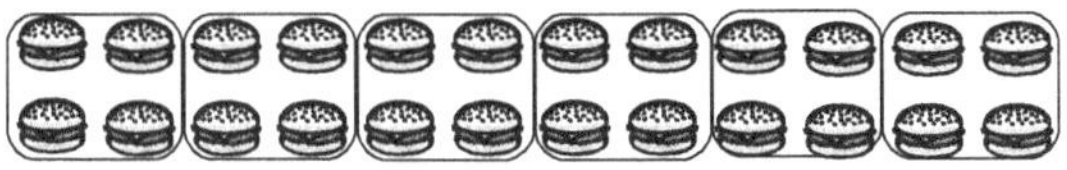

24, 24, 6, 6, 4, 4

❿ a 9 b 18 c 9 ⓫ 34 L ⓬ 5 ⓭ 3 rectangles will be coloured

⓮ 20 ⓯ 33

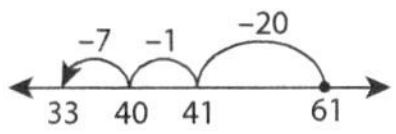

⓰ 4291

Activity

(9) even (10) odd (11) ordinal numbers (12) digits

(18) number line (19) number sentence (20) numeral expander

(21) abacus

26:3

❶ 39 L ❷ a $\frac{1}{4}$ b $\frac{2}{4}$ or $\frac{1}{2}$ ❸ a 20, 20, 5, 5 b 18, 18, 6, 6
❹ a Pa b Nanna c Alan d Diane e Lyn
❺ a 6, 6 b 9, 9 c 8, 8 d 6, 6

26:4

❶ a 12 b 9 ❷ a 51 b 32 ❸ 114 ❹ 50, 200 ❺ 20
❻ a 3 b 7

Challenge

a 3 × 5 = 15, 15 ÷ 3 = 5, 5 × 3 = 15, 15 ÷ 5 = 3
b 2 × 9 = 18, 18 ÷ 2 = 9, 9 × 2 = 18, 18 ÷ 9 = 2
c 3 × 8 = 24, 24 ÷ 3 = 8, 8 × 3 = 24, 24 ÷ 8 = 3

Activity

a 18, 18, 9, 2
b 24, 24, 4, 6
c 30, 30, 5, 6
d 30, 30, 10, 3

27:1

❶ 4 ❷ 4 ❸ 2 ❹ 2 ❺ 50 ❻ 3 ❼ 3 ❽ 10 ❾ 10
❿ 70 ⓫ 8321
⓬ a [abacus: Th H T U] b 1644 ⓭ a 16, 8, 8 b 10, 2, 2
⓮ 3, 3 ⓯ a 190 b 208
⓰ a 5, 5 b 5, 5 c 9, 9 d 9, 9
⓱ a 3 spaceships will be coloured. b $\frac{5}{8}$ c no

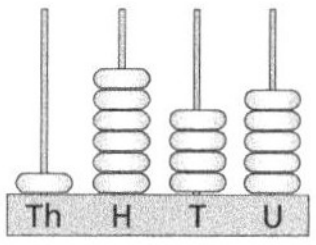

27:2

❶ 8 ❷ 8 ❸ 9 ❹ 9 ❺ 250 ❻ 6 ❼ 6 ❽ 8 ❾ 8
❿ 420 ⓫ 1569 ⓬ 2585 ⓭ 7, 7
⓮ a 7000 (or 7 thousands) b 70 (or 7 tens)
⓯ a 24, 8, 8 b 24, 6, 6 ⓰ five thousand one hundred and ninety
⓱ 459 ⓲ a 190 b 45 c 28 d 293 ⓳ 1 2 5 tens 6 ones

Activity

(19) line of symmetry (21) corner (22) edge (23) face (24) cube (25) prism (26) pyramid (27) base (28) cylinder (29) cone (30) sphere

27:3

❶ a 1 4 hundreds 7 tens 9 ones
b 1 4 7 tens 9 ones ❷ 1062 ❸ 1999
❹ 6789 ❺ 819 ❻ a 190 b 19, 79 c 74 d 643
❼ a 77 b 44 ❽ 2002
❾ four thousand and twenty ❿

⓫ a 38 b 45

27:4

❶ 60c ❷ 10 ❸ a $1.85 b 55c ❹ 97 ❺ 24 ❻ 0 ❼ 140
❽ a 91 b 90 c 92 d 92

Challenge

a 6, 20, 20, 10, 12, 10
b 60, 25, 40, 16, 10, 36

Activity

a 6, 6, 6 b 7, 7, 7 c 7, 7, 7 d 9, 9, 9

28:1

❶ 10 ❷ 10 ❸ 3 ❹ 3 ❺ 2 ❻ 2 ❼ 2 ❽ 2
❾ a 82 b 76 c 51 d 43 ❿ 1324, 3599 ⓫ 4
⓬ 20c and 10c coins will be circled. ⓭ $44 ⓮ 4
⓯ 59 ⓰ a 39 b 47

28:2

❶ 5 ❷ 10 ❸ 4 ❹ 5 ❺ 550 ❻ 79 ❼ 60 ❽ 67 ❾ 16
❿ 674 ⓫ 5243 ⓬ This is a trapezium. It has 4 vertices and 4 sides.
⓭ 59 ⓮ 13 ⓯ a 530 b 65 c 33 d 375 ⓰ 6 ⓱ $1.35
⓲ a 349 – 200 = 149 b 673 – 300 = 373
⓳ [clock] quarter to 6 or 5:45

Activity

(8) rhombus (or diamond) (9) trapezium (10) parallelogram
(11) quadrilaterals (12) pentagons (13) hexagons
(16) regular shapes (17) irregular shapes

28:3

❶ 9, 9 ❷ 3545 ❸ 4052 ❹ 302
❺ a 57 b 52 c 838 d 322 ❻ 50c and 5c coins will be circled.
❼ right angle ❽ more ❾ 8, 12, 16, 20, 24, 28 ❿ a 77 b 74

28:4

❶ a 6 b 11 c 51 ❷ square, rectangle, parallelogram, rhombus
❸ 7004 ❹ A black rectangle ❺ 36

Challenge

Answers will vary. One answer could be: It has 4 equal sides, 4 corners and 4 angles. Its opposite sides are parallel.

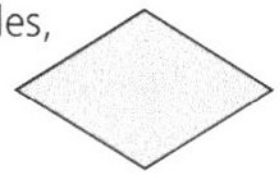

Activity

3, 6, 1, 9, 5, 8, 0, 7, 4, 10
3, 1, 7, 5, 2, 8, 6, 10, 4, 9

29:1

❶ 55 ❷ 69 ❸ 45 ❹ 46 ❺ 69 ❻ 60 ❼ 15 ❽ 3 ❾ 12
❿ 89 ⓫ a 90 b 36 c 59 d 33 ⓬ 70c ⓭ square metres
⓮ yes ⓯ 28 + 7 = 35 ⓰ 2421 ⓱ yes
⓲ 2nd shape will be circled. ⓳ 12, 15, 18, 21, 24, 27

29:2

1 64 **2** 81 **3** 50 **4** 52 **5** 89 **6** 40 **7** 10 **8** 12

9 3 **10** 106 **11** square metres **12** 7268, 7278 **13** 85c

14 46 + 36 = 82 **15** a 54 – 39 = 55 – 40 = 15
b 62 – 28 = 64 – 30 = 34 c 75 – 47 = 78 – 50 = 28
d 68 – 27 = 71 – 30 = 41

16 6 thousand + 4 tens + 3 ones, 73 hundreds + 2 ones **17** 10

Activity

a 5188, 5178, 5278
b 4502, 4562, 2562, 2565, 2265
c 8543, 8943, 3943, 3948, 3998

29:3

1 43 **2** 62 **3** 59 + 46 =105 **4** 1st shape will be ticked

5 a 58 – 29 = 59 – 30 = 29 b 54 – 18 = 56 – 20 = 36
c 61 – 33 = 68 – 40 = 28 d 73 – 48 = 75 – 50 = 25

6 hexagon

7 Answers will vary. Shapes that may be drawn include: square, rectangle, rhombus, trapezium, parallelogram, kite, irregular quadrilateral.

8 a 46 – 32 = 16 – 2 = 14 b 72 – 49 = 32 – 9 = 23

29:4

1 a 30c b 105c or $1.05 **2** 200c or $2 **3** a 301 b 101

4  **5** 18

Challenge

Answers will vary.

Activity

70, 63, 44, 59, 77, 23, 28, 57, 80, 74
71, 64, 45, 60, 78, 24, 29, 58, 81, 75

30:1

1 5 **2** 3 **3** 4 **4** 1 **5** 76 **6** 72 **7** 6 **8** 50 **9** 10

10 75 **11** 36 + 38 = 74 **12** 31 **13** 60 **14** no **15** a 20, 4, 20, 5, 4
b 30, 3, 30, 10, 3 **16** a 46 b 48 **17** a 23 b 27

30:2

1 8 **2** 8 **3** 11 **4** 6 **5** 42 **6** 8 **7** 5 **8** 18 **9** 8

10 103 **11** a unlikely b even chance c very likely
d certain **12** 500 **13** a 53 b 62 c 587 d 65 **14** a 70 b 90

15 Answers will vary, e.g. 1, 4, 9, 16, 25

Activity

a no b even chance c less

30:3

1 562 **2** 401 **3** yes **4** 54 **5** a yes b 4 **6** 15c

7 a 56 – 28 = 36 – 8 = 28 b 75 – 28 = 55 – 8 = 47 **8** a 61 b 52

9 30

30:4

1 cube, or square prism **2** 9755, 9745, 9735 **3** yes **4** 95

5 5

Challenge

Answers will vary and may include: It is an odd number and has 4 digits. It is higher than 3013 and lower than 3034. It rounds to 3030 (to the nearest 10) and 3000 (to the nearest 1000). It can be written as three thousand and twenty-five, 3000 + 20 + 5 or (3 × 1000) + (2 × 10) + (5 × 1). The number before is 3024 and the number after is 3026. It can be represented using 3 thousand blocks, 2 tens blocks and 5 ones blocks. It is in the pattern 3005, 3015, 3025, 3035. 3035 – 10 = 3025, 3005 + 20 = 3025

Activity

a 35 + 37 = 72 b 54 + 28 = 82 c 60 + 40 = 100

31:1

1 39 **2** 51 **3** 49 **4** 69 **5** 625 **6** 53 **7** 16 **8** 6

9 70 **10** 923 **11** a 81, 91, 101, 111 b 60, 65, 70, 75
c 12, 15, 18, 21 d 460, 470 **12** A **13** 4 rectangles will be coloured.

14 7250 **15** a 62 b 90 **16** 3:15 or quarter past 3

31:2

1 345 **2** 161 **3** 43 **4** 25 **5** 261 **6** 28 **7** 14 **8** 3

9 60 **10** 913 **11** 45 + 35 = 80 **12** a grey b no

13 28 **14** Answers will equal 15. **15** a 93 b 78

Activity

8, 4, 10, 6, 9, 5, 7, 11, 3, 1
9, 5, 14, 7, 10, 6, 8, 12, 4, 2

31:3

1 a 90 b 104 **2** 4, 4, opposite sides will be the same colour

3 Estimates will vary. 15

4 a $\frac{3}{5}$ b $\frac{2}{5}$ **5** 428 **6** 12, 12, 4, 3 **7** 91

31:4

1 yes **2** a 174 b 177 **3** 156 **4** a 1.5 b 3 c 6

5 104 (number line: 69 +30 → 99 +1 → 100 +4 → 104) **6** a 35 b 34

Challenge

Answers will vary. One example is that you may see a crocodile at school tomorrow.

Activity

a total of 7 b Answers will vary.

32:1

1 78 **2** 59 **3** 6 **4** 3 **5** 64 **6** 53 **7** 25 **8** 8 **9** 70

10 76 **11** 300 m **12** 4 cm, 40 mm **13** 12 **14** 30 **15** $1.25 or 125c

16 a 76 – 35 = 71 – 30 = 41 b 45 – 28 = 25 – 8 = 17

17 3521 **18** 14 **19** August **20** 12, 15, 18, 21, 24 **21** a 63 b 64

32:2

1 429 **2** 172 **3** 31 **4** 25 **5** 53 **6** 4 **7** 14 **8** 8

9 60 **10** 39 **11** 25 m **12** a 1 fifty-two b 52 minutes past 1

13 2 cm, 20 mm **14** 92 **15** The top and bottom sides of the trapezium will be traced. Two sets of parallel lines in the rectangle will be traced: the top and bottom sides, and the left and right sides.

16 10

17 a 61 b 81 **18** 59 – 30 = 29

Activity

a 6148, 6158, 6157

b 8381, 8081, 8061, 8065

c 9027, 9427, 7427, 7422, 7482

32:3

1 33 **2** 51 **3** 77 **4** triangular pyramid, 4, 6, 4, triangle

5 a 35 mm b 15 mm c 45 mm **6** 2 past 4 b 36 past 10, 24 to 11

7 9427 **8** no **9** a 82 b 73 **10** 76 – 50 = 26

32:4

1 a 100 b 100 c 500 d 1000 **2** 4 **3** a 2 cm b 5 cm

Challenge

Answers will vary.

Activity

10, 30, 50, 70, 100, 80, 20, 60, 40, 90

0, 15, 25, 35, 50, 40, 10, 30, 20, 45

2, 6, 10, 14, 20, 16, 4, 12, 8, 18

33:1

1 33 **2** 3 **3** 20 **4** 10 **5** 14 **6** 42 **7** 4 **8** 5 **9** 4

10 28 **11** 80 cm **12** 8 cm **13** 4 trapeziums **14** yes **15** **B, D, C, A**

16 6239 **17** no **18** 4 **19** Answers will equal 6.

33:2

1 79 **2** 32 **3** 27 **4** 69 **5** 35 **6** 36 **7** 4 **8** 5

9 4 **10** 25 **11** 34 cm **12** a 1 cm 7 mm b 2 cm 6 mm

13 81, 45 **14** a even chance b impossible c unlikely d certain

15 4538 **16**

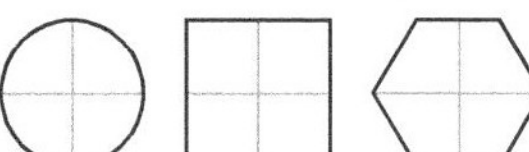

Activity

2, 6, 10, 14, 20, 16, 4, 12, 8, 18

0, 12, 20, 28, 40, 32, 8, 24, 16, 36

5, 15, 25, 35, 50, 40, 10, 30, 20, 45

33:3

1 38 **2** 48 **3** 68 **4** $97 **5** $84 **6** 81, 52

7 Each quarter has 2 rectangles. 2 rectangles will be coloured. $\frac{3}{4}$ or $\frac{6}{8}$

8 no **9** 7 cm, 70 mm **10** no **11** 5048 **12** 90 or 91

13 a 30 b 46 c 51 d 76

33:4

1 90 cm **2** 55 **3** a 13 km b 37 km c 24 km **4** A

Challenge

Answers will vary.

Activity

84, 61, 48, 46, 42, 59, 75, 43, 57, 40

82, 59, 36, 64, 50, 57, 83, 61, 65, 48

34:1

1 5 **2** 2 **3** 7 **4** 9 **5** 12 **6** 24 **7** 10 **8** 8 **9** 15

10 18 **11**

A								
B								
C								

12 3 layers of 6 = 18 boxes **13** $\frac{6}{8}$

14 1 layer of 7 = 7 cubic centimetres **15** 13, 32 **16** November

34:2

1 14 **2** 15 **3** 2 **4** 3 **5** 15 **6** 38 **7** 28 **8** 16

9 40 **10** 26 **11** a 14 b 8 **12** 60 cm

13 data **14** 2 layers of 6 = 12 cubic centimetres

15 15, 54 **16** 4:22 or 22 minutes past 4 **17** 601

Activity

(1) metre (2) centimetre (3) millimetre (4) litre (5) kilogram

(6) minute (7) square centimetre (8) cubic centimetre

34:3

1 18 **2** $26 **3** 3 layers of 10 = 30 cubic centimetres

4 The 'Total' column is 22, 8, 19, 28 b 20

5 3 out of 4, $\frac{3}{4}$ **6** a 7 squares will be coloured.

b 5 squares will be coloured.

34:4

1 6 **2** a 6 cm^2 b 12 cm **3** 6 **4** 5

Challenge

First clock will be coloured up to 4, second clock will be coloured up to 2.

$\frac{1}{3}$ is larger than $\frac{1}{6}$.

Activity

a 6028, 6128, 6118 b 9341, 9541, 6541, 6511, 6513

c 5033, 5833, 2833, 2837, 2877

35:1

1 16 2 20 3 30 4 3 5 49 6 8 7 19 8 5
9 7 10 19 11 **B** and **C** 12 a $\frac{3}{8}$ b 4 rectangles will be coloured, $\frac{4}{8}$
13 465 780 14 Answers could include: It is a sphere. It has one curved surface, no edges, no corners. It can roll. 15 5 16 a 7 b 2

35:2

1 14 2 40 3 7 4 5 5 23 6 31 7 83 8 72
9 7 10 18 11 B will be ticked, C will be crossed, A will be circled
12 31 13 830 871 will be circled. 14 6 15 34 321 16 a 2 parts will be coloured, $\frac{2}{4}$ b parallelogram 17 3 layers of 6 = 18 cubic centimetres
18 12, 15, 18, 21, 24

Activity

(21) abacus (22) table (23) picture graph (24) tally
(25) column graph (26) sector graph (27) digital watch
(28) analog clock (29) calendar (30) balance scales

35:3

1 a 73 741 b 90 639

2

	Thousands	Hundreds	Tens	Units
a	567	6	0	3
b	380	6	8	9
c	293	0	0	4

3 no 4 4 layers of 4 = 16 cubic centimetres
5 Answers will vary 6 a Diane b 12 c 11 7 31

35:4

1 a 2 cm b 6 cm 2 6 faces + 8 corners – 12 edges = 2
3 560 963 will be circled. 4 970 630 5 3
6 a 8 b 67

Challenge

Answers will vary.

Activity

(20) net of a cube (24) cube (25) prism (26) pyramid
(28) cylinder (29) cone (30) sphere

	Faces	Edges	Corners
Number	6	12	8

36:1

1 20 2 30 3 40 4 50 5 67 6 2 7 3 8 12 9 13
10 39 11 cube and cylinder 12 a rhombus b hexagon c 3 d 7
13 991 567 will be circled. 14 6 15 22

36:2

1 45 2 145 3 24 4 38 5 748 6 458 7 84
8 64 9 20, 4 10 a ÷ b ∟ c 2B d 1B 11 metres
12 95 (number line: 67 +20 → 87 +3 → 90 +5 → 95) 13 153 14 prism 15 599 16 a 6 b 3

Activity

4, 7, 10, 3, 8, 5, 12, 11, 6, 9
14, 8, 11, 5, 9, 6, 13, 4, 7, 10

36:3

1 753 200 2 a 41 b 33 c 63 d 72
3 a cube b square c 4A d 1B 4 litres
5 a 85 (number line: 49 +30 → 79 +1 → 80 +5 → 85) b 38 (number line: 72 – 30 → 42 –2 → 40 –2 → 38)
6 a circle b square c circle

36:4

1 508 076 2 5 3 a 15 b 27
4 B - more than half

Challenge

Answers will vary.

Activity

a 12, 12, 6, 2
b 36, 36, 4, 9
c 40, 40, 5, 8
d 90, 90, 10, 9

37:1

1 23 2 33 3 43 4 53 5 38 6 4 7 14 8 16 9 6
10 48 11 a D b A 12 no 13 30 14 439 017
15 4320, 65 195, 71 920 16 6 17 a 18th December (or December 18) b 13th December (or December 13)

37:2

1 25 2 35 3 45 4 55 5 33 6 16 7 13 8 16
9 35 10 36 11 a 7 b 14 c 31 d 30 12 yes 13 562 092
14 a pansies b 15 c 5 15 a 603 079 b 906 051
16 a 69 – 40 = 29 b 88 – 40 = 48

Activity

1, 4, 7, 2, 9, 6, 3, 8, 5, 10
7, 4, 9, 0, 8, 2, 5, 10, 3, 6

37:3

1 77 2 31 3 18.02.26 4 14 5 a centimetres b litres
6 The $1, 20c, 10c and 5c coins will be circled. Change = $1.35
7 a 6 b emu c 4 8 40

37:4

❶ 10 ❷ 25 ❸ 50 ❹ 100 ❺ 45 ❻ 6 boats will be circled.

❼ 45, 60, 75, 90, 105 ❽ 28 ❾ $8:40

Challenge

(1, 1 and 5), (1, 2 and 4), (1, 3 and 3), (2, 2 and 3)

Activity

Answers will vary.

17:3 out of 9

1. Colour 4 sixths of this rectangle.

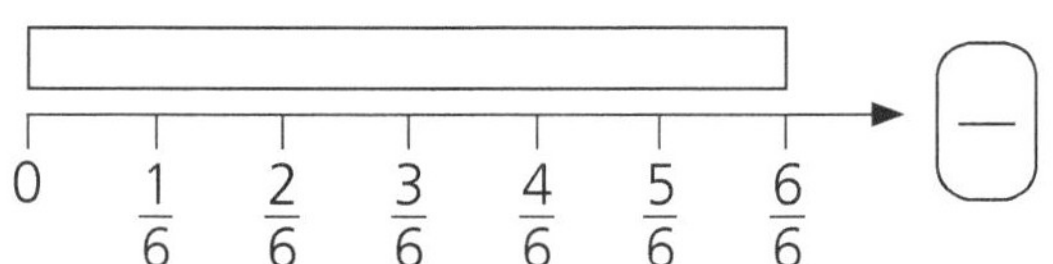

2. Do we measure mass with centimetres, grams or litres? ______

3. Is a mug more than 1 kg? ______

4. What analog time is shown?

______

5. Write the time that is four minutes after 7 to 5. ______

6. 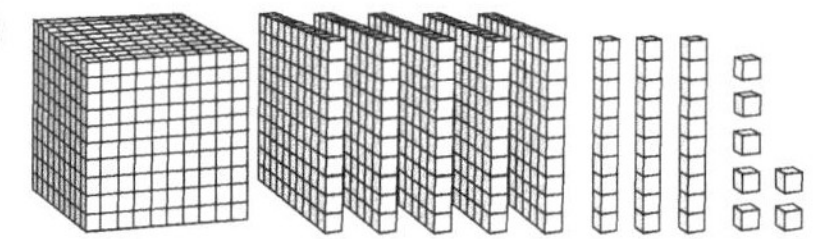

The number modelled here is ______.

7. Would you use metres (m) or centimetres (cm) to measure the length of a truck? ______

8. Write 3 metres 35 centimetres in short form. ______

9. Write in words: 14, 40, 44.

______

______

17:4 out of 8

Extension

1. How many different odd pairs could I make from 3 odd socks? ______

2. Circle $\frac{1}{4}$.

3. True or false?
$\frac{1}{4}$ is more than $\frac{1}{8}$. ______

4. a Colour 5 sixths red and 1 sixth blue.
   b 5 sixths + 1 sixth ______

5. Twelve bolts have the same mass as 2 shoes. How many bolts have the same mass as 4 shoes? ______

6. Write the time that is 1 hour and 4 minutes before 4 thirty-six. ______

7. 12 △ 8 = 20 △ = ______

8. Would 6 pencils weigh more than 3 maths textbooks? ______

Challenge

Draw and label items that weigh less than 1 kg.

0 5 10 15 20 25 30 35 40 45 50 55

In each case, skip count, writing in the numbers as you go. Use the number line to help you.

× tables

Skip count by 3.	3 → 6 → ☐ → ☐ → ☐ → ☐ → ☐
Skip count by 4.	4 → 8 → ☐ → ☐ → ☐ → ☐ → ☐
Skip count by 5.	5 → ☐ → ☐ → ☐ → ☐ → ☐ → ☐ → ☐

18:1 ☐ out of 18

1. 2 × 2 ____
2. 2 × 4 ____
3. 3 × 2 ____
4. 3 × 10 ____
5. 7 × 5 ____
6. Half of 20. ____
7. Half of 8. ____
8. Double 6. ____
9. 53 + 25 ____
10. 63 + 36 ____
11. Would a chair weigh more than 1 kilogram? ____
12. Join the dots. This is a regular ____.
13. Would the mass of potatoes be measured in centimetres, litres or kilograms? ____
14. 5 × 4 = ____ 4 × 5 = ____
15. A B C D

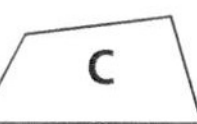

Which shape does not have opposite sides parallel? ____
16. This shows ____ groups of ____.

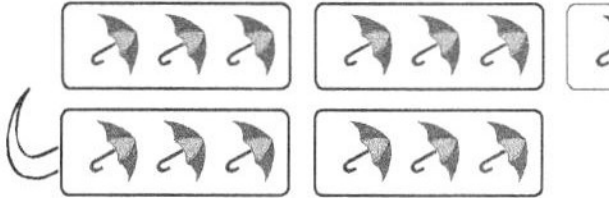

17. 2 × 3 = ____ 3 × 3 = ____ 4 × 3 = ____
18. 23 – 14 = ____ – ____

The answer to this is ____.

18:2 ☐ out of 16

1. 8 × 10 ____
2. 3 × 10 ____
3. 8 × 2 ____
4. 6 × 10 ____
5. $\begin{array}{r} 55 \\ +\ 22 \\ \hline \end{array}$
6. 3 × 4 ____
7. 4 × 4 ____
8. 8 × 5 ____
9. 3 × 5 ____
10. $\begin{array}{r} 45c \\ -\ 24c \\ \hline \end{array}$
11. Use the short form to write 8 kilograms. ____
12. How many wheels on 4 cars? ____
13. Which picture shows lines that are:

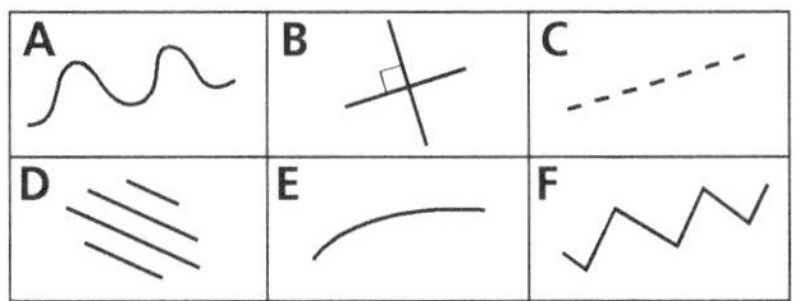

a parallel? ____ b perpendicular? ____
14. How many animals in:

a 32 pairs? ____
b 46 pairs? ____
c 84 pairs? ____
15. Which quadrilaterals have all sides equal?

____
16. Join the dots.

This is a regular ____.

A coin is to be tossed 10 times.

a How many *heads* would be most likely? ____

b Toss a coin 10 times and show the results in this graph. Colour a circle for each toss.

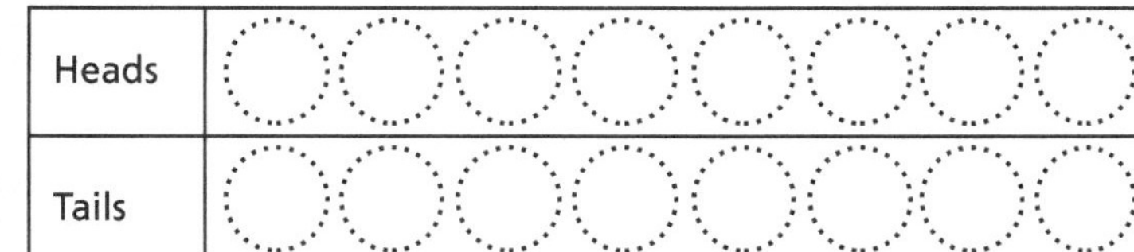

Heads	○ ○ ○ ○ ○ ○ ○ ○
Tails	○ ○ ○ ○ ○ ○ ○ ○

18:3 ☐ out of 8

❶ How many legs would there be on 6 dogs? ______

❷ Does $4 \times 6 = 6 \times 4$? ______

❸ 3 rows of 3 = ______

$3 \times 3 =$ ______

Is 9 a square number? ______

❹ Does: **a** $4 + 4 + 4 = 3 \times 4$? ______

b $10 \times 2 = 2 \times 10$? ______

c $78 + 34 = 34 + 78$? ______

❺ ______ rows of ______ = ______

______ $\times$ ______ = ______

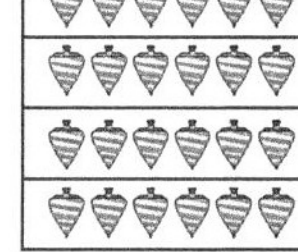

❻ Is 3×5 half of 3×10? ______

❼ Use this picture to complete the graph.

Kangaroos	Emus	Rabbits

❽ Follow the rule to continue each pattern.

a Add 5. 15, ______, ______, ______

b Subtract 2. 20, ______, ______, ______

c Add 10. 4, ______, ______, ______

d Subtract 10. 60, ______, ______, ______

18:4 Extension ☐ out of 5

❶ This pyramid is made of 3 layers of 10c coins. What is the total value if it is:

a 3 layers high? ______

b 7 layers high? ______

❷ If 2 non-parallel lines are drawn to cross these parallel lines, at how many points would lines cross altogether? ______

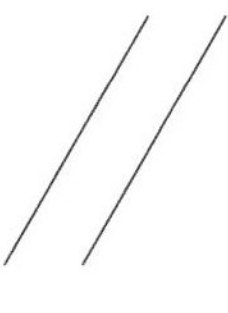

❸ 5 pentagons have ______ sides.

❹

1	3	9	10	12	7

Which three of these numbers add to give:

a 17? ______ **b** 19? ______

❺ 6 △ 8 = 14 △ = ______

Challenge

List number sentences that are equal to 17.

× tables

6 groups of 2 is the same as **3 rows of 4**.

	2	4	6	8	10
× 2					

	1	2	3	4	5
× 4					

19:1 ☐ out of 14

1. 2 × 4 ______
2. 3 × 4 ______
3. 10 × 4 ______
4. 5 × 4 ______
5. $\begin{array}{r} 27 \\ +\ 12 \\ \hline \end{array}$
6. Double 9. ______
7. Half of 18. ______
8. 33 + 22 ______
9. 44 + 11 ______
10. $\begin{array}{r} \$56 \\ -\ \$11 \\ \hline \end{array}$
11. Start at 40. Count by 4s.

    40, ______, ______, ______, ______, ______
12. Six teams of 4 children.

    How many children altogether? ______
13. Baskets Thrown

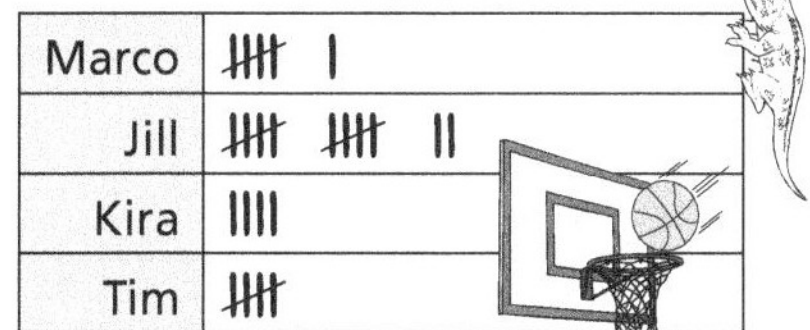

Baskets Thrown	
Marco	𝍸 I
Jill	𝍸 𝍸 II
Kira	IIII
Tim	𝍸

  a Who threw the most baskets? ______

  b Who threw the least baskets? ______

  c How many more did Jill score than Tim? ______

  d How many more did the girls score than the boys? ______

  e How many baskets were thrown altogether? ______

14. This shape is a ______________.

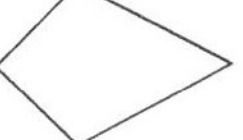

19:2 ☐ out of 16

1. 6 × 4 ______
2. 8 × 4 ______
3. 9 × 4 ______
4. 6 × 4 ______
5. $\begin{array}{r} 53 \\ +\ 41 \\ \hline \end{array}$
6. 30 take away 3. ______
7. Add 25 to 34. ______
8. 48 minus 35. ______
9. 45 plus 44. ______
10. $\begin{array}{r} \$44 \\ -\ \$34 \\ \hline \end{array}$
11. True or false?

  a 3 × 9 = 9 × 3 ______

  b 3 × 9 = 9 + 9 + 9 ______

12. 5 flowers in each bunch.

    How many in 4 bunches? ______
13. a 28, 24, 20, ______, ______, ______, ______

    b 76, 66, 56, ______, ______, ______, ______

    c 64, 54, 44, ______, ______, ______, ______
14. A B C

    Which group shows parallel lines? ______
15. This shape is a

    ______________.

16. These shapes are

    r______________ shapes.

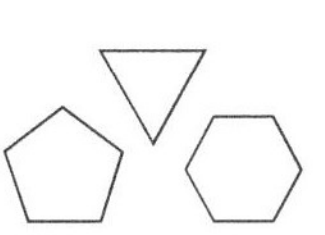

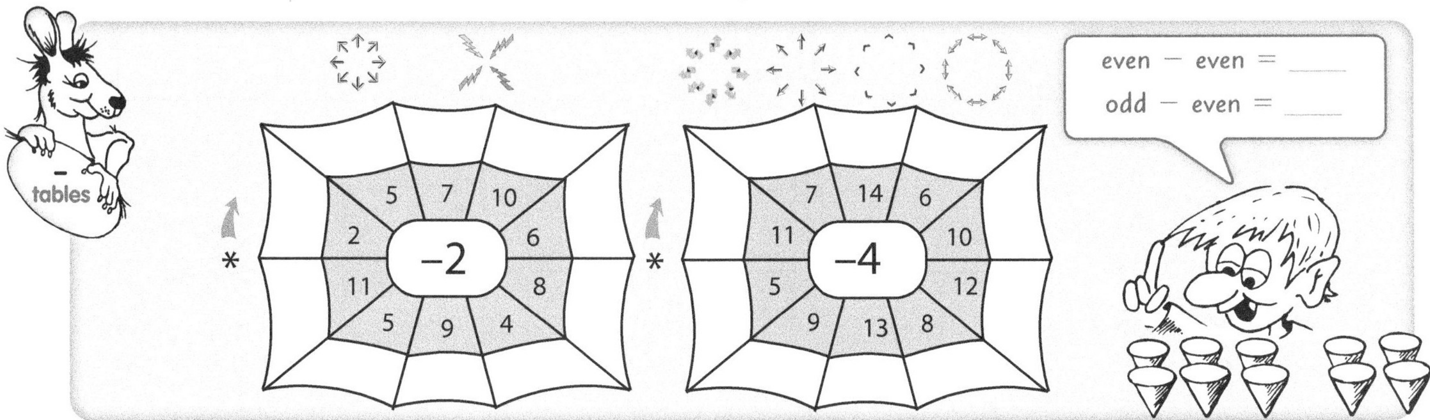

19:3 ☐ out of 8

1.
$$\begin{array}{r} 3 \\ 4 \\ 8 \\ 6 \\ +\ 9 \\ \hline \end{array}$$

2.
$$\begin{array}{r} 9 \\ 2 \\ 4 \\ 1 \\ +\ 3 \\ \hline \end{array}$$

3.
$$\begin{array}{r} 8 \\ 6 \\ 2 \\ 1 \\ +\ 4 \\ \hline \end{array}$$

4. Follow the rule to continue each pattern.
   - a Add 3. 3, ______, ______, ______
   - b Subtract 2. 19, ______, ______, ______
   - c Add 10. 23, ______, ______, ______
   - d Subtract 10. 96, ______, ______, ______

5. Use the tally in 19:1 question 13, on the opposite page, to complete this column graph.

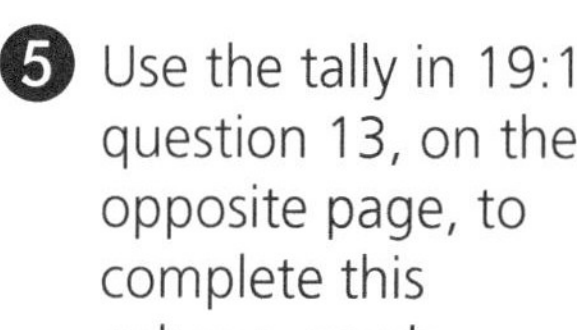

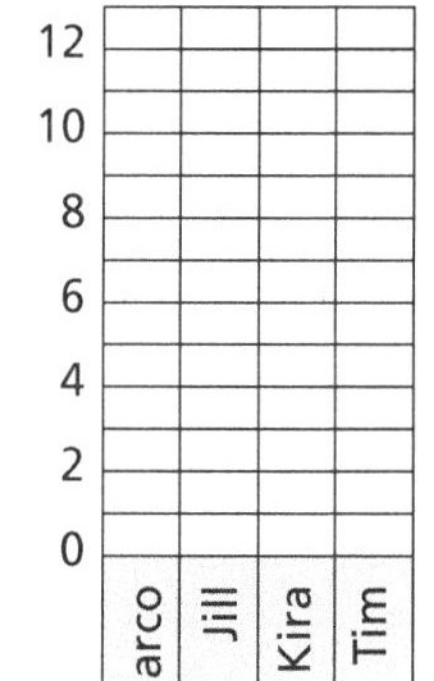

6. Start at 40 and count by 5s.

   40, ______, ______, ______, ______

7. Does 5 × 4 = 4 × 5? ______

8.
   - a 10 dogs have ______ legs.
   - b 5 dogs have ______ legs.
   - c 7 dogs have ______ legs.
   - d Does a group of 10 dogs have twice as many legs as a group of 5 dogs? ______

19:4 ☐ out of 4

Extension

1. What shape would you get if you fold the shape along the dotted line?

   a  ______

   b 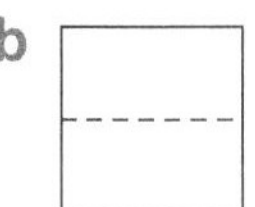 ______

2. 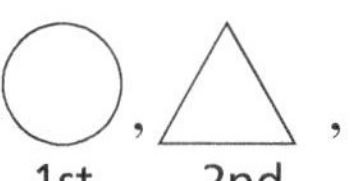 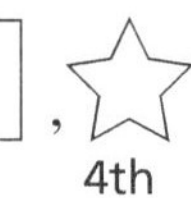 

   If this pattern were repeated, what would be the 13th shape? ______

3.
   - a How many quarters in 5 oranges? ______
   - b $\frac{1}{4} + \frac{1}{4} + \frac{1}{4} + \frac{1}{4} + \frac{1}{4} + \frac{1}{4}$ ______
   - c I had 3 oranges cut into quarters. I ate 2 pieces. How much is left? ______

4. How many legs on 5 cats and 3 birds? ______

Challenge

Write number sentences that are equal, for example, 54 – 42 = 52 – 40.

______

______

______

______

______

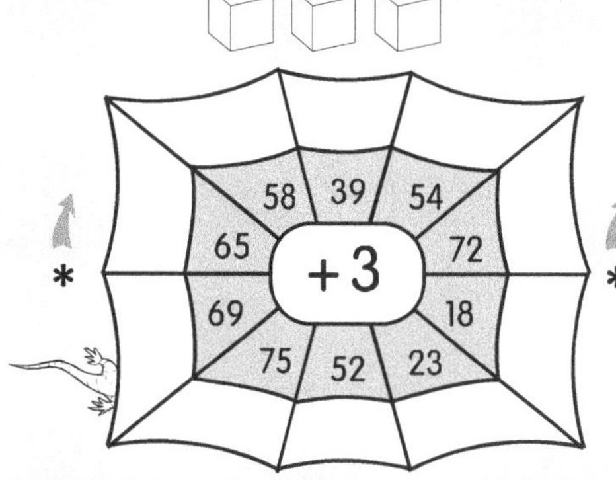

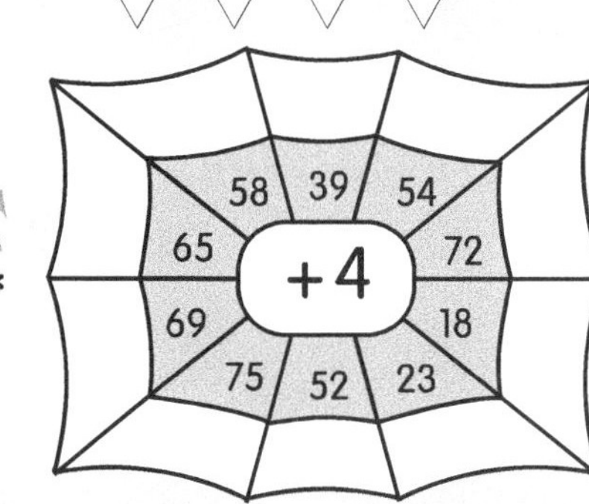

 • *AUSTRALIAN SIGNPOST MATHS NSW 3 MENTALS* • ISBN 978 0 6557 0910 7

20:1 out of 18

1. 3×4 ____
2. 4×4 ____
3. 2×3 ____
4. 5×3 ____
5. $\begin{array}{r} 32 \\ +\ 11 \\ \hline \end{array}$
6. 4 less than 12. ____
7. 4 less than 16. ____
8. 3 less than 12. ____
9. 3 less than 9. ____
10. $\begin{array}{r} \$41 \\ -\ \$31 \\ \hline \end{array}$
11. Write the name and the number of edges.

a 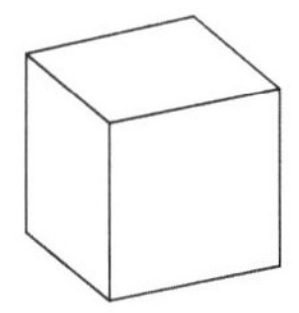

b 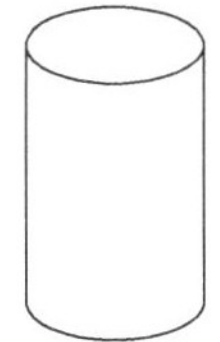

12. a 5 children have ______ toes.

    b 3 children have ______ toes.

13. Does $4 \times 9 = 9 \times 4$? ____
14. I made towers using 3 blocks for each tower. How many blocks would I need for 4 towers? ____

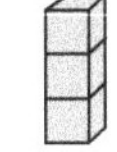

15. 3, 6, 9, ____, ____, ____, ____
16. How many sides on 3 triangles? ____

17. a Draw a kite.

    b How many sides? ____

    c How many corners? ____
18. I had \$10 and was given \$15 more.

    How much money do I have now? ____

20:2

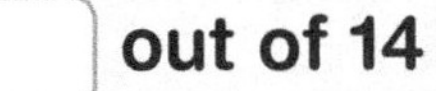

out of 14

1. 7×4 ____
2. 9×4 ____
3. 6×3 ____
4. 7×3 ____
5. $\begin{array}{r} 50 \\ +\ 47 \\ \hline \end{array}$
6. 3 less than 51. ____
7. 3 less than 42. ____
8. 4 less than 22. ____
9. 4 less than 33. ____
10. $\begin{array}{r} \$87 \\ -\ \$67 \\ \hline \end{array}$
11. Describe this object.

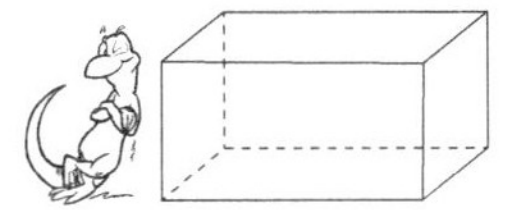

12. Add 10 to complete these patterns.

    a 546, ____, ____, ____, ____

    b 789, ____, ____, ____, ____

    c 2460, ____, ____, ____
13. a How many faces has this pyramid? ____

    b How many corners has this pyramid? ____

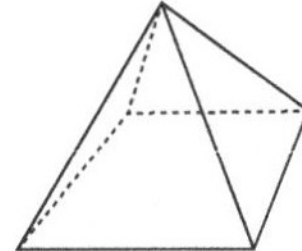

14. 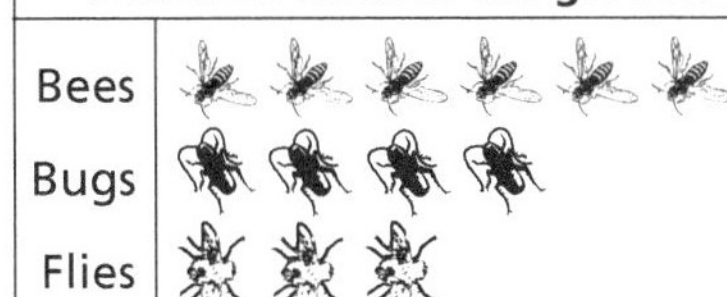

Creatures seen in the garden	
Bees	🐝🐝🐝🐝🐝🐝
Bugs	🪳🪳🪳🪳
Flies	🪰🪰🪰

Each picture = 2 creatures

    a How many more bees than flies were seen? ____

    b How many creatures were seen altogether? ____

Turn to ID card B on page 7.

Give the answers for these numbers.

(3) ____ lines (4) ____ lines

(8) ____ (11) ____

(12) ____ (13) ____

(16) ____ shapes (17) ____ shapes

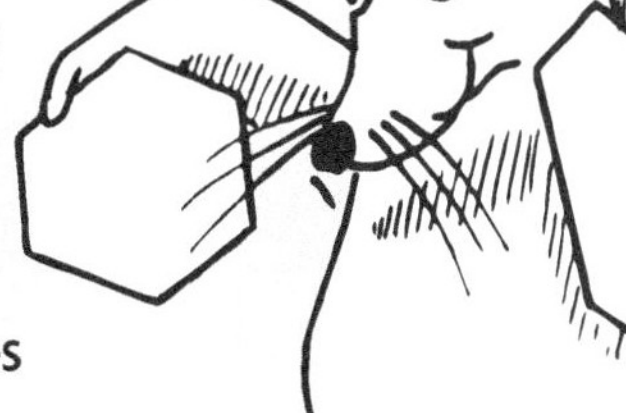

20:3 out of 11

❶
$$\begin{array}{r} 6 \\ 2 \\ 3 \\ 4 \\ 9 \\ +\ 1 \\ \hline \end{array}$$

❷
$$\begin{array}{r} 5 \\ 4 \\ 3 \\ 2 \\ 1 \\ +\ 6 \\ \hline \end{array}$$

❸
$$\begin{array}{r} 9 \\ 2 \\ 1 \\ 8 \\ 6 \\ +\ 2 \\ \hline \end{array}$$

❹ Is 4 × 10 twice 2 × 10? ______

❺ Follow the rule to complete these patterns.

a Subtract 10. 96, ______, ______, ______

b Add 3. 9, ______, ______, ______, ______

c Add 100. 45, ______, ______, ______

d Add 5. 12, ______, ______, ______, ______

❻ I bought 32 apples and 16 were eaten.

______ − ______ = ______

How many were left? ______

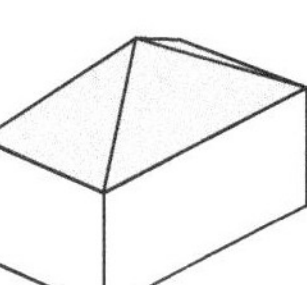

❼ Name the two solids in this model. ______

______

❽ These lines are

______.

❾ I made 7 towers each with 5 blocks.

How many blocks did I use? ______

❿ How many corners has a kite? ______

⓫ ⬠ A pentagon has ____ sides.

20:4 out of 5

Extension

❶ How many pairs of different counting numbers add to give 16? ______

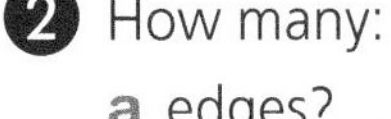

❷ How many:

a edges? ______

b faces + corners? ______

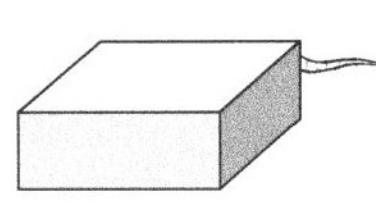

❸ a The line parallel to **E**. ______

b The lines parallel to **A**. ______

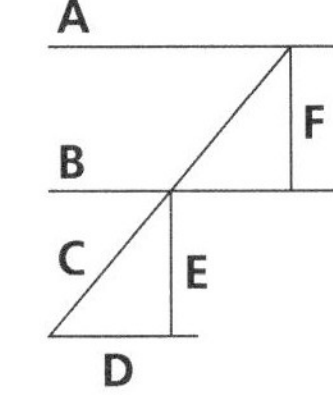

❹ Guess my 3D object.
It has 5 faces. It has 8 edges.
The cross-section is a square.

______

Draw the object.

❺ I have 13 fewer cards than my friend.

They have 52 cards.

How many cards do we have altogether?

______ + ______ = ______

Challenge

Rewrite these number sentences by subtracting 10, 20 or 30 from each side, for example 36 − 16 = 26 − 6. Then write the answer.

a 47 − 29 = ______ − ______ = ______

b 56 − 38 = ______ − ______ = ______

c 53 − 36 = ______ − ______ = ______

d 65 − 27 = ______ − ______ = ______

Strategy Time

Complete each pattern and write the rule.

a 34, 37, 40, ____, ____, ____, ____, ____, ____, ____, ____ Rule: ______

b 47, 45, 43, ____, ____, ____, ____, ____, ____, ____, ____ Rule: ______

c 538, 548, 558, ____, ____, ____, ____, ____, ____ Rule: ______

d 889, 789, 689, ____, ____, ____, ____, ____, ____ Rule: ______

e 1230, 1330, 1430, ____, ____, ____, ____ Rule: ______

Ask, 'How much is added or taken away each time?'

21:1 ☐ out of 17

1. 0 × 5 ____
2. 4 × 10 ____
3. 2 × 5 ____
4. 4 × 4 ____
5. 66 + 11
6. 3 less than 6. ____
7. 3 less than 3. ____
8. 22 − 11 ____
9. 55 − 11 ____
10. $44 − $11

11. Which shapes will roll? ____________.

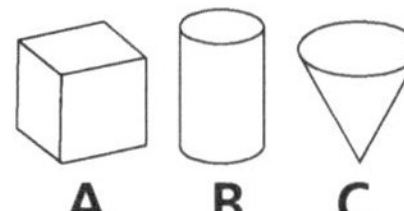

12. 5 groups of 4 = ____
13. 60 – 5 – 5 – 5 = ____
14. This is called an ____________.

15. This is a ____________.
It has ____ faces,
____ edges
and ____ corners.
The cross-section shape is a ____________.

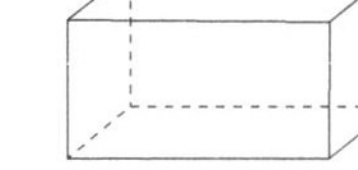

16. I had 3 rows of 5 stickers.
How many stickers did I have? ____
17. Arrange these angles in order of size, from smallest to largest. ____

21:2 ☐ out of 19

1. 3 × 5 ____
2. 3 × 10 ____
3. 3 × 2 ____
4. 3 × 4 ____
5. 39 + 50
6. 4 less than 40. ____
7. 3 less than 30. ____
8. Digits in 4032. ____
9. Half of 24. ____
10. $95 − $45

11. **a** 30 − 3 − 3 − 3 − 3 = ____
b 40 − 4 − 4 − 4 − 4 − 4 − 4 = ____
12. Write these angles in order, smallest to largest. ____

13. Round 44 to the nearest 10. ____
14. Round 546 to the nearest 100. ____
15. Is there an equal chance of throwing each number on a dice? ____
16. How many flat surfaces are on a cylinder? ____

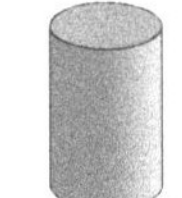

17. Write the even numbers between 43 and 48. ____
18. Use the jump strategy to find 64 − 36.
19. Which is larger, 382, 372 or 375? ____

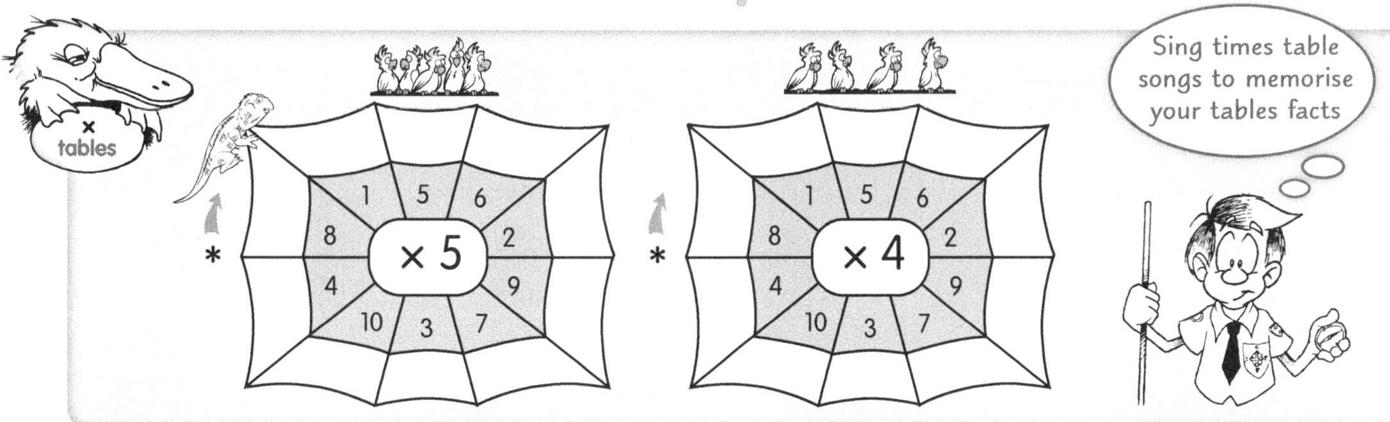

21:3 ☐ out of 5

1 Write two different number sentences that are equal to 17.

__________ = __________

2

A	B	C	D
E	F	G	H

a How many angles on shape **C**? ______

b How many faces on shape **D**? ______

c Name shape **E**. ______

d Which are 2D shapes? ______

e Which are solid objects? ______

3

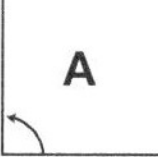

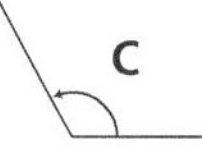

a Which is a right angle? ______

b Which is the largest angle? ______

4 I saw 29 kangaroos and 15 wallabies.
How many did I see altogether?

_____ + _____ = _____

5 This is a __________.

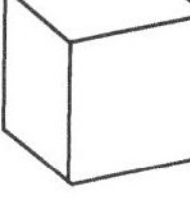

It has ____ faces, ____ edges and ____ corners.

The cross-section is a __________.

21:4 ☐ out of 6

Extension

1 How many faces on 3 cubes? ______

How many edges on 3 cubes? ______

How many vertices on 3 cubes? ______

2 How many 60c stamps could you buy for $2? ______

3 38 + 23 ______

38 ⟶

4 How many sides are there on 5 hexagons and 4 kites? ______

5 I have 17 fewer stickers than my friend.
She has 35 stickers.
How many stickers do we have altogether?

_____ + _____ = _____

6 a 40 + 6 + 4 + 8 + 2 + 1 + 7 = ______

b 30 + 17 + 11 + 13 + 19 + 8 = ______

Challenge

Write a pattern with the rule:

a *Add 2.* __________

b *Subtract 3.* __________

c *Add 4.* __________

d *Subtract 2.* __________

e *Write a pattern using only numbers ending in 0.*

____

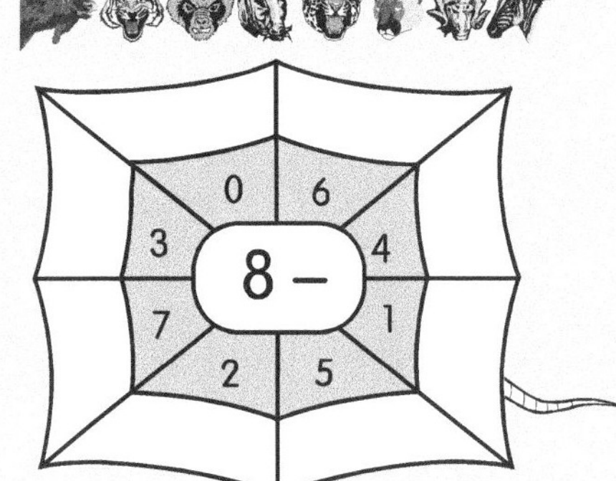

22:1 out of 18

1. 3 × 10 ____
2. 6 × 4 ____
3. 1 × 4 ____
4. 4 × 5 ____
5. Half of 12. ____
6. Double 6. ____
7. Half of 20. ____
8. Double 11. ____
9. Is each shape a prism, a pyramid or neither?

   a 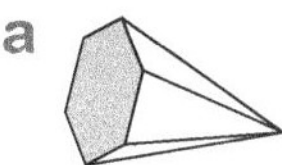 ____

   b 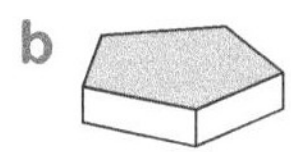 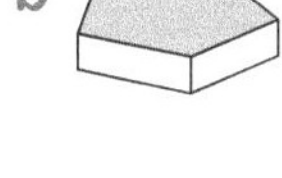 ____

10. This is called an ____________ .

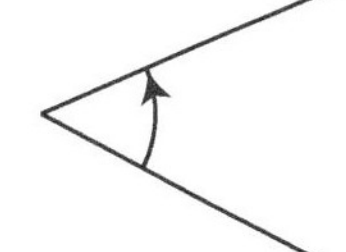

11. 5 kites have ____ sides.
12. Is the corner of this page a right angle? ____
13. The number after 5005 is ________.
14. Would a tennis ball have a mass greater than 1 kg? ____
15. Use the short form to write 3 kilograms. ____
16. 4500 = ____ thousands + ____ hundreds
17. Circle the smallest area.

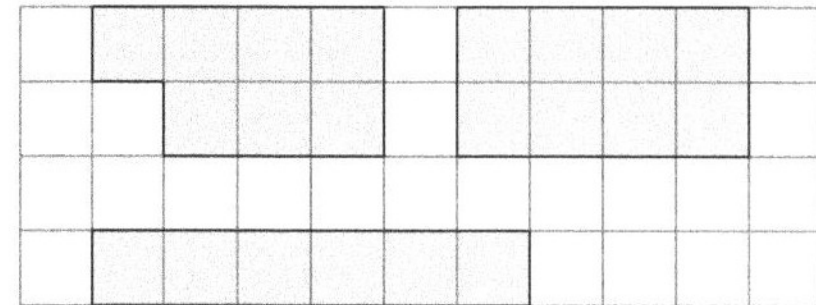

18. 7420, 7430, 7440, ____, ____, ____

22:2 out of 14

1. 10 × 4 ____
2. 9 × 4 ____
3. 8 × 4 ____
4. 7 × 4 ____
5. 54 + 10 ____
6. 39 + 10 ____
7. 88 − 45 ____
8. 79 − 25 ____
9. Write the names of 2 shapes that always have right angles.

   ____
10. Use a ruler to draw two right angles on this grid.
11. My mass is 23 kg and Tom's mass is 34 kg.

    a What is our total mass? ____

    b What is the difference between our mass? ____
12. Draw a line that is a quarter turn anticlockwise.

What number is your line pointing to? ____

13. A rhombus has ________ angles.
14. Use a ruler to copy this angle.

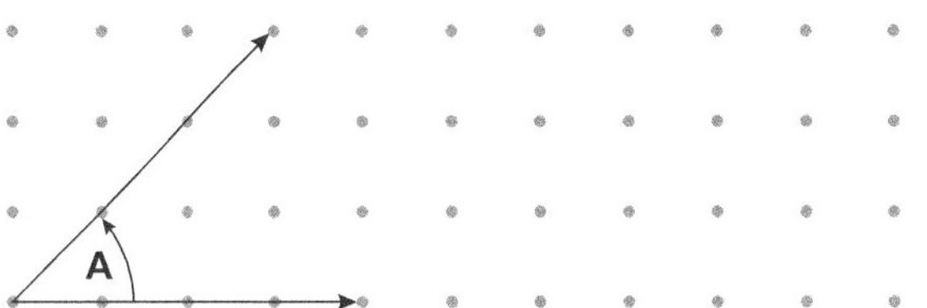

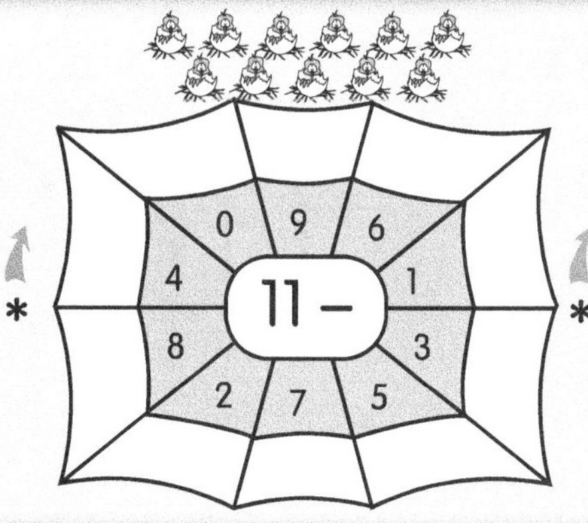

22:3 ☐ out of 11

1. 3
   4
   8
   6
   + 9

2. 9
   2
   4
   1
   + 3

3. 8
   6
   2
   1
   + 4

4. 5735 = _____ thousands + _____ hundreds + _____ tens + _____ ones

5. Write six thousand and thirty-one as a numeral. _____

6. Would a brick have a mass greater than 1 kg? _____

7. 3205, 3305, 3405, _____, _____, _____

8. Use the short form to write 7 kilograms. _____

9. Write the number before and after:
   a _____, 4638, _____
   b _____, 9204, _____

10. Which angle is larger than a right angle? _____

    A B C

11. a The number shown on the abacus. _____

    b How many are in the tens column? _____

    Th H T U

Extension

22:4 ☐ out of 8

1. The total value of Australia's:
   a 2 gold coins _____
   b 4 silver coins _____

2. How many hexagons would be in row:

   a 4? _____ b 10? _____

3. Colour 1 quarter of this rectangle.

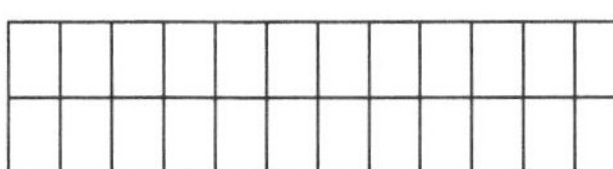

4. Round off 3239 to the nearest hundred. _____

5. I have twelve 10 dollar notes. How much money do I have? _____

6. Which is larger, $\frac{1}{2}$ or $\frac{2}{3}$? _____

7. I had 35 apples. I ate some and had 19 left. How many did I eat? _____

8. 200 + 5000 + 8 + 20 + 60 = _____

Challenge

Rewrite each problem in 3 different ways so that the answer to each is the same.

a 56 – 34 b 47 – 36 c 74 – 45

_____ _____ _____

(+6) (+6)

_____ _____ _____

_____ _____ _____

tables

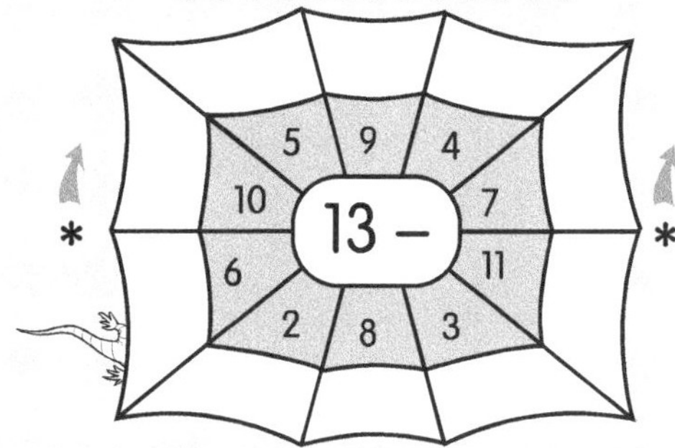

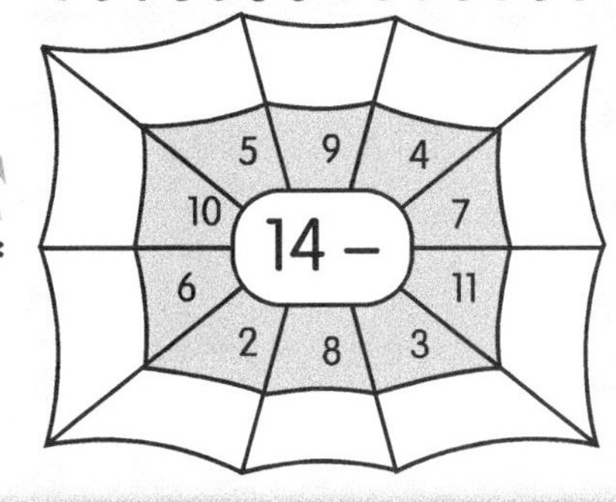

 AUSTRALIAN SIGNPOST MATHS NSW 3 MENTALS • ISBN 978 0 6557 0910 7

23:1   ___ out of 16

1. 4×5 ______
2. 3×2 ______
3. $20 - 2$ ______
4. $20 - 5$ ______
5. Six times two. ______
6. $18 - 9$ ______
7. $5 + $5 + $5 ______
8. $4 + $4 + $4 ______
9. This rectangle is 1 row of ______ or ______ square centimetres.
10. If the clock's hand turns a three-quarter turn clockwise, what does it point to? ______

11. 7294 = ______ thousands + ______ hundreds + ______ tens + ______ ones
12. Which is the largest area? ______

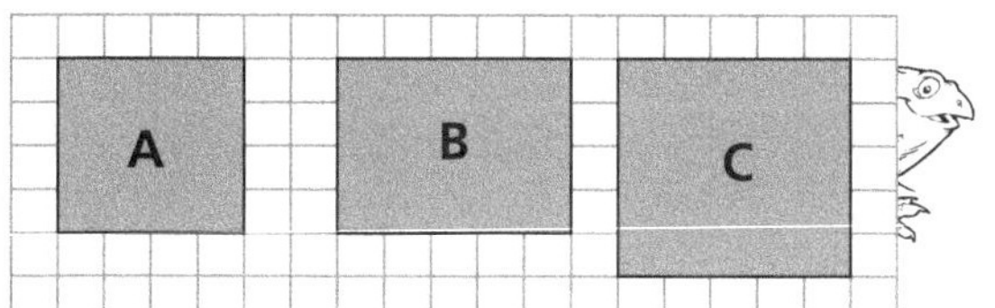

13. Circle the larger fraction.

$\frac{5}{8}$ **or** $\frac{4}{8}$

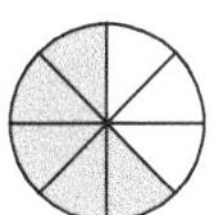

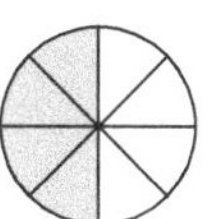

14. How many days in September? ______
15. Days in one week. ______
16. 5, 10, 15, ______, ______, ______, ______, ______

23:2   ___ out of 20

1. $40 - 6$ ______
2. $50 - 8$ ______
3. $70 - 3$ ______
4. $90 - 7$ ______
5. Total of 4 and 3. ______
6. To 24 add 31. ______
7. 23 less than 50. ______
8. Sum of 34 and 4. ______
9. My Dad's mass is 57 kg more than my mass. What is his mass, if my mass is 28 kg? ______
10. Circle the larger fraction. written here. $\frac{2}{4}$ or $\frac{3}{4}$

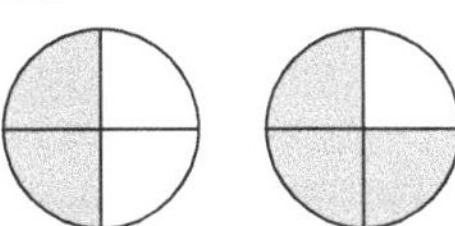

11. 9729 = ______ thousands + ______ hundreds + ______ tens + ______ ones
12. How many days in July and August? ______
13. Name the months in autumn.

______

______

14. Minutes in 1 hour. ______
15. 56 kg – 28 kg = ______
16. Write the short date for 13th April, 2026. ______
17. $3000 + 200 + 70 + 8$ ______
18. Does $4 \times 7 = 7 \times 4$? ______
19. Fill these in for 1479.

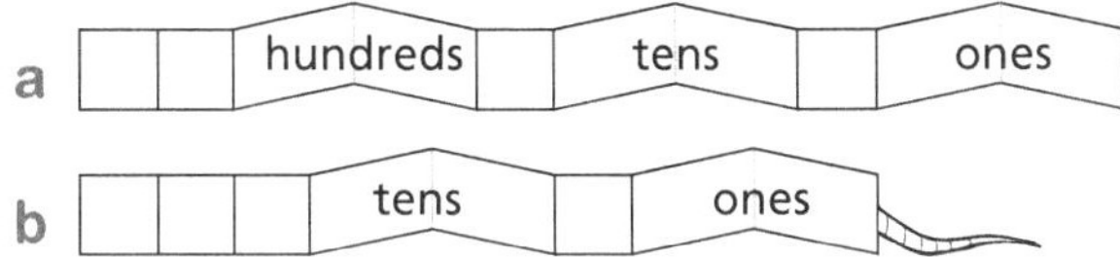

20. 98, 88, 78, ______, ______, ______, ______, ______

○○○○○   ☆☆☆☆☆

– tables

*	+5	5, 10, 15, 20, 25, 30, 35, 40, 45, 50
*	+5	6, 11, 16, 21, 26, 31, 36, 41, 46, 51

Can you see a pattern?

23:3 out of 4

1 a What fraction has been coloured?

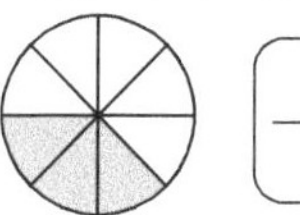
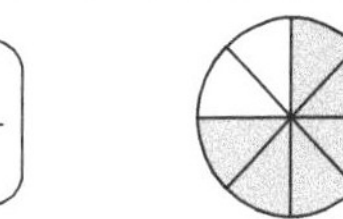

b Colour 7 eighths. Write the fraction.

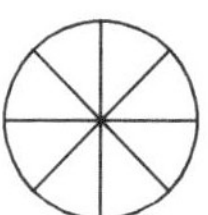

c Tick the largest of the 3 fractions above.

2 a What month is this? ______

October

S	M	T	W	T	F	S
	1	2	3	4	5	6
7	8	9	10	11	12	13
14	15	16	17	18	19	20
21	22	23	24	25	26	27
28	29	30	31			

Note: The calendar for October changes each year.

b How many Tuesdays? ______

c What day is the 12th? ______

d How many days in this month? ______

e What is the date of the first Sunday? ______

f What is the date of the last Saturday? ______

3 This area is

3 rows of ______.

Area = ______

square centimetres

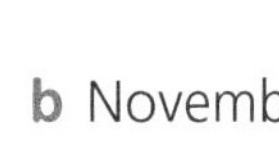

4 How many days in:

a August? ______ b November? ______

23:4 out of 5

Extension

1 Here are 2 desks drawn from above. If 2 sheets of paper can cover one desk, how much paper is needed to cover each group of desks?

a 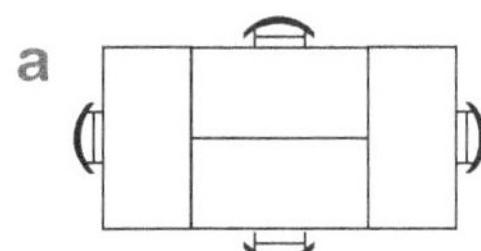 ______

b 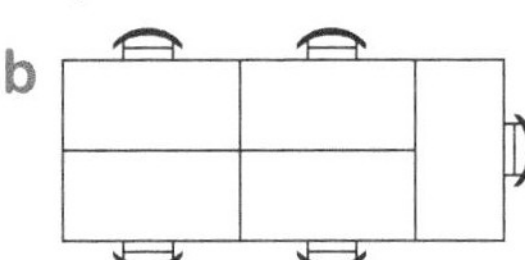 ______

2 This pyramid is made of 20-cent coins.

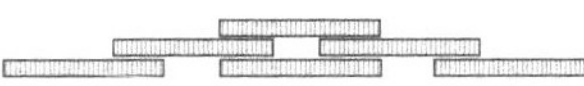

What is the total value if it is:

a 3 layers high? ______

b 5 layers high? ______

3 50 + 2000 + 40 + 1000 + 300 = ______

4 Write a large fraction that is less than 1.

5 I had 12 oranges. A quarter of them were eaten. How many are left? ______

Challenge

List number sentence that are equal to:

a 43 – 28

______

______

b 75 – 39

______

______

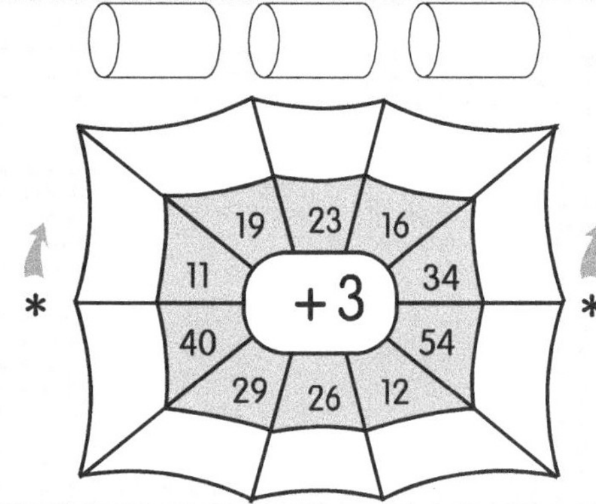

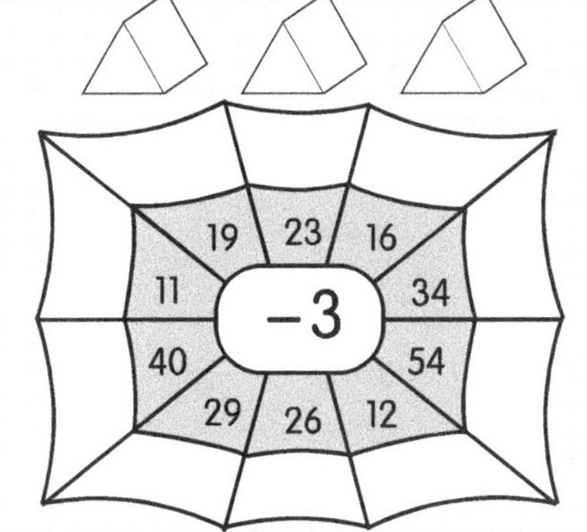

24:1   ☐ out of 14

1. 3×5 ____
2. 0×5 ____
3. 5×5 ____
4. 10×5 ____
5. Two times five. ____
6. 5c + 5c + 5c ____
7. \$2 + \$2 + \$2 ____
8. $10 \div 2 \times 2$ ____
9. **a** What fraction is shaded? ☐

   b Write a fraction that is smaller than $\frac{3}{4}$. ☐
10. 8002 = ____ thousands + ____ ones
11.

   a Who sits in front of **L**? ____

   b Who sits behind **S**? ____

   c Who sits to the right of **G**? ____

   d Who sits to the left of **P**? ____

   e Who sits in the back right corner? ____
12. 4000 + 900 + 30 + 1 = ____
13.

	3	7	4	5	2	10	6	9
× 2								

14. What is the change from \$20 if I spend \$12? ____

24:2   ☐ out of 14

1. 3×4 ____
2. 0×4 ____
3. 3×2 ____
4. 3×4 ____
5. Two times five. ____
6. 20c − 5c ____
7. \$10 − \$8 ____
8. $6 \div 2 \times 2$ ____
9. 3 months before March is ____.
10. **a** How many Mondays? ____

   b The last day is a ____.

   c What day is it 3 days after the 4th of June? ____

June

S	M	T	W	T	F	S
	1	2	3	4	5	6
7	8	9	10	11	12	13
14	15	16	17	18	19	20
21	22	23	24	25	26	27
28	29	30				

Note: The calendar for June changes each year.

11. **a**

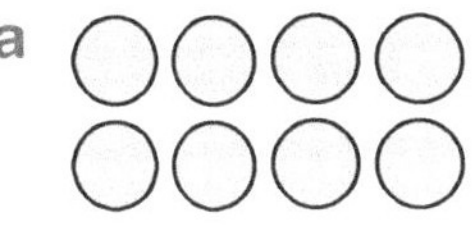

   $2 \times 4 =$ ____

   $4 \times 2 =$ ____

   $8 \div 2 =$ ____

   $8 \div 4 =$ ____

   b

   $2 \times 5 =$ ____

   $5 \times 2 =$ ____

   $10 \div 2 =$ ____

   $10 \div 5 =$ ____
12. How many people can each be given 4 lollies? ____

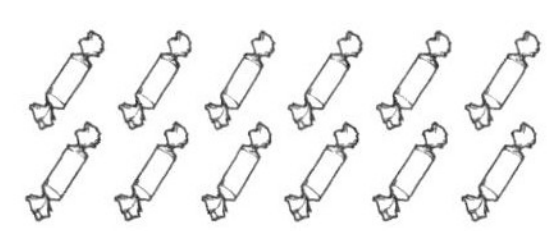

   $12 \div 4 =$ ____
13. 3000 + 200 + 7 = ____
14. **a** 35 + 24 = ____   **b** 51 + 23 = ____

   c 72 + 16 = ____   **d** 43 + 22 = ____

a How many **rows of 10** coins? ____

$3 \times 10 =$ ____ $10 \times 3 =$ ____

$30 \div 3 =$ ____ $30 \div 10 =$ ____

b How many **groups of 5** cones? ____

$4 \times 5 =$ ____ $5 \times 4 =$ ____

$20 \div 4 =$ ____ $20 \div 5 =$ ____

 • *AUSTRALIAN SIGNPOST MATHS NSW 3 MENTALS* • ISBN 978 0 6557 0910 7

24:3 ☐ out of 6

1 a Shade $\frac{3}{4}$. b Shade $\frac{1}{2}$.

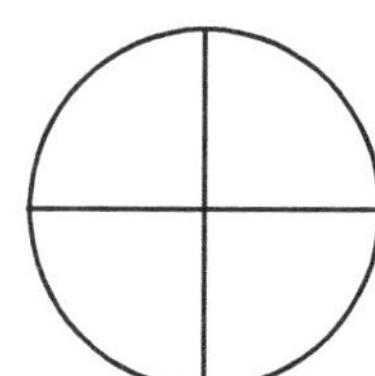

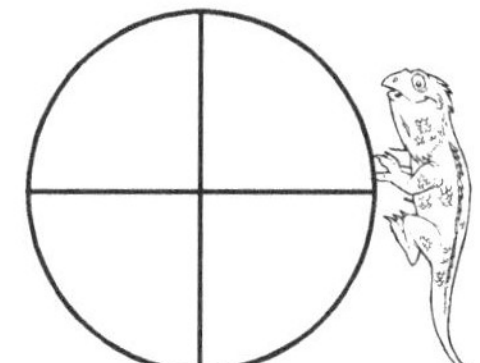

c Which is larger, $\frac{3}{4}$ or $\frac{1}{2}$? ☐

2 Follow the directions and colour the path of the counter.

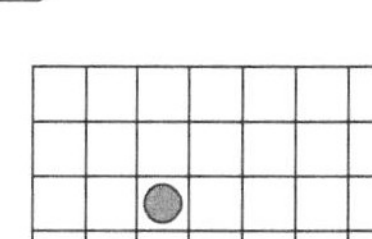

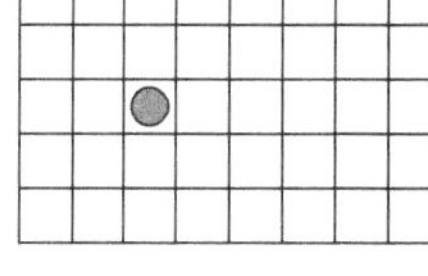

Move 2 up, then 2 left, then 4 down, then 5 right, then 3 up.

3 The area is

______ rows of ______.

Area = ______ square centimetres

4 a Months in one year. ______

b The month before March is ______.

c The month after December is ______.

d November is the ______ month of the year.

e Write the short date for 5th May, 2026. ______

5

	3	7	4	5	2	10	6	9
× 4								

6 Use this table to find:

a 12 ÷ 4 = ______ b 8 ÷ 4 = ______

24:4 Extension ☐ out of 8

1 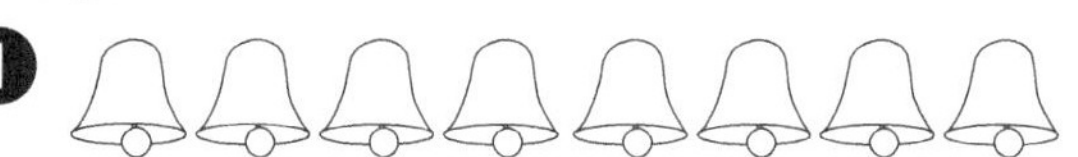

Colour one quarter of the bells red and one half of them blue. What fraction have you coloured? ______

2 What fraction of $1 is:

a 20 cents? ______ b 5 cents? ______

3 70 + 5 + 9000 + 4 + 10 = ______

4 Hours in 3 days. ______

5 Months in 5 years. ______

6 Today is Monday, What day will it be:

a in 6 days time? ______

b 2 weeks from tomorrow? ______

7 a Days in 5 weeks. ______

b Days in 10 weeks. ______

8 I was given $1 on Monday. Each day I was given double the amount I was given the day before.

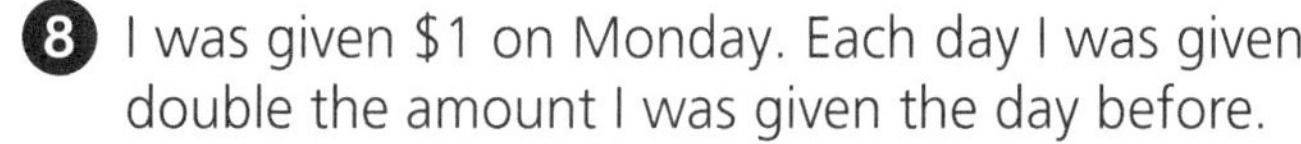

a How much was I given on Friday? ______

b How much money would I have been given altogether once I got to the 7th day? ______

Challenge

Starting at the circle, colour squares to make a path that ends at the triangle.

Write the directions for the path.

See 24:3, question 2.

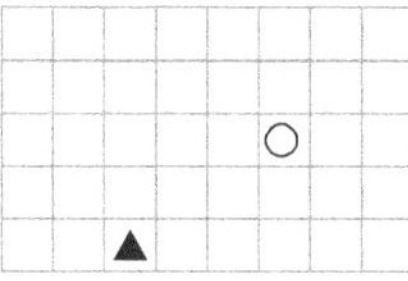

______

______

______

Complete each multiplication fact family.

a 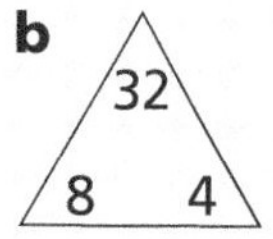

b 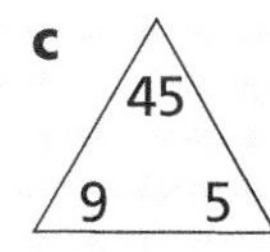

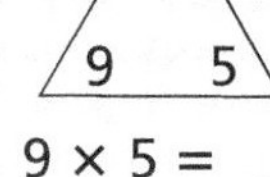

c 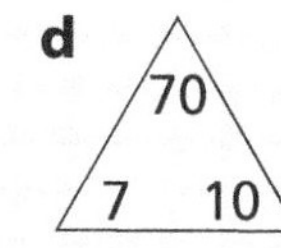

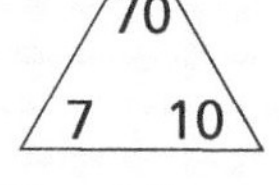

d 70, 7, 10

a	b	c	d
2 × 7 = ___	8 × 4 = ___	9 × 5 = ___	7 × 10 = ___
7 × 2 = ___	4 × 8 = ___	5 × 9 = ___	10 × 7 = ___
14 ÷ 2 = ___	32 ÷ 8 = ___	45 ÷ 9 = ___	70 ÷ 7 = ___
14 ÷ 7 = ___	32 ÷ 4 = ___	45 ÷ 5 = ___	70 ÷ 10 = ___

25:1 out of 14

❶ 8 + 12 ____

❷ 15 + 5 ____

❸ 17 + 3 ____

❹ 11 + 9 ____

❺ 9 + 9 + 9 + 9 ____

❻ 3 + 3 + 3 + 3 ____

❼ 20 − 5 ____

❽ 20 − 7 ____

❾ How many days in:

a April? ____ b November? ____

c May? ____ d October? ____

❿ a How many groups of 5 hooks?

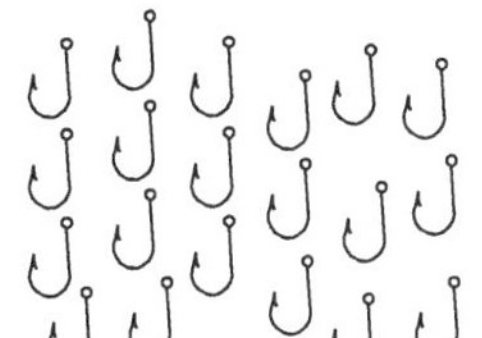

b 4 × 5 ____

c 5 × 4 = ____

d 20 ÷ 5 ____

e 20 ÷ 4 = ____

⓫ 

a 2 × 4 = ____

b 8 ÷ 2 = ____

c 2 × ____ = 8

d 8 ÷ 4 = ____

⓬ Area = ____ square centimetres

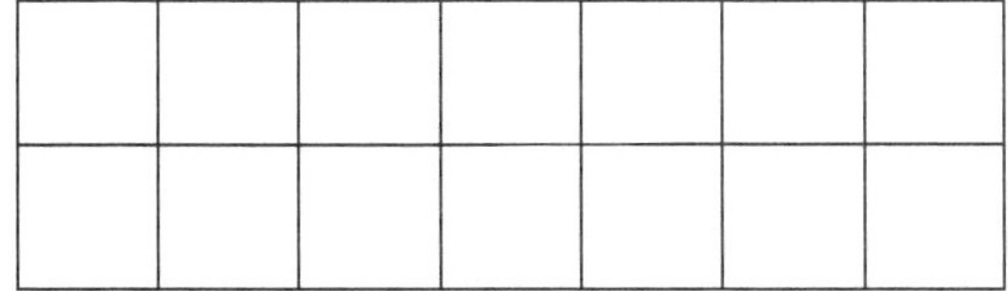

⓭ 0, 3, 6, ____, ____, ____, ____, ____

⓮ Bridge to 10 to find:

a 26 + 9 ____ b 32 − 5 ____

c 38 + 6 ____ d 51 − 6 ____

25:2   out of 12

❶ 23 − 10 ____

❷ 46 + 10 ____

❸ 15 + 15 ____

❹ 19 + 19 ____

❺ Double 29. ____

❻ Halve 68. ____

❼ Halve 46. ____

❽ Double 35. ____

❾ 3 × 5 = 15 so 15 ÷ 5 = ____

6 × 2 = 12 so 12 ÷ 6 = ____

❿ I have 28 toys. To how many children can I give 4 toys?

____

28 ÷ 4 = ____

⓫ 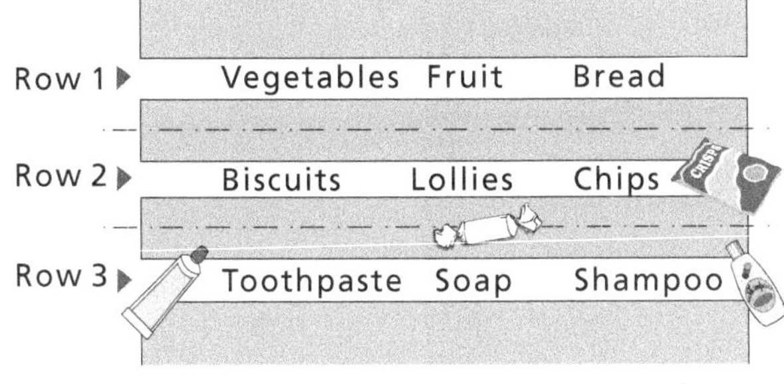

a Which row has chips in it? ____

b What is found between bread and vegetables? ____

c What is found next to the toothpaste? ____

d Which row has bread in it? ____

e What is between the biscuits and chips? ____

⓬ 67, 77, 87, ____, ____, ____, ____

a 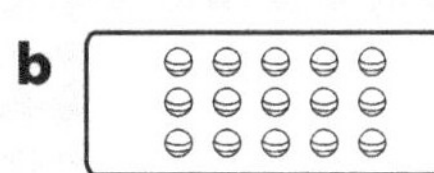 2 rows of 4 = ____ How many 2s in 8? = ____

2 × 4 = ____ so 8 ÷ 4 = ____

b 3 rows of 5 = ____ How many 5s in 15? = ____

3 × 5 = ____ so 15 ÷ 3 = ____

c  3 groups of 2 = ____ How many 2s in 6? = ____

3 × 2 = ____ so 6 ÷ 3 = ____

 ISBN 978 0 6557 0910 7

25:3 ☐ out of 7

1. ____ × 2 = 16 so 16 ÷ 2 = ____

2. How many ears would 10 children have? ____

10 × 2 = ____ 20 ÷ 2 = ____

3. **a** 4 × 10 = ____
   b 40 ÷ 10 = ____
   c 4 × ____ = 40
   d 40 ÷ 4 = ____

4.

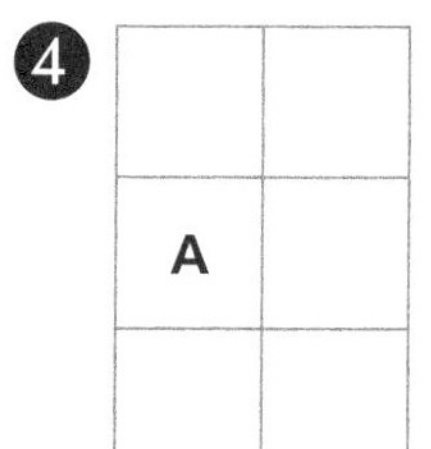

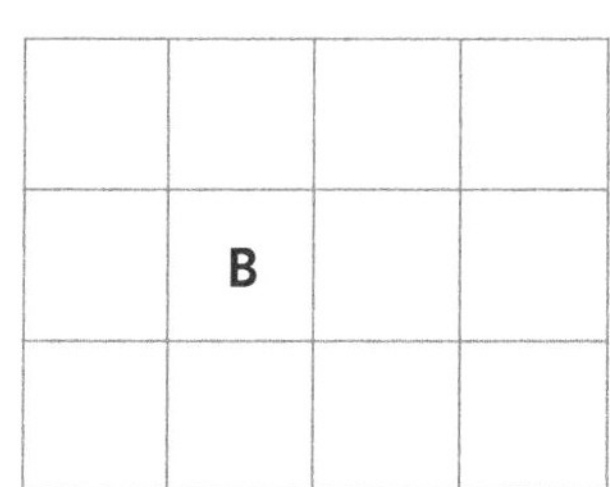

Area = ____ square centimetres   Area = ____ square centimetres

5. 56 hundreds + 34 ones = ____

6. **a** 2 × 3 = ____
   b 6 ÷ 2 = ____
   c ____ × 3 = 6

7. Use the jump strategy to find:

47 + 38 = ____

25:4 Extension ☐ out of 7

1. 5 sheets of paper can make a book.
   How many books can I make if I have:
   a 20 sheets? ____ **b** 17 sheets? ____

2. 8 × 4 ÷ 4 × 5 ÷ 5 = ____

3. If 23 × 4 = 92 then 92 ÷ 4 = ____

4. 15 hundreds + 3 hundreds + 72 ones = ____

5. I doubled a number and then added 5.
   My answer was 23.
   What number did I start with? ____

6. A bottle balanced 12 bolts.
   A book balanced 4 bolts.
   a Does the bottle have the same mass as 12 bolts? ____
   b How many books would balance the bottle? ____

7. **a** 1000 − 401 ____ **b** 1000 − 704 ____

Challenge

Draw a path on the grid from the counter to the triangle. Describe the path.

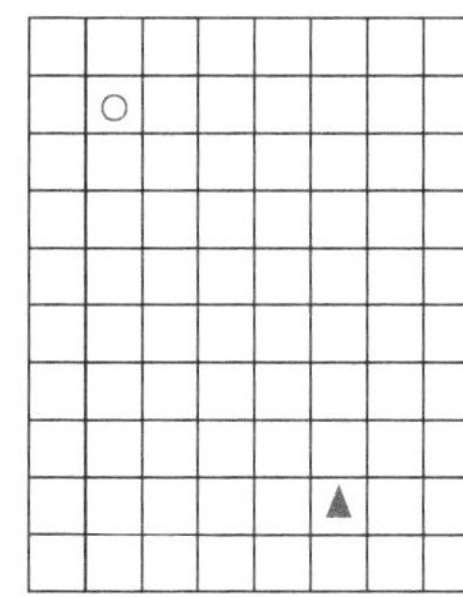

____
____
____
____
____

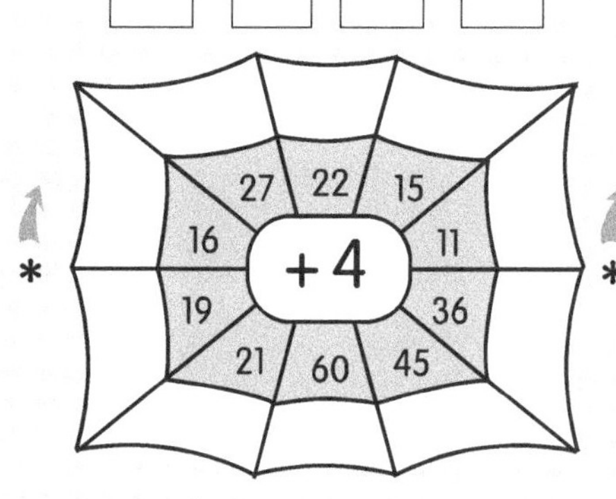

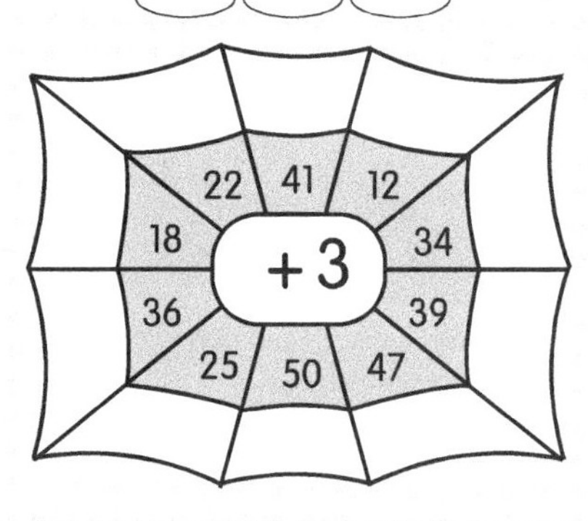

Use your number facts.

 • *AUSTRALIAN SIGNPOST MATHS NSW 3 MENTALS* • ISBN 978 0 6557 0910 7

26:1 out of 18

1. $6 \times 2 =$ ____
2. $12 \div 2 =$ ____
3. $9 \times 2 =$ ____
4. $18 \div 2 =$ ____
5. $5 \times 10 =$ ____
6. $50 \div 10 =$ ____
7. $3 \times 5 =$ ____
8. $15 \div 5 =$ ____
9. Circle groups of 5 balls.
   What is 4 groups of 5? ____ $4 \times 5 =$ ____
   How many 5s in 20? ____ $20 \div 5 =$ ____
   Share 20 among 4. ____ $20 \div 4 =$ ____
10. Write 18 litres using short form. ____
11. Would a bucket hold more than 1 L? ____
12. 5 children shared 10 books.
    How many did each child get? ____
13. I baked 12 biscuits on one tray and 15 on another. How many biscuits did I bake? ____
14. Use ____ $\times 2 = 12$ to find $12 \div 2 =$ ____.
15. Six people shared 18 pencils. How many did each person get? ____

16. What is the value of the 2 in
    a 3203? ____ b 8024? ____
17. Is 5273 larger than 5198? ____
18. a $15 + 8 = 20 +$ ____ b $19 + 6 = 20 +$ ____

26:2 out of 16

1. $4 \times 5 =$ ____
2. $20 \div 5 =$ ____
3. $4 \times 4 =$ ____
4. $16 \div 4 =$ ____
5. $9 \times 10 =$ ____
6. $90 \div 10 =$ ____
7. $7 \times 2 =$ ____
8. $14 \div 2 =$ ____
9. 
   Circle groups of 4 hamburgers.
   What is 6 groups of 4? ____ $6 \times 4 =$ ____
   How many 4s in 24? ____ $24 \div 4 =$ ____
   Share 24 among 6. ____ $24 \div 6 =$ ____
10. a Half of 18 is ____. b Double 9 is ____.
    c $9 \times 2 \div 2 =$ ____
11. Write 34 litres using short form. ____
12. How many 2 L containers of water would I need to fill a 10 L bin? ____
13. Colour 3 fifths of this rectangle.

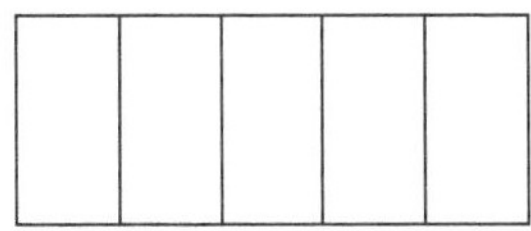

14. How many sides on 5 kites? ____.
15. Use the jump strategy to find:
    $61 - 28 =$ ____

16. $4000 + 200 + 90 + 1 =$ ____

Turn to ID card A on page 6.
Give the answers for these numbers.

(9) ____ numbers (10) ____ numbers

(11) ____ numbers (12) ____

(18) ____ (19) ____

(20) ____ (21) ____

26:3

 out of 5

1. Write thirty-nine litres using short form. ______

2. **a** (a bar of 4 equal parts, 1 shaded) $\frac{\square}{\square}$ is coloured.
   b (a bar of 4 equal parts, 2 shaded) $\frac{\square}{\square}$ is coloured.

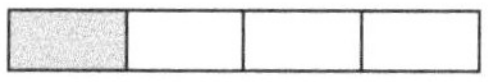

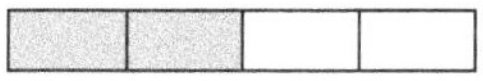

3. **a** 5 × 4 ______
   4 × 5 ______
   20 ÷ 4 ______
   5 × 4 ÷ 4 ______

   b 6 × 3 ______
   3 × 6 ______
   18 ÷ 3 ______
   6 × 3 ÷ 3 ______

4.

Diane

Pa

Alan

Lyn

Nanna

Whose photo is:
a in the middle? ______
b at the bottom left? ______
c at the top right? ______
d above Nanna's photo? ______
e below Alan's photo? ______

5. **a** ____ × 5 = 30 so 30 ÷ 5 = ____
   b ____ × 3 = 27 so 27 ÷ 3 = ____
   c ____ × 4 = 32 so 32 ÷ 4 = ____
   d ____ × 10 = 60 so 60 ÷ 10 = ____

26:4

Extension

out of 6

1. If 12 × 9 = 108, find:
   a 108 ÷ 9 ______ **b** 108 ÷ 12 ______

2. If 32 + 19 = 51 then:
   a 19 + 32 = ______ **b** 51 − 19 = ______

3. How many shoes are in 57 pairs? ______

4. Half of 100? ______ Half of 400? ______

5. Lachlan shared 60 grapes with 2 of his friends. How many did each child get? ______

6. Ten pens fill one box.
   How many boxes can be filled with:
   a 30 pens? ______ **b** 70 pens? ______

Challenge

Write multiplication fact families for:

a
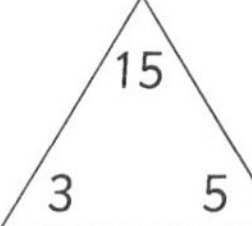

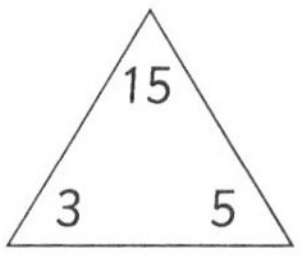

3 × 5 = ______ 15 ÷ 3 = ______
5 × 3 = ______ 15 ÷ 5 = ______

b
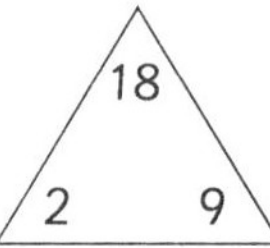

______ ______
______ ______

c
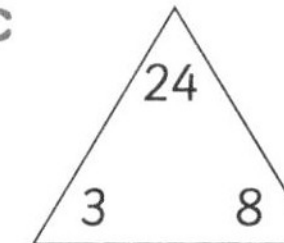

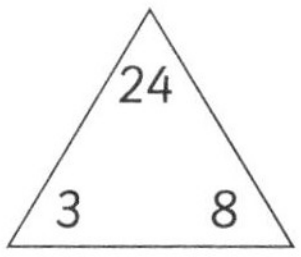

______ ______
______ ______

Concept

Complete each multiplication fact family.

a
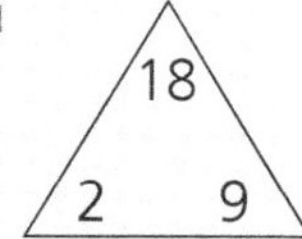

2 × 9 = ______
9 × 2 = ______
18 ÷ 2 = ______
18 ÷ 9 = ______

b
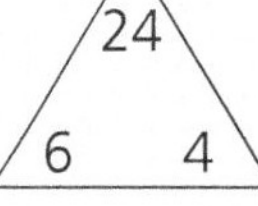

6 × 4 = ______
4 × 6 = ______
24 ÷ 6 = ______
24 ÷ 4 = ______

c
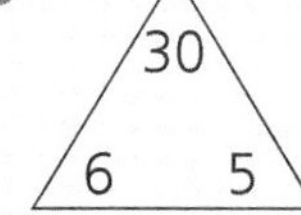

6 × 5 = ______
5 × 6 = ______
30 ÷ 6 = ______
30 ÷ 5 = ______

d
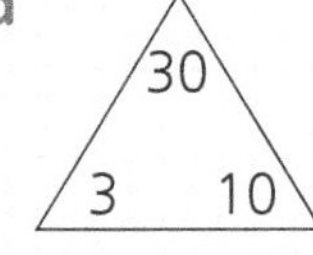

3 × 10 = ______
10 × 3 = ______
30 ÷ 3 = ______
30 ÷ 10 = ______

27:1

out of 17

1. ____ × 3 = 12
2. 12 ÷ 3 ____
3. ____ × 5 = 10
4. 10 ÷ 5 ____
5. 43 + 7 = ____
6. ____ × 10 = 30
7. 30 ÷ 10 ____
8. ____ × 2 = 20
9. 20 ÷ 2 ____
10. 61 + 9 = ____
11. 8000 + 300 + 20 + 1 = ____
12. a Show the number 1645 on this abacus.

    b One less than 1645 is ____.

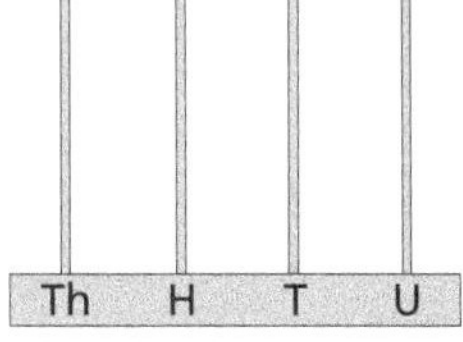

13. a 8 × 2 ____
    16 ÷ 2 ____
    8 × 2 ÷ 2 ____

    b 2 × 5 ____
    10 ÷ 5 ____
    2 × 5 ÷ 5 ____
14. Use ____ × 3 = 9 to find 9 ÷ 3 = ____.
15. a 4 + 6 = 10 so 184 + 6 = ____

    b 14 − 6 = 8 so 214 − 6 = ____
16. a ____ × 5 = 25 so 25 ÷ 5 = ____

    b ____ × 3 = 15 so 15 ÷ 3 = ____

    c ____ × 4 = 36 so 36 ÷ 4 = ____

    d ____ × 10 = 90 so 90 ÷ 10 = ____
17. a Colour three eighths.

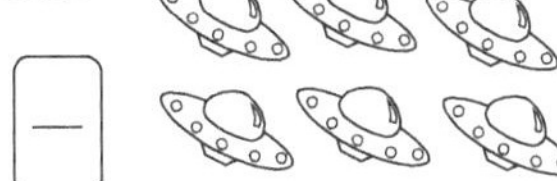

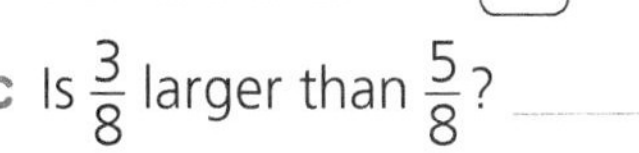

    b What fraction is not coloured? $\frac{\square}{\square}$

    c Is $\frac{3}{8}$ larger than $\frac{5}{8}$? ____

27:2

out of 19

1. ____ × 5 = 40
2. 40 ÷ 5 ____
3. ____ × 3 = 27
4. 27 ÷ 3 ____
5. 243 + 7 = ____
6. ____ × 10 = 60
7. 60 ÷ 10 ____
8. ____ × 2 = 16
9. 16 ÷ 2 ____
10. 415 + 5 = ____
11. 1000 + 500 + 60 + 9 = ____
12. One more than 2584 is ____.
13. Use ____ × 4 = 28 to find 28 ÷ 4 = ____.
14. What is the value of the 7 in:

    a 7320? ____ b 2072? ____
15. a 8 × 3 = ____
    24 ÷ 3 = ____
    8 × 3 ÷ 3 = ____

    b 6 × 4 = ____
    24 ÷ 4 = ____
    6 × 4 ÷ 4 = ____
16. Write 5190 in words.

    ____

    ____

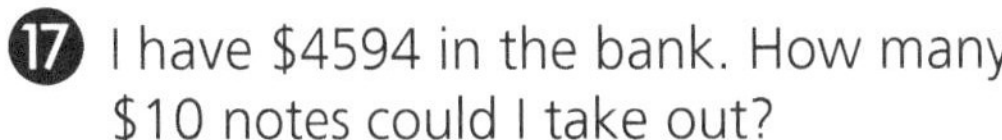

17. I have $4594 in the bank. How many $10 notes could I take out? ____
18. a 3 + 7 = 10 so 183 + 7 = ____

    b 23 − 8 = 15 so 53 − 8 = ____

    c 34 − 6 = 34 − 4 − 2 = ____

    d 288 + 5 = 288 + 2 + 3 = ____
19. 1256 = ☐ ☐ ☐ tens ☐ ones

Turn to ID card B on page 7.
Give the answers for these numbers.

(19) line of ____ (21) ____

(22) ____ (23) ____ (24) ____

(25) ____ (26) ____ (27) ____

(28) ____ (29) ____ (30) ____

 AUSTRALIAN SIGNPOST MATHS NSW 3 MENTALS • ISBN 978 0 6557 0910 7

27:3 ☐ out of 11

1. Fill these in for 1479.

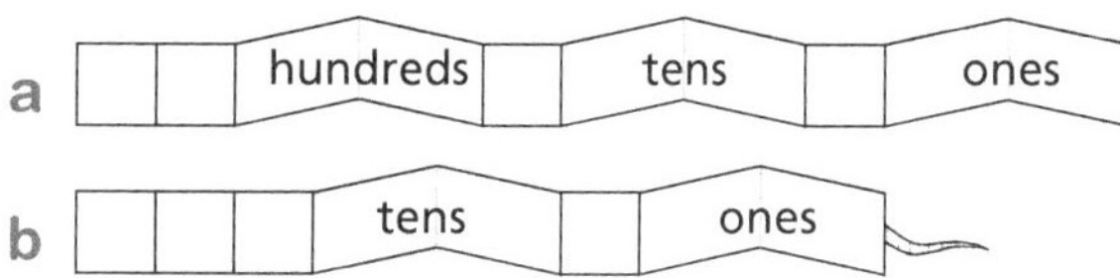

2. Write the numeral for one thousand and sixty-two. ______
3. The year before 2000. ______
4. 6000 + 700 + 80 + 9 = ______
5. I have $8192 in the bank. How many $10 notes could I take out? ______
6. a 183 + 7 = ______
   b 12 + 7 = ______ so 72 + 7 = ______
   c 82 − 8 = 82 − 2 − 6 = ______
   d 637 + 6 = 637 + 3 + 3 = ______
7. a 100 − 23 = ______ b 100 − 56 = ______
8. 3 more than 1999. ______
9. Write 4020 in words. ______

______

10. Show the time 3:34 on the clock face.

11. a 25 + 13 = ______ b 30 + 15 = ______

27:4 Extension ☐ out of 8

1. Four identical books cost $2.40 altogether. How much for one book? ______
2. How many hundreds in 1000? ______
3. A  B 

   a The total value of the coins in **A** and **B**. ______
   b The difference in value of the coins in **A** and **B**. ______
4. One zoo has 82 monkeys. Another zoo has 15 monkeys. How many monkeys in both zoos? ______
5. Months in 2 years. ______
6. 30 − 6 − 6 − 6 − 6 − 6 ______
7. 20 + 30 + 40 + 50 ______
8. In a non-leap year, how many days are there in:
   a spring? ______ b summer? ______
   c autumn? ______ d winter? ______

Challenge

Complete each column as quickly as you can. Once finished, check your answers. Record your time.

a		b	
3 × 2	______	6 × 10	______
5 × 4	______	5 × 5	______
2 × 10	______	8 × 5	______
2 × 5	______	4 × 4	______
3 × 4	______	1 × 10	______
5 × 2	______	9 × 4	______

Time = ______ seconds

Multiplication linked with division

☐ groups of 6 = 24
☐ × 6 = 24
The answer is 4.

a ☐ groups of 5 = 30
☐ × 5 = 30
How many groups of 5 in 30?
______.

b 4 shares of ☐ = 28
4 × ☐ = 28
28 shared among 4 boys = ______

c ☐ rows of 6 = 42
☐ × 6 = 42
How many rows of 6 in 42?
______.

d 3 shares of ☐ = 27
3 × ☐ = 27
27 shared among 3 girls = ______

28:1 ☐ out of 16

1. ______ × 5 = 50
2. 50 ÷ 5 ______
3. ______ × 2 = 6
4. 6 ÷ 2 ______
5. ______ × 10 = 20
6. 20 ÷ 10 ______
7. ______ × 2 = 4
8. 4 ÷ 2 ______
9. Use a mental strategy to find:

   a 69 + 13 = ______ b 66 + 10 = ______

   c 37 + 14 = ______ d 33 + 10 = ______

10. 

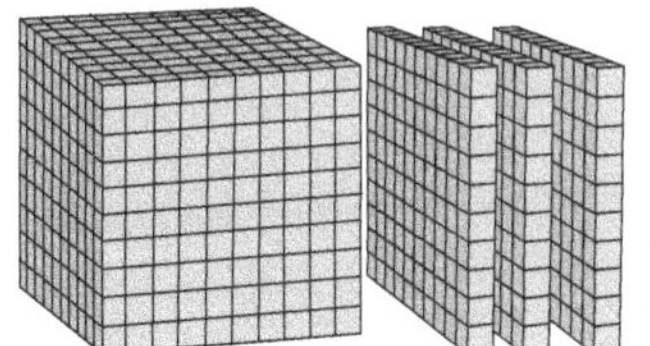

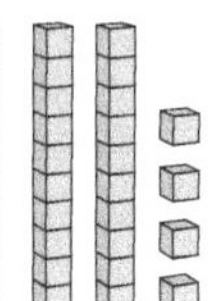

The number modelled above. ______

The number before 3600. ______

11. A trapezium has ______ sides.
12. Circle the change I would get from 50 cents when I spend 20 cents.

13. I spent $31 on fish and $13 on bread.

    How much did I spend? ______

14. 10 – 2 – 2 – 2 ______
15. There were 24 white sheep and 35 black sheep. How many sheep altogether? ______
16. 

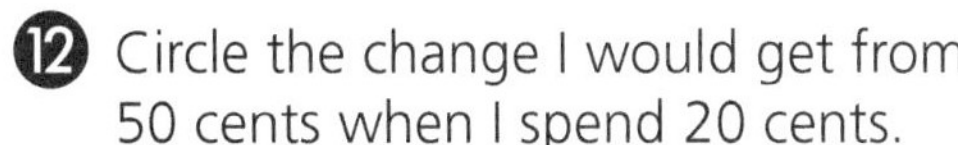

a 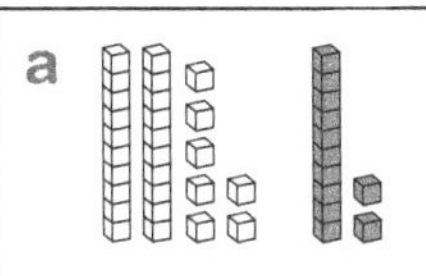

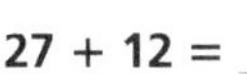

27 + 12 = ______

b 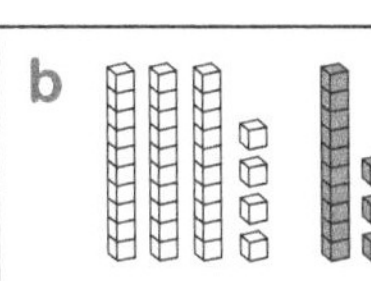

34 + 13 = ______

28:2 ☐ out of 19

1. 10 ÷ 2 ______
2. 50 ÷ 5 ______
3. 40 ÷ 10 ______
4. 25 ÷ 5 ______
5. 546 + 4 ______
6. 56 + 23 ______
7. 83 − 23 ______
8. 48 + 19 ______
9. 45 − 29 ______
10. 667 + 7 ______
11. 5000 + 200 + 40 + 3 = ______
12. This is a ______.

    It has ______ vertices and ______ sides.

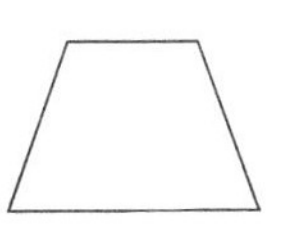

13. I saw 34 galahs and 25 cockatoos.

    How many birds did I see? ______

14. 56 forks and 43 knives.

    How many more forks? ______

15. a 526 + 4 = ______

    b 13 − 8 = 5 so 73 − 8 = ______

    c 42 − 9 = 42 − 2 − 7 = ______

    d 367 + 8 = 367 + 3 + 5 = ______

16. A cube has ______ faces.
17. I had $2 and spent 65 cents.

    My change was ______.

18. Add to both numbers to make these easier.

    a 348 − 199 = ______ − ______ = ______

    b 671 − 298 = ______ − ______ = ______

19. Show the time 25 minutes to 6. What is the time 10 minutes after this?

    ______

Turn to ID card B on page 7.

Give the answers for these numbers.

(8) ______ (9) ______

(10) ______ (11) ______

(12) ______ (13) ______

(16) ______ shapes (17) ______ shapes

Make up a study card for any mistakes.

Study card

Put questions on one side and answers on the other.

28:3 ___ out of 10

1. Use _____ × 5 = 45 to find 45 ÷ 5 = _____.
2. 3000 + 500 + 40 + 5 = _____
3. Write the numeral for the number shown. _____

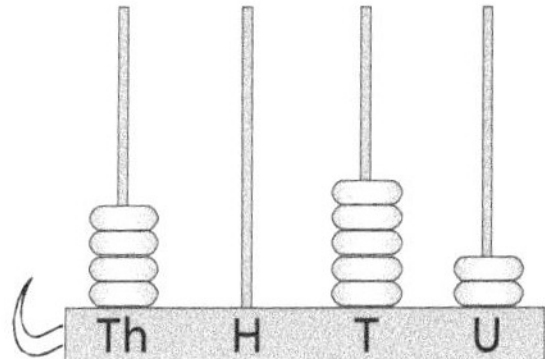

4. I have $3028 in the bank. How many $10 notes could I take out? _____
5. Bridge to the next ten to find:
   a 49 + 8 _____ b 45 + 7 _____
   c 829 + 9 _____ d 317 + 5 _____
6. Circle the change I would get from $2 when I spend $1.45.

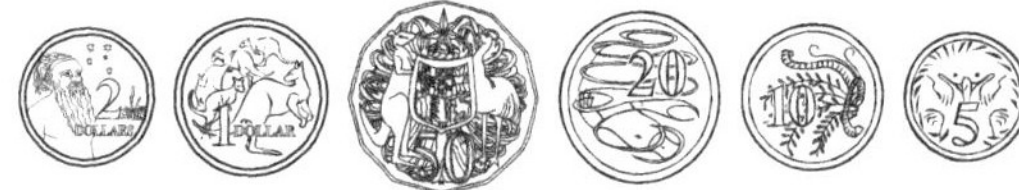

7. This is called a r_____ angle.

8. Is the area of your classroom more or less than 3 square metres? _____
9. The first 7 multiples of 4 are

   4, ___, ___, ___, ___, ___, ___
10.

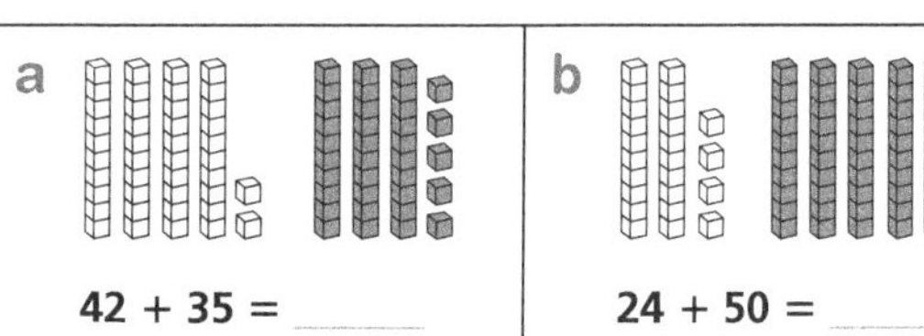

a	b
42 + 35 = _____	**24 + 50 =** _____

28:4 Extension ___ out of 5

1. If this pattern continues, how many hexagons will be in row:

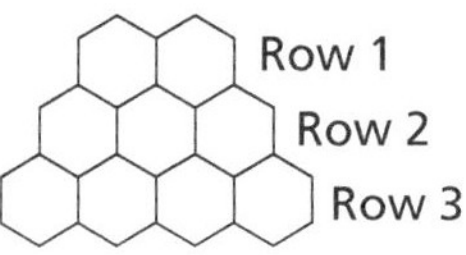

   a 5? _____
   b 10? _____ c 50? _____
2. List four 2D shapes that always have parallel lines. _____
3. Write the numeral seven thousand and four. _____
4. 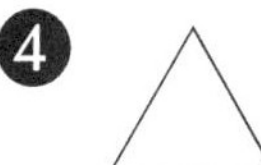 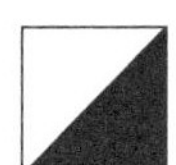 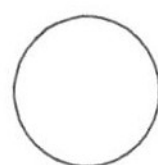  

   If this pattern were repeated, what would the 19th shape be? _____
5. Luke has 12 books. Kim has 3 times as many. How many has Kim? _____

Challenge

Draw a rhombus and describe it.

29:1 out of 19

1. 35 + 20 ____
2. 28 + 41 ____
3. 56 − 11 ____
4. 68 − 22 ____
5. 27 + 42
6. 64 subtract 4. ____
7. 3 × 5 ____
8. 15 ÷ 5 ____
9. 6 × 2 ____
10. 69 + 20

11. a 5 + 5 = 10 so 85 + 5 = ____
    b 21 − 5 = 16 so 41 − 5 = ____
    c 26 − 7 = 19 so 66 − 7 = ____
    d 28 + 5 = 28 + 2 + 3 = ____
12. I had $1 and spent 30c.
    My change was ____.
13. Would you measure the area of a wall using square centimetres or square metres?
    ____
14. Does 34 − 19 = 35 − 20? ____
15. How many birds were there if there were 28 budgies and 7 quails?
    ____ + ____ = ____
16. 2000 + 400 + 20 + 1 = ____
17. Is 5270 an even number? ____
18. Circle the parallelogram.

19. 3, 6, 9, ____, ____, ____, ____, ____, ____

29:2 out of 17

1. 45 + 19 ____
2. 62 + 19 ____
3. 74 − 24 ____
4. 83 − 31 ____
5. 77 + 12
6. 4 × 10 ____
7. 40 ÷ 4 ____
8. 3 × 4 ____
9. 12 ÷ 4 ____
10. 49 + 57

11. Would you measure the area of a court using litres, square metres or metres?
    ____
12. 7238, 7248, 7258, ____, ____
13. I had $2 and spent $1.15.
    My change was ____.
14. There were 46 seagulls and 36 magpies.
    How many birds altogether?
    ____ + ____ = ____
15. Rewrite these number sentences. Add the same number to each side to bridge the second number to 10.
    a 54 − 39 = ____ − ____ = ____
    b 62 − 28 = ____ − ____ = ____
    c 75 − 47 = ____ − ____ = ____
    d 68 − 27 = ____ − ____ = ____
16. 6043 = ___ thousands + ___ tens + ___ ones
    7302 = ___ hundreds + ___ ones
17. 20 balls shared by 2 kids. How many each? ____

Use place value to change these numbers.

a
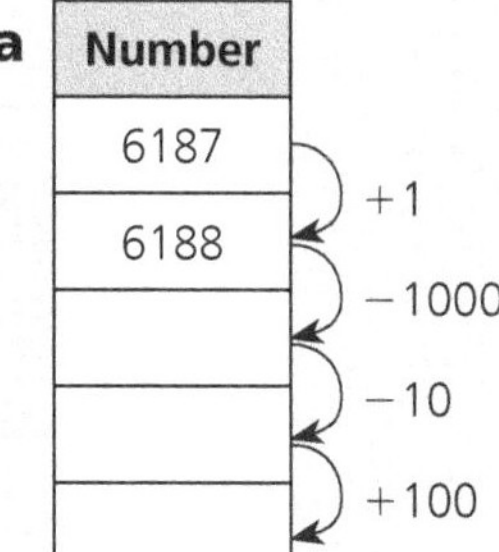

b
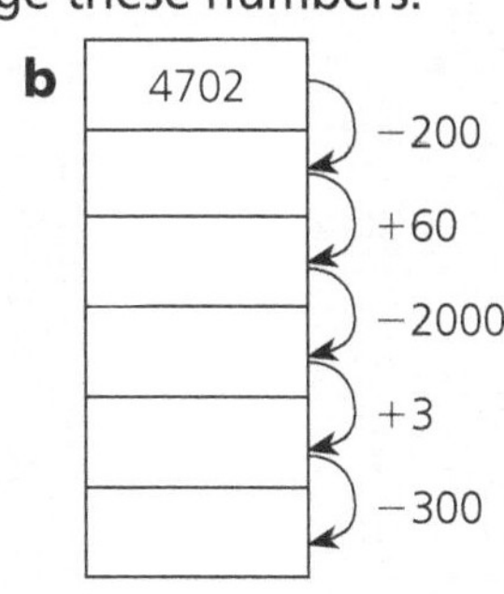

c
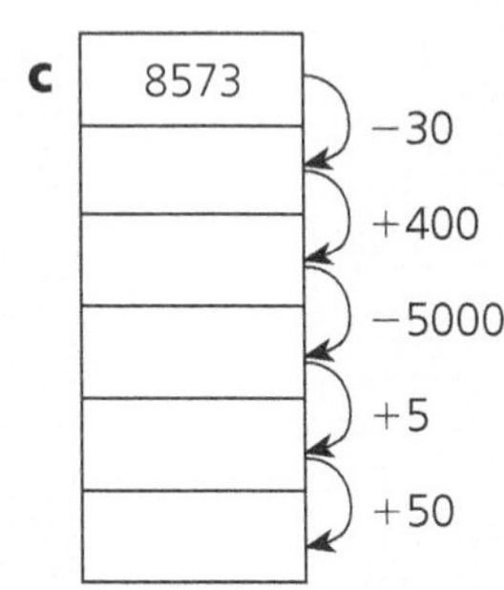

Understanding place value is important.

29:3

out of 8

1

tens	ones
3	8
+	5

2

tens	ones
5	7
+	5

3 There were 59 rosellas and 46 kookaburras.

How many birds altogether?

_____ + _____ = _____

4 Tick the trapezium.

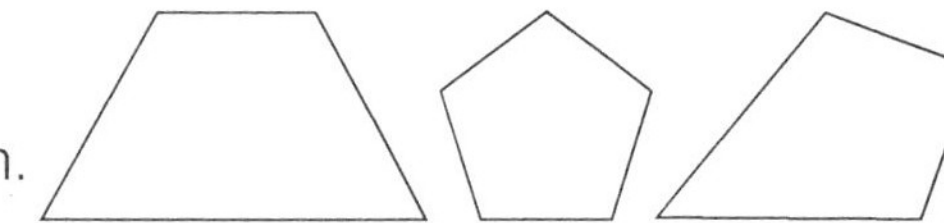

5 Rewrite these number sentences. Add the same number to each side to bridge to 10.

a 58 − 29 = _____ − _____ = _____

b 54 − 18 = _____ − _____ = _____

c 61 − 33 = _____ − _____ = _____

d 73 − 48 = _____ − _____ = _____

6 Guess my shape: I have 6 sides and 6 vertices. I am a _____________.

7 On this grid, draw and label 2 quadrilaterals.

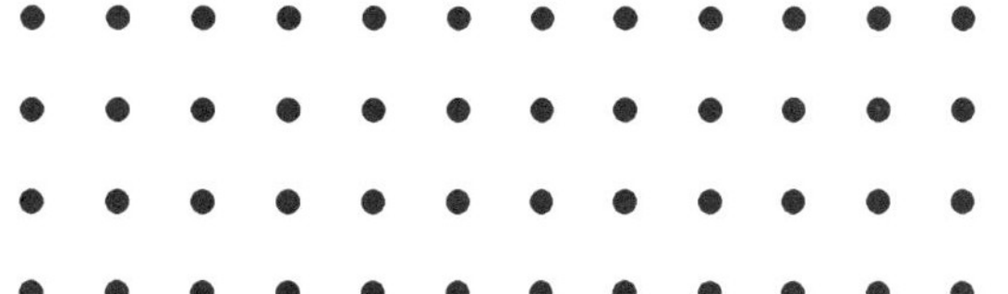

8 Subtract tens to make these easier.

a 46 − 32 = _____ − _____ = _____

b 72 − 49 = _____ − _____ = _____

29:4

out of 5

1 This pyramid is made of 3 layers of 5c coins.

What is the total value if it is:

a 3 layers high? _____

b 6 layers high? _____

2 One banana costs 50 cents.

How much do four cost? _____

3 **a** 1000 − 699 = _____ **b** 1000 − 899 = _____

4

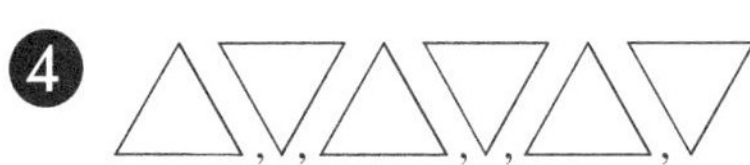

If this pattern continues, what will the 26th triangle look like? _____

5 Mum grew 36 roses and cut 18.

How many were not cut? _____

Challenge

Write 6 more questions that are equal to:

a 65 − 38

b 43 − 29

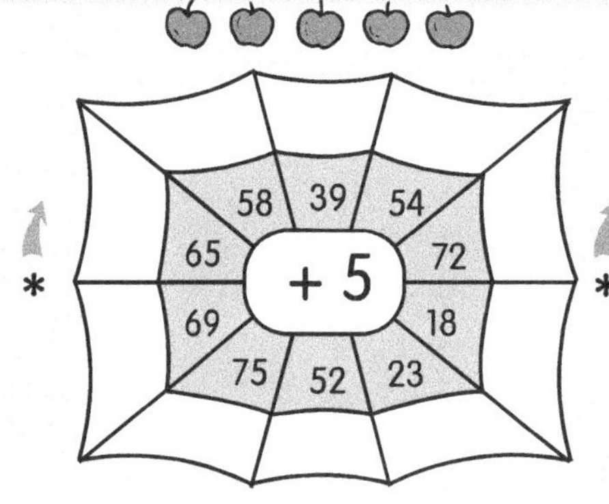

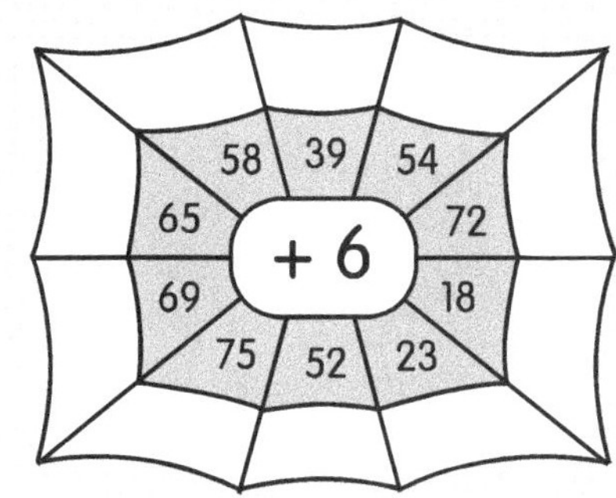

Bridge to 10 and use addition facts to answer these quickly.

 • *AUSTRALIAN SIGNPOST MATHS NSW 3 MENTALS* • ISBN 978 0 6557 0910 7

30:1 ☐ out of 17

1. 15 + ____ = 20
2. 27 + ____ = 30
3. 26 + ____ = 30
4. 39 + ____ = 40
5. 56 + 20 ____
6. 60 plus 12. ____
7. 2 × 3 ____
8. 10 × 5 ____
9. 50 ÷ 5 ____
10. 45 + 30 ____
11. I saw 36 snakes and 38 lizards.
    How many did I see altogether?
    ____ + ____ = ____
12. How many days in May? ____
13. How many minutes in an hour? ____
14. If I toss a coin in the air, would heads be more likely than tails? ____

15. Write the multiplication tables for:

a

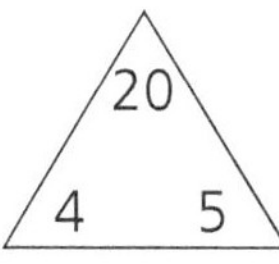

4 × 5 = ____
5 × ____ = ____
20 ÷ 4 = ____
20 ÷ 5 = ____

b

30, 3, 10

3 × 10 = ____
10 × ____ = ____
30 ÷ 3 = ____
30 ÷ 10 = ____

16.

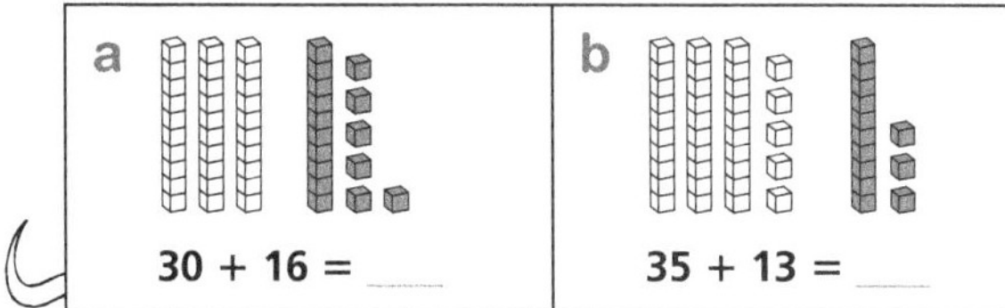

a 30 + 16 = ____

b 35 + 13 = ____

17. **a** If 6 + 7 = 13 then 16 + 7 = ____
    b If 8 + 9 = 17 then 18 + 9 = ____

30:2 ☐ out of 15

1. 34 + ____ = 42
2. 28 + ____ = 36
3. 56 + ____ = 67
4. 79 + ____ = 85
5. $\begin{array}{r} 29 \\ +\ 13 \\ \hline \end{array}$
6. 2 × 4 ____
7. 10 ÷ 2 ____
8. 9 × 2 ____
9. 16 ÷ 2 ____
10. $\begin{array}{r} 58 \\ +\ 45 \\ \hline \end{array}$
11. **impossible** **unlikely** **even chance** **very likely** **certain**

I throw a standard die once. Choose a label for the chance that the die shows:

a a three ____
b an odd number ____
c larger than two ____
d a number ____

12. Round 453 to the nearest hundred. ____
13. Bridge to the next ten to find:
    a 46 + 7 ____ **b** 56 + 6 ____
    c 579 + 8 ____ **d** 57 + 8 ____

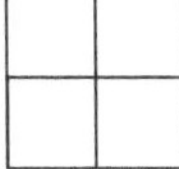

14.

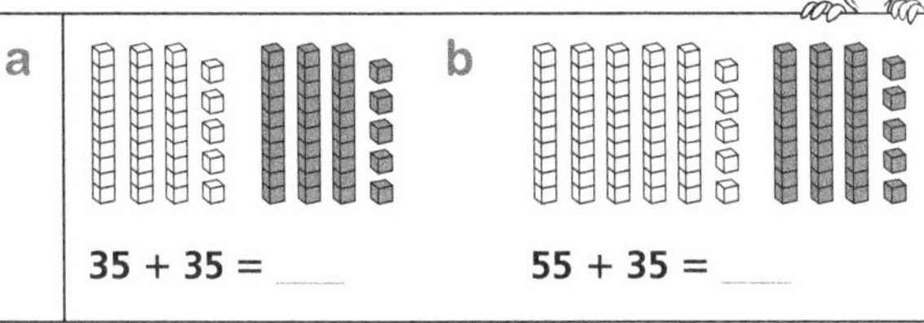

a 35 + 35 = ____

b 55 + 35 = ____

15. Write 5 square numbers.
    ____

This is a class lucky dip.

a Is Gino likely to pick the pen? ____
b What is the chance that Gino will pick something starting with 'c'? ____
c If we add another different prize to the lucky dip, will Gino have more or less chance of picking the pen? ____

30:3 out of 9

1

hund	tens	ones
1	2	5
4	3	7

2

hund	tens	ones
2	0	8
+ 1	9	3

3 Is there an even chance of spinning a **B**? ________

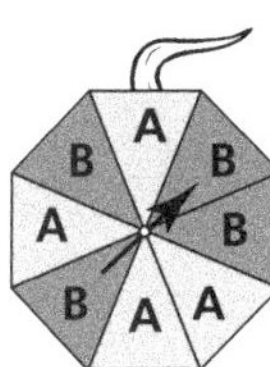

4 I saw 38 wombats and 16 echidnas.

How many did I see altogether? ________

5 a Are these numbers equally likely to be spun? ________

b How many 2s are most likely in 12 spins? ________

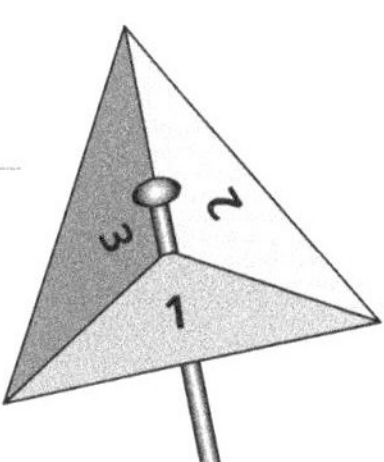

6 I had $2 and spent $1.85.

My change is ________.

7 Subtract 20 from each numeral on the left of the = sign to make these easier to answer.

a 56 – 28 = 36 – ________ = ________

b 75 – 28 = ________ – ________ = ________

8

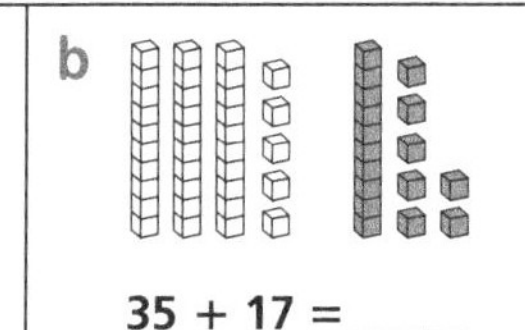

a 43 + 18 = ________

b 35 + 17 = ________

9 How many days in June? ________

30:4 out of 5

Extension

1 Guess my 3D object.

It has 6 faces. It has 12 edges.

The cross-section is a square.

____

Draw the object.

2 9785, 9775, 9765, ________, ________, ________

3 ● ○ ● ○ ● ○

1st 2nd 3rd 4th 5th 6th

If this pattern continues, will the 41st circle be shaded? ________

4 I scored 56 goals this season. My sister scored 17 fewer goals. How many goals did we score altogether? ________

5 1 4 2 4 3

Two of these cards are to be drawn from a hat and added. What is the most likely total? ________

Challenge

What do you know about the number 3025?

____

Complete these cards.

a

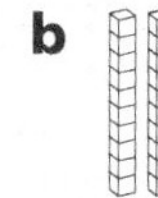

☐ + ☐ = ☐

b

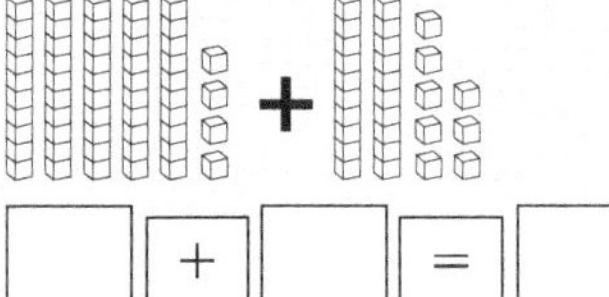

☐ + ☐ = ☐

c

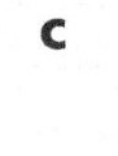

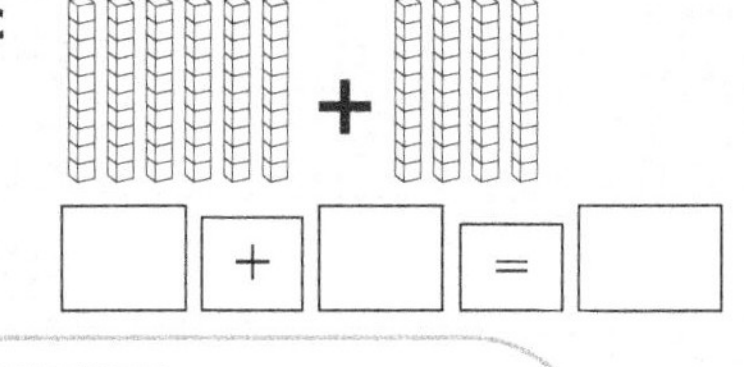

☐ + ☐ = ☐

10 ones can be traded for **1 ten**.

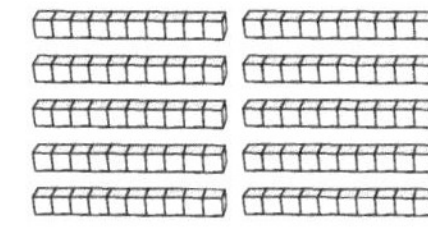

10 tens can be traded for **1 hundred**.

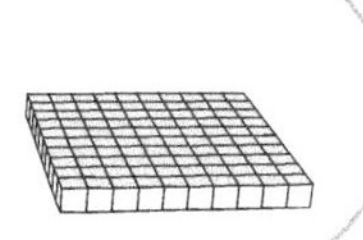

31:1

out of 16

1. 19 + 20 ____
2. 30 + 21 ____
3. 61 − 12 ____
4. 82 − 13 ____
5. 572 + 53 ____
6. 67 minus 14. ____
7. 8 × 2 ____
8. 12 ÷ 2 ____
9. 7 × 10 ____
10. 672 + 251 ____
11. a 51, 61, 71, ____, ____, ____, ____
    b 45, 50, 55, ____, ____, ____, ____
    c 3, 6, 9, ____, ____, ____, ____
    d 430, 440, 450, ____, ____
12. A 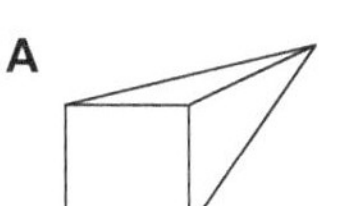 B 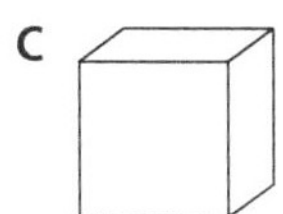 C

    Which shape is a pyramid? ____
13. Colour 4 fifths of this rectangle.

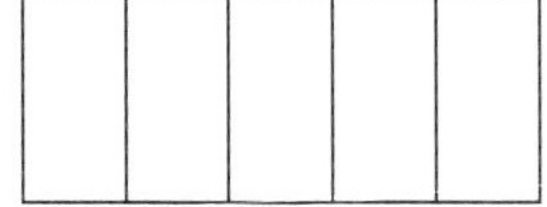

14. Is 7205 or 7250 larger? ____
15. 

    a 23 + 39 = ____

    b 60 + 30 = ____
16. What is the time 15 minutes after 3 o'clock? ____

31:2

out of 15

1. 300 + 45 ____
2. 120 + 41 ____
3. Half of 86 ____
4. 60 − 35 ____
5. 193 + 68 ____
6. 62 minus 34. ____
7. 7 × 2 ____
8. 15 ÷ 5 ____
9. 6 × 10 ____
10. 739 + 174 ____
11. 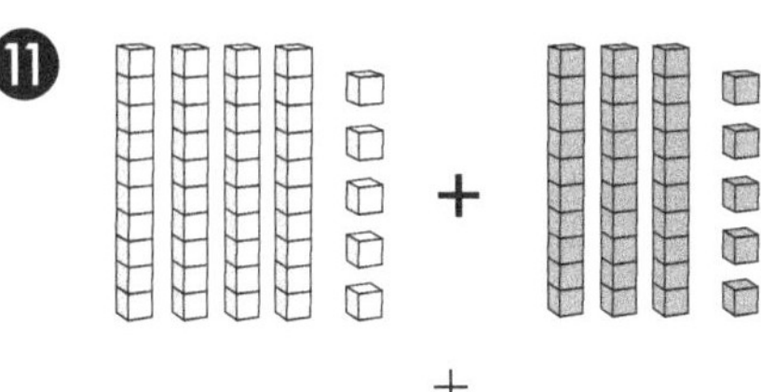

    ____ + ____ = ____
12. If I take a ball without looking:

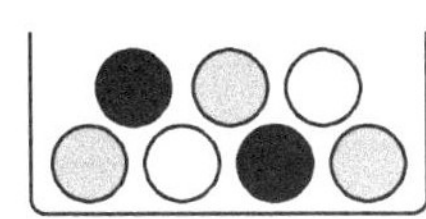

    a Am I more likely to pick a black or grey ball? ____

    b Is there an equal chance of picking black, white and grey? ____.
13. Jason drew 2 blue monsters.
    He gave each one 14 legs.
    How many legs were there altogether? ____
14. Write a problem that is equal to 56 – 41, then write the answer.
    ____
15. 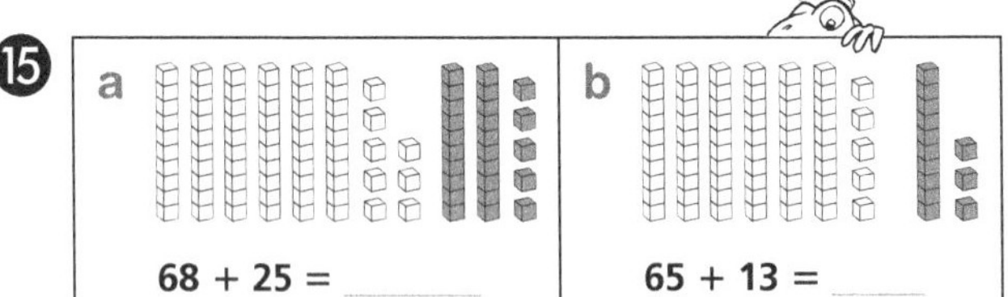

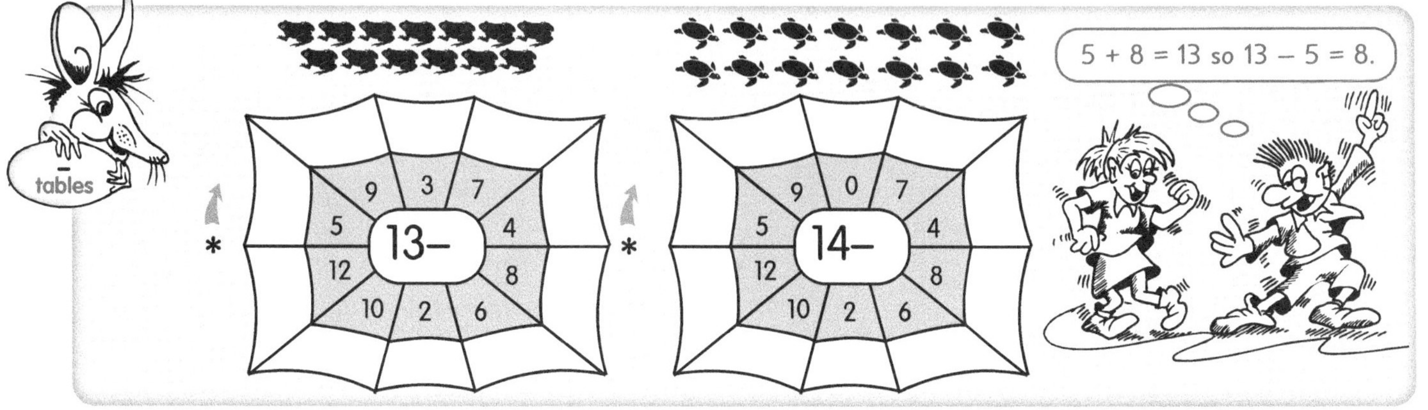

31:3

out of 7

1 a 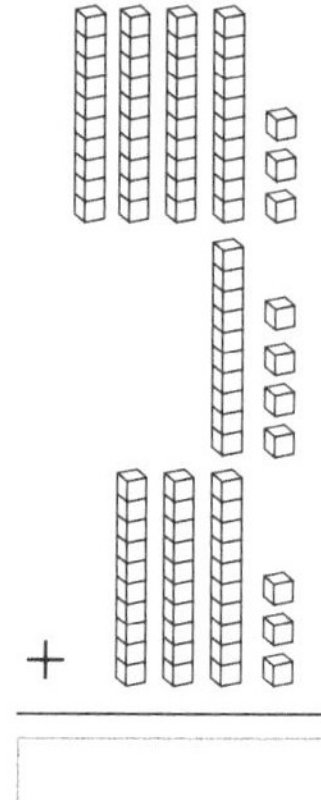 b 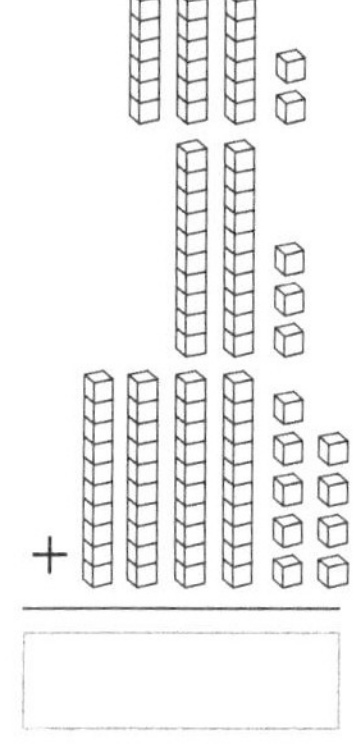

2 This parallelogram has _____ sides and _____ vertices. Trace each pair of parallel lines in a different colour.

3 Estimate the number of times 'p' is used on this page. Check by counting.

Estimate = _____ Number = _____

4 a What fraction is white? _____

b What fraction is shaded? _____

5 Jim collected 134 stamps and Jean collected 294 stamps. How many had they collected altogether? _____

6 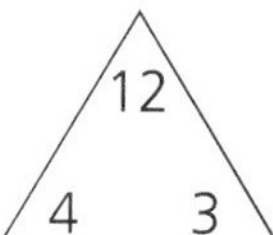

$4 \times 3 =$ _____ $3 \times 4 =$ _____

$12 \div 3 =$ _____ $12 \div 4 =$ _____

7 How many days in spring? _____

31:4

Extension

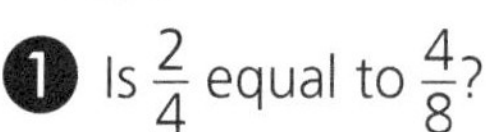

out of 6

1 Is $\frac{2}{4}$ equal to $\frac{4}{8}$? _____

2 a 53 more than 121. _____

b 44 more than 133. _____

3 How many full weeks in 3 years? _____

4 For music notes (♩ = 1, 𝅗𝅥 = 2, 𝅝 = 4) putting a dot after the symbols adds an extra half of its value. Write the value of:

a ♩. _____ c 𝅝. _____

b 𝅗𝅥. _____

5 69 + 35 _____

69

6 How many angles are in

a 5 squares and 5 triangles? _____

b 4 rhombuses and 3 hexagons? _____

Challenge

Write a list of events that are very unlikely to happen but not impossible.

a When we throw two dice, would a total of 4 or a total of 7 occur more often? _____

b Toss two dice 50 times. When a total of 4 or 7 is thrown, colour a square in the graph below.

Total thrown																	
	4																
	7																

32:1

out of 21

1. 33 + 45 ____
2. 29 + 30 ____
3. 12 ÷ 2 ____
4. 6 ÷ 2 ____
5. $\begin{array}{r} 70 \\ -\ \ 6 \\ \hline \end{array}$
6. 67 minus 14. ____
7. 5 less than 30. ____
8. 13 subtract 5. ____
9. 7 groups of 10. ____
10. $\begin{array}{r} 83 \\ -\ \ 7 \\ \hline \end{array}$
11. I ran 100 metres 3 times. How far did I run? ____
12. How long is this line: in cm? ____ in mm? ____
13. How many months in a year? ____
14. How many days in September? ____
15. The value of these coins is ____.

16. a 76 – 35 = ____ – ____ = ____

    b 45 – 28 = ____ – ____ = ____
17. 3000 + 500 + 20 + 1 = ____
18. How many days in 2 weeks? ____
19. The 8th month of the year is ____.
20. 3, 6, 9, ____, ____, ____, ____, ____
21. 

    a 25 + 38 = ____ 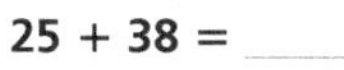

    b 25 + 39 = ____

32:2

out of 18

1. 400 + 29 ____
2. 140 + 32 ____
3. Half of 62. ____
4. 40 – 15 ____
5. $\begin{array}{r} 90 \\ -\ 37 \\ \hline \end{array}$
6. 16 ÷ 4 ____
7. 7 × 2 ____
8. 16 ÷ 2 ____
9. 6 × 10 ____
10. $\begin{array}{r} 47 \\ -\ \ 8 \\ \hline \end{array}$
11. I walked along the balance beam 5 times. If it is 5 metres long, how far did I walk? ____
12. a The time is: ____.

    b It means ____ minutes past ____.
13. How long is this line: in cm? ____ in mm? ____
14. How many days in winter? ____
15. Trace the parallel lines on these shapes.
16. 30 balls are shared equally between 3 groups. Each group gets ____ balls.
17. 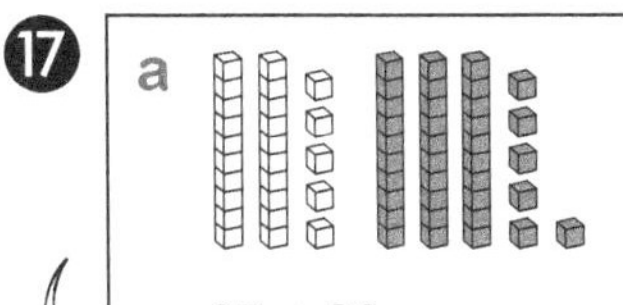

    a 25 + 36 = ____

    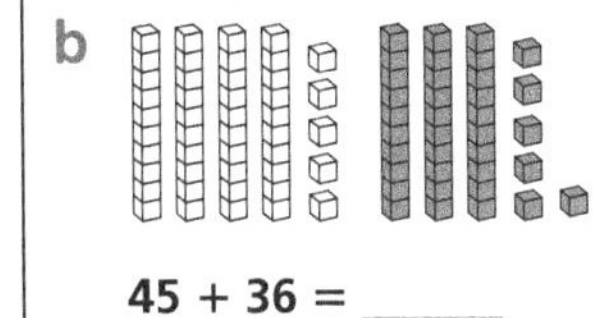

    b 45 + 36 = ____
18. 56 – 27 = ____ – ____ = ____

Use place value to change these numbers.

a

Number	
5248	+1000
6248	–100
	+10
	–1

b

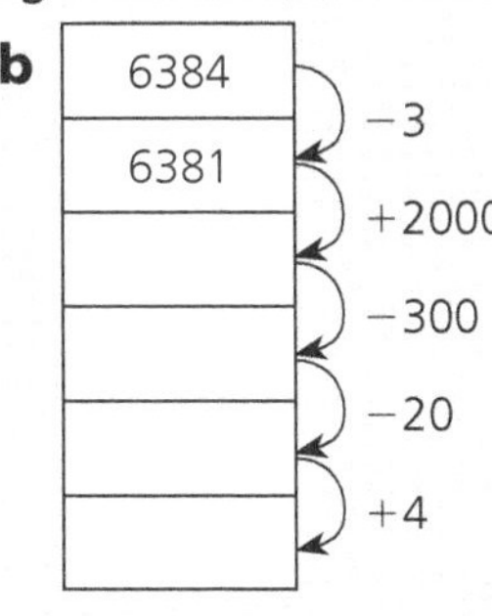

6384	
6381	–3
	+2000
	–300
	–20
	+4

c

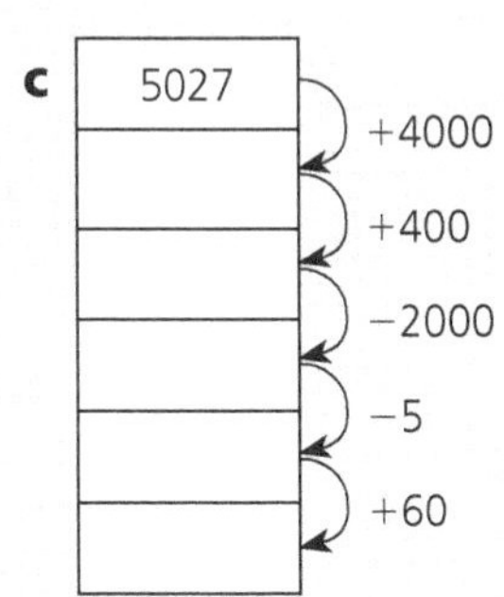

5027	
	+4000
	+400
	–2000
	–5
	+60

32:3 ☐ out of 10

1. 40 − 7
2. 60 − 9
3. 80 − 3

4. This is a ________________.
   It has _____ faces, _____ edges and _____ corners.
   The cross-section is a ________________.

5. Measure the lines in millimetres.
   a ________
   b ________
   c ________

6. Complete the labels.

a 

_____ past _____

b 

_____ past _____
_____ to _____

7. 9000 + 400 + 20 + 7 ________
8. Is 3405 higher than 3412? ________
9.

a	b
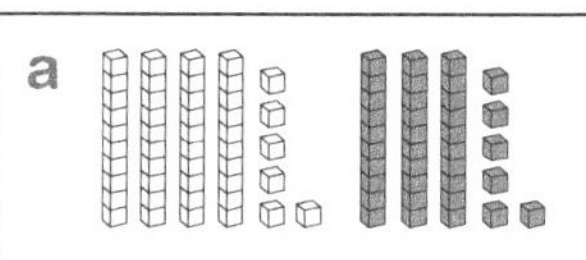 46 + 36 = _____	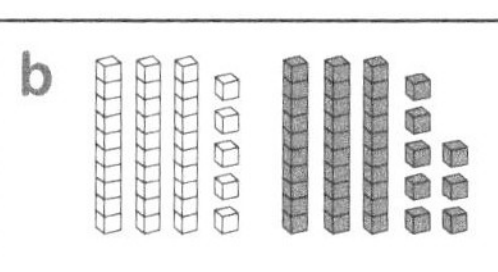 35 + 38 = _____

10. 72 – 46 = _____ – _____ = _____

32:4 ☐ out of 3 Extension

1. a How many centimetres in 1 m? ________
   b How many millimetres in 10 cm? ________
   c How many millimetres in 50 cm? ________
   d How many millimetres in 1 m? ________

2. 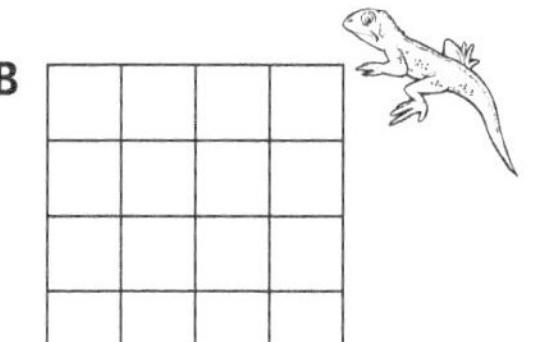

   What is the most number of shape A that could be cut from shape B? ________

3. Cailin is 113 cm and Felicity is 115 cm.
   a How much taller is Felicity? ________
   b Cailin grew 16 cm taller and Felicity grew 19 cm taller. What is the difference between their heights now? ________

Challenge

Use a ruler to measure objects. List the name and length of each object.

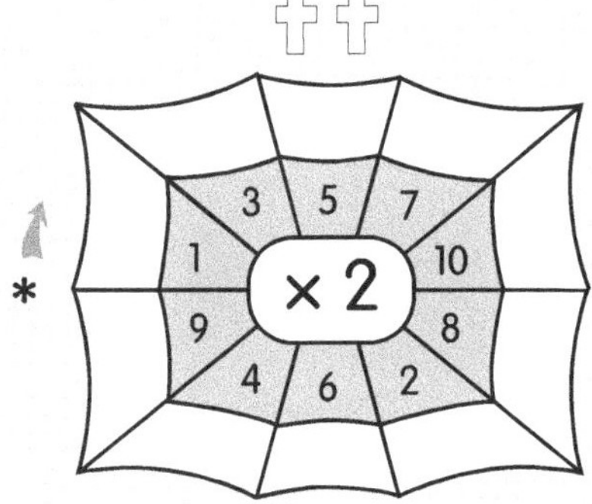

33:1 out of 19

1. 20 + 13 ____
2. 20 − 17 ____
3. 2 × 10 ____
4. 20 ÷ 2 ____
5. 42 − 28
6. 54 minus 12. ____
7. 9 × 2 ____
8. 3 × 4 ____
9. 10 ÷ 2 ____
10. 53 − 25
11. The length of my foot is 20 cm. If the length of my chair was four lengths of my feet, how long is my chair? ____
12. 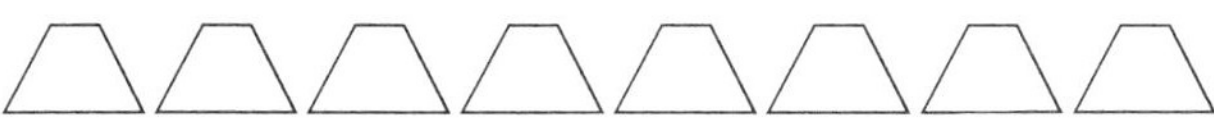

    This line is ____ cm long.
13. What is $\frac{1}{2}$ of 8 trapeziums? ____
14. Is addition the opposite of subtraction? ____
15. List these angles in order of size, from smallest to largest. ____

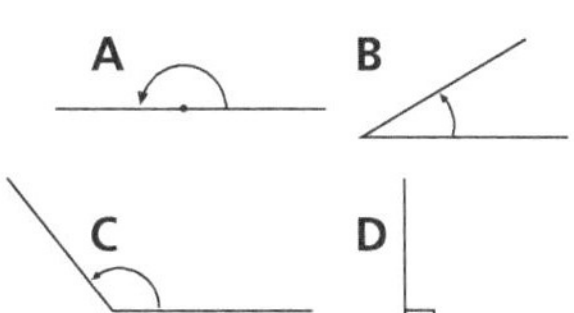

16. 6000 + 200 + 30 + 9 ____
17. Is 4609 lower than 4099? ____
18. How many digits in 4703? ____
19. Write another problem that is equal to 24 – 18. ____

33:2 out of 16

1. 56 + 23 ____
2. 16 + 16 ____
3. 40 − 13 ____
4. 80 − 11 ____
5. 50 − 15
6. Double 18. ____
7. 16 ÷ 4 ____
8. 20 ÷ 4 ____
9. 40 ÷ 10 ____
10. 61 − 36

11. My ribbon is 68 cm. If I cut it in half, how long will each piece be? ____
12. Measure the length of:
    - a ____ cm ____ mm
    - b ____ cm ____ mm
13. 45 + 36 = ____ so 81 − 36 = ____
14. **impossible** **unlikely** **even chance** **likely** **certain**

    I throw a standard die once. Choose a label for the chance that the die shows:
    - a an even number ____
    - b a seven ____
    - c smaller than two ____
    - d 1, 2, 3, 4, 5 or 6 ____
15. 45 hundreds + 38 ones ____
16. Draw lines to cut these shapes into quarters.

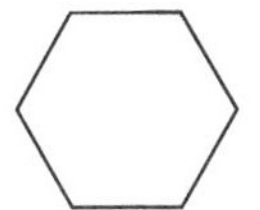

× tables

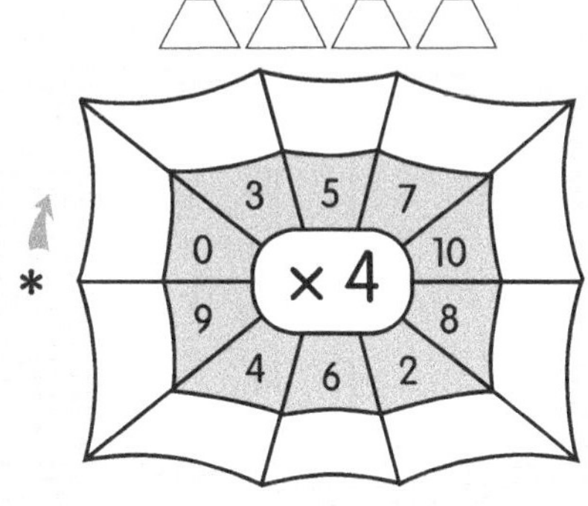

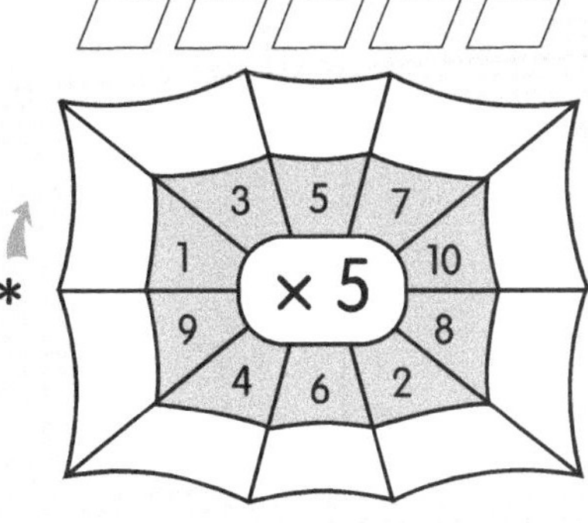

 • *AUSTRALIAN SIGNPOST MATHS NSW 3 MENTALS* • ISBN 978 0 6557 0910 7

33:3 ☐ out of 13

1. 42 − 4 =

2. 51 − 3 =

3. 73 − 5 =

4.

tens	ones
$4	4
+$5	3

5.

tens	ones
$6	3
+$2	1

6. 52 + 29 = ______ so 81 − 29 = ______

7. Draw lines to cut this group into quarters.

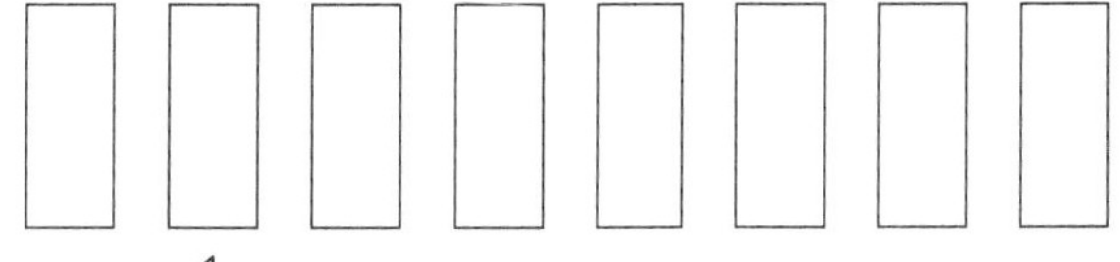

Colour $\frac{1}{4}$.

What fraction is not coloured? $\frac{\square}{\square}$

8. Is there an even chance of landing on **A**?

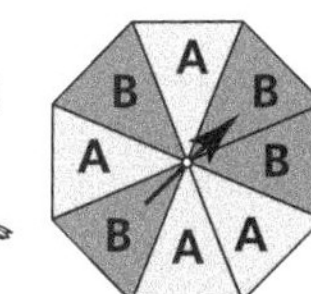

______

9. This line is ____ centimetres long.

This line is ________ millimetres long.

10. Is 5091 larger than 5901? ______

11. 54 hundreds + 8 ones = ______

12. How many days in summer? ______

13. Lee is 9 years old. How old will he be in:

a 21 years? ______ b 37 years? ______

c 42 years? ______ d 67 years? ______

33:4 Extension ☐ out of 4

1. I placed 6 square tiles in a long line with no gaps or overlaps. If each tile was 15 cm, how far was my line of tiles? ______

2. How many blocks are needed to make a staircase of ten steps?

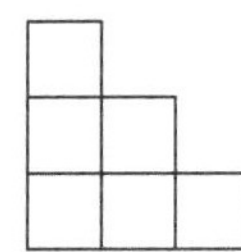

______

3. Use the sign to find the distance from:

a Minden to Ironbark ______

b Minden to Goodna ______

c Ironbark to Goodna ______

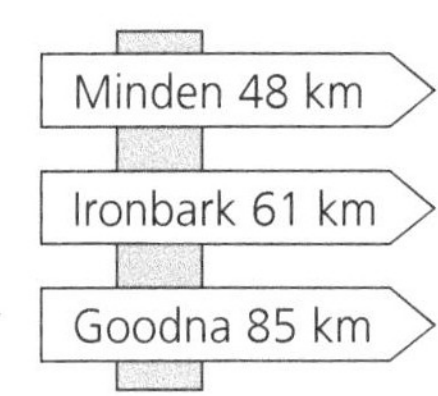

4. Which has the greatest area? ______

A 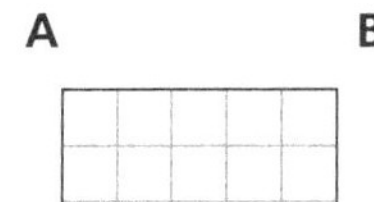

B 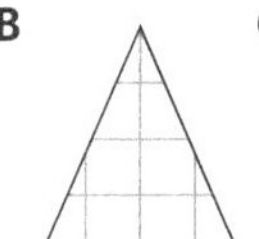

C 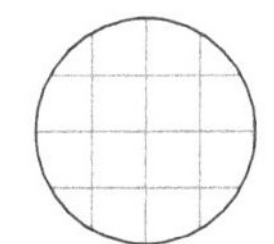

Challenge

Draw and label some fractions of your own.

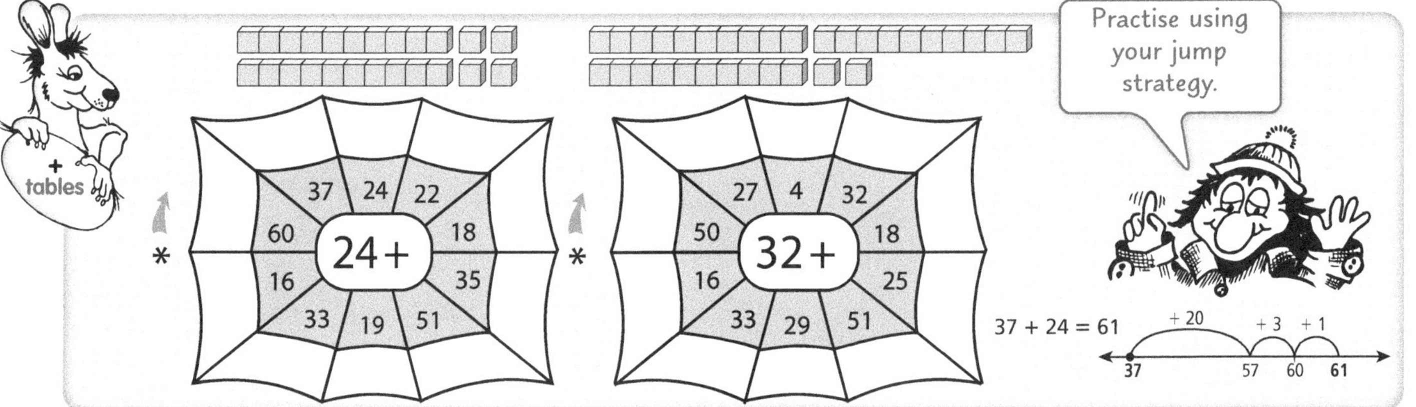

 • *AUSTRALIAN SIGNPOST MATHS NSW 3 MENTALS* • ISBN 978 0 6557 0910 7

34:1 ☐ out of 16

1. 15 + ____ = 20
2. 28 + ____ = 30
3. 14 ÷ 2 ____
4. 18 ÷ 2 ____
5. $\begin{array}{r} 41 \\ -\ 29 \\ \hline \end{array}$
6. Double 12. ____
7. Halve 20. ____
8. 4 × 2 ____
9. 3 × 5 ____
10. $\begin{array}{r} 36 \\ -\ 18 \\ \hline \end{array}$
11. Draw a column graph for this tally.

A	𝍸 ||
B	||||
C	𝍸 |

A								
B								
C								

12. How many boxes are in this stack?

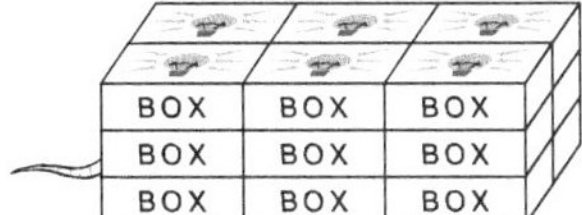

____ layers of ____

= ____ boxes

13. What fraction has been coloured?

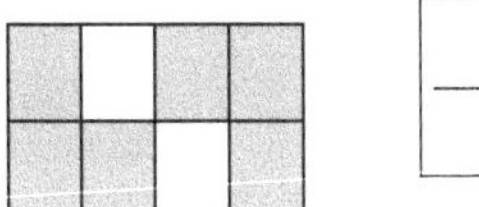

14.

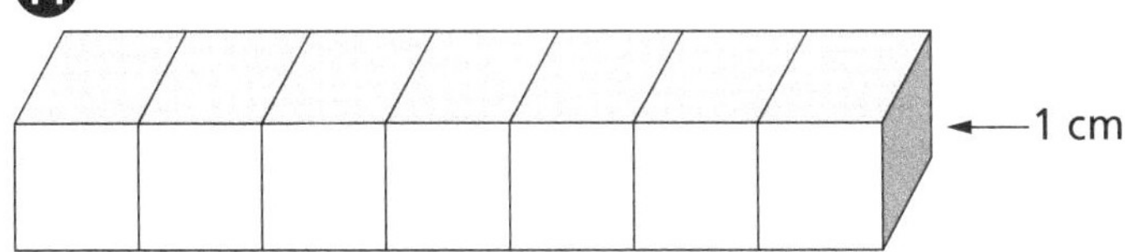

What is the volume of this model?

____ layer of ____ = ____ cubic centimetres.

15. 32 − 19 = ____ so 13 + 19 = ____
16. The 11th month of the year is ____________.

34:2 ☐ out of 17

1. 18 + ____ = 32
2. 21 + ____ = 36
3. 20 ÷ 10 ____
4. 12 ÷ 4 ____
5. $\begin{array}{r} 52 \\ -\ 37 \\ \hline \end{array}$
6. Double 19. ____
7. Halve 56. ____
8. 8 × 2 ____
9. 8 × 5 ____
10. $\begin{array}{r} 51 \\ -\ 25 \\ \hline \end{array}$
11.

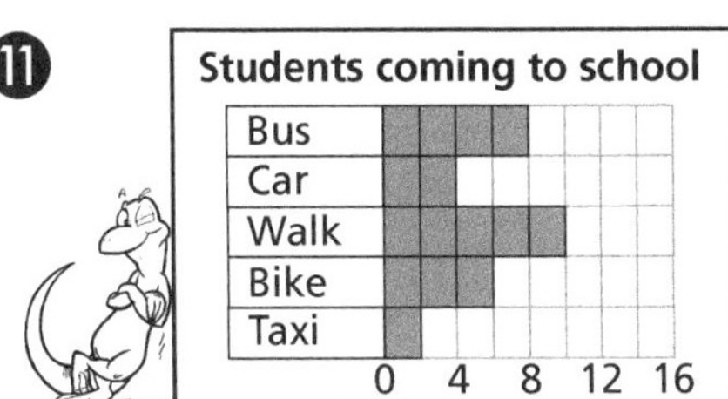

a How many students came to school by bus or bike? ____

b How many more students walked to school than came to school by taxi? ____

12. My handspan is 15 cm. I measured my table and it was 4 handspans wide.

How wide is my table? ____

13. Surveys are used to collect ____________.
14. The volume of this model

= ____ layers of ____

= ____ cubic centimetres

15. 54 − 39 = ____ so 15 + 39 = ____
16. What is the time 30 minutes after 3 fifty-two?

____

17. 1000 – 399 ____________

Turn to ID card A on page 6.

Give the answers for these numbers.

(1) ____________ (2) ____________

(3) ____________ (4) ____________

(5) ____________ (6) ____________

(7) ____________ (8) ____________

 • *AUSTRALIAN SIGNPOST MATHS NSW 3 MENTALS* • ISBN 978 0 6557 0910 7

34:3

out of 6

1.

tens	ones
4	6
− 2	8

2.

tens	ones
$7	5
−$4	9

3. The volume of this model

= ______ layers of ______

= ______ cubic centimetres

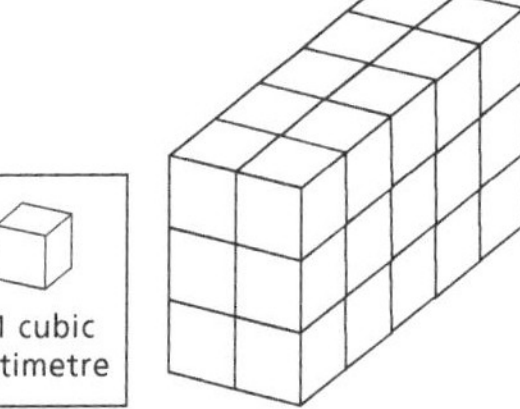

4. **Animals seen**

Name	Tally	Total
Koala	𝍸 𝍸 𝍸 𝍸 II	
Bilby	𝍸 III	
Emu	𝍸 𝍸 𝍸 IIII	
Possum	𝍸 𝍸 𝍸 𝍸 𝍸 III	

a Fill in the last column of the tally above.

b How many more possums than bilbies were seen? ______

5.    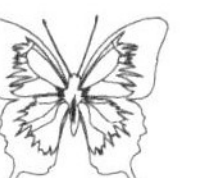 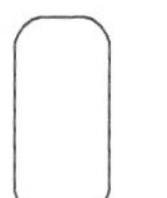

What part is shaded? ______ out of ______

6. a Colour $\frac{7}{8}$.

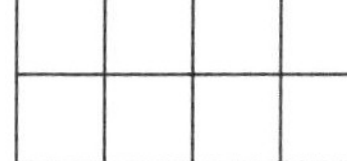

b Colour $\frac{5}{8}$.

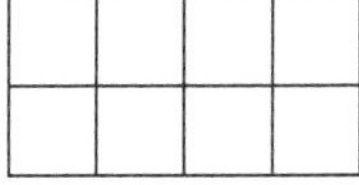

34:4

out of 4

1. 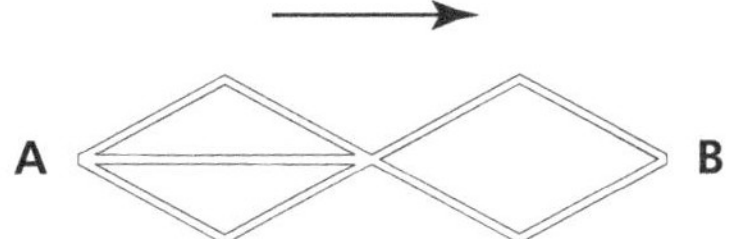

How many different ways are there of going from A to B? ______

2. a Find the total area of the faces. ______

b Find the total length of the edges. ______

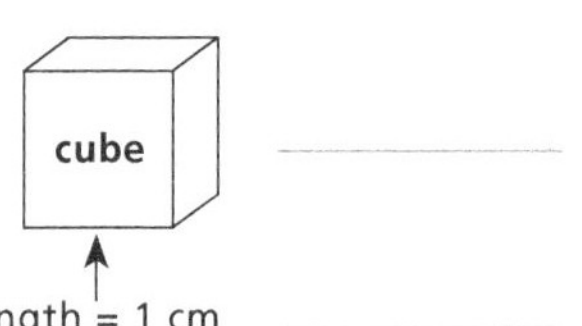

3. In how many different orders can you write the letters A, B and C? (You could make a list.) ______

4. How many place-value ones blocks do you need to cover this area?

Area = ______ blocks

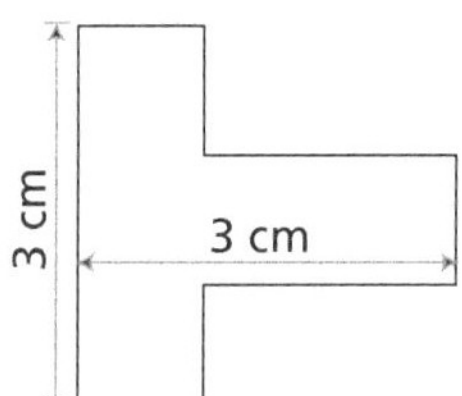

Challenge

- Colour:

one third one sixth

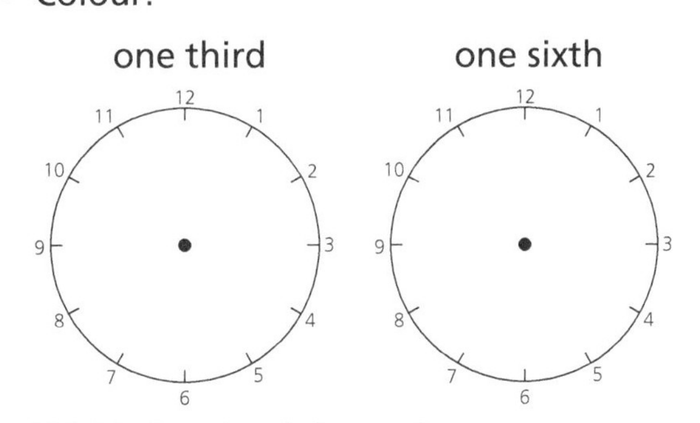

- Which fraction is larger? ______________

a 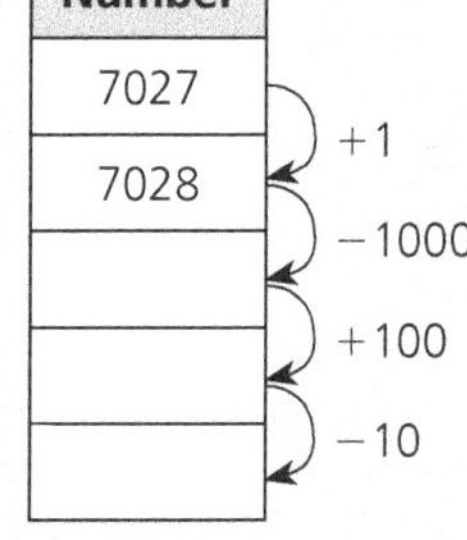

Number	
7027	+1
7028	−1000
	+100
	−10

b 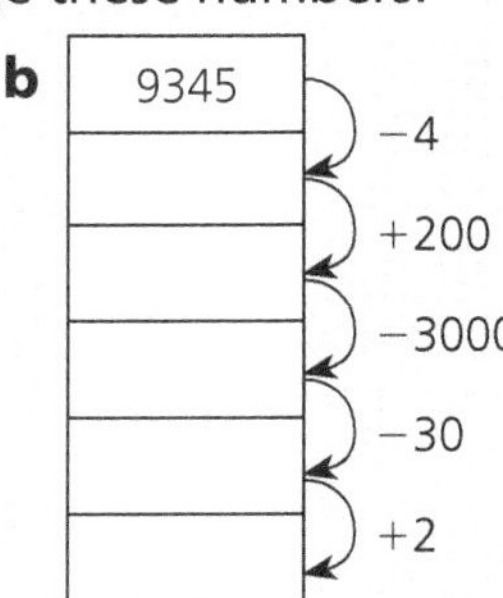

9345	−4
	+200
	−3000
	−30
	+2

c 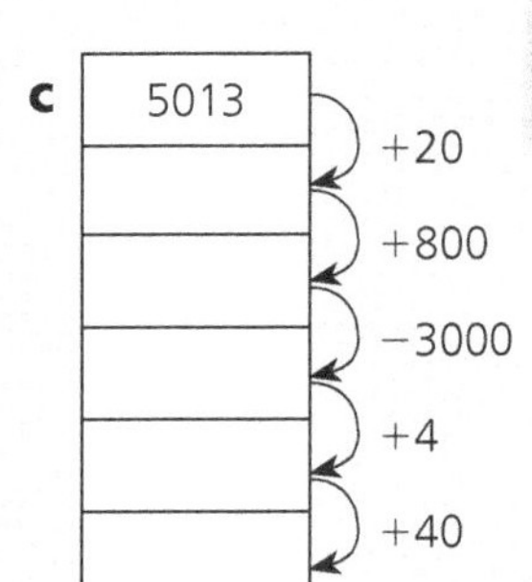

5013	+20
	+800
	−3000
	+4
	+40

35:1 [ ] out of 16

1. 8 × 2 ____
2. 4 × 5 ____
3. 3 × 10 ____
4. 6 ÷ 2 ____
5. $\begin{array}{r} 62 \\ -\ 13 \\ \hline \end{array}$
6. Half of 16. ____
7. 4 less than 23. ____
8. 10 shared by 2. ____
9. 14 shared by 2. ____
10. $\begin{array}{r} 48 \\ -\ 29 \\ \hline \end{array}$
11. Which of these objects have only flat surfaces? ____

A  B 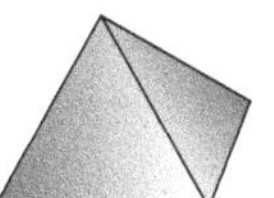 C  D 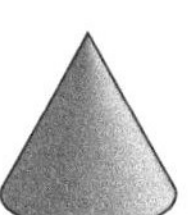

12. a What fraction has been coloured?

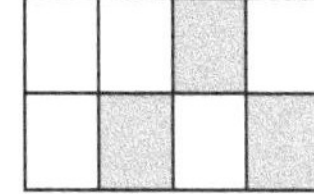 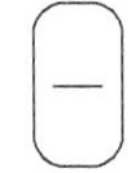

b Colour 4 eighths. Write the fraction.

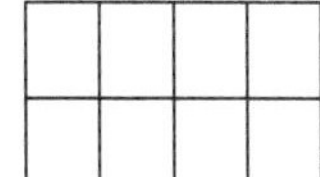 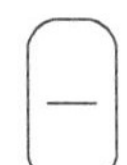

13. Circle the largest number.

456 701 465 780 456 710

14. Describe this 3D object.

____

____

15. A pentagon has ____ sides.
16. a 19 + 8 = 20 + ____

b 28 + 4 = 30 + ____

35:2 [ ] out of 18

1. 7 × 2 ____
2. 8 × 5 ____
3. 35 ÷ 5 ____
4. 25 ÷ 5 ____
5. $\begin{array}{r} 51 \\ -\ 28 \\ \hline \end{array}$
6. Half of 62. ____
7. 9 less than 92. ____
8. 35 + 37 ____
9. 42 − 35 ____
10. $\begin{array}{r} 65 \\ -\ 47 \\ \hline \end{array}$
11. Tick the sphere. Cross the cube. Circle the pyramid.

A 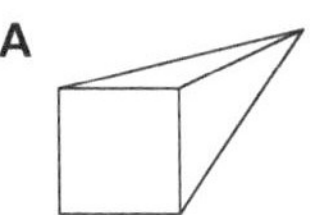 B C 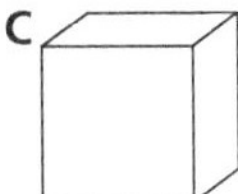 

12. How many days in March? ____
13. Circle the largest number.

830 871, 830 781, 830 187

14. How many digits in 756 430? ____
15. 30 000 + 4000 + 300 + 20 + 1 = ____
16. a Colour and label 2 quarters of this shape.

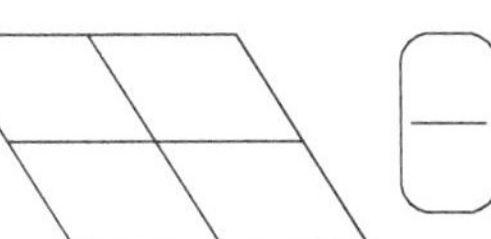

b This shape is a ____.

17. The volume of this model

= ____ layers of ____

= ____ cubic centimetres

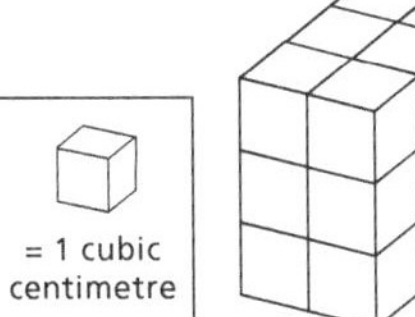

18. 3, 6, 9, ____, ____, ____, ____, ____

Turn to ID card A on page 6.
Give the answers for these numbers.

(21) ____		(22) ____	
(23) ____	graph	(24) ____	
(25) ____	graph	(26) ____	graph
(27) ____	watch	(28) ____	clock
(29) ____		(30) ____	scales

35:3 out of 7

1. a 70 000 + 3000 + 700 + 40 + 1 = ______
   b 90 000 + 600 + 30 + 9 = ______

2. Write these numbers on the place-value chart.
   a 567 603   b 380 689   c 293 004

	Thousands	Hundreds	Tens	Units
a	567	6	0	3
b				
c				

3. Is 678 342 larger than 678 451? ______

4. The volume of this model
   = ______ layers of ______
   = ______ cubic centimetres

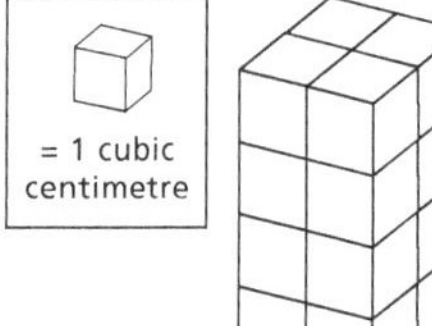

5. List objects that look like a sphere.
   ______

6. Goals kicked this year

Kym	𝍸 𝍸 𝍸 𝍸
Lisa	𝍸 ||||
Diane	𝍸 𝍸 |||
Marta	𝍸 𝍸 ||

   a Who kicked 13 goals? ______
   b How many did Marta kick? ______
   c How many more goals did Kym kick than Lisa? ______

7. How many days in May? ______

35:4 out of 6

Extension

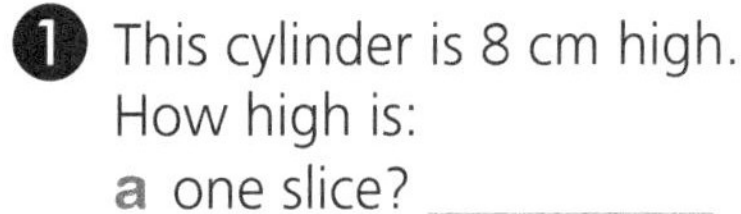

1. This cylinder is 8 cm high. How high is:
   a one slice? ______
   b three slices? ______

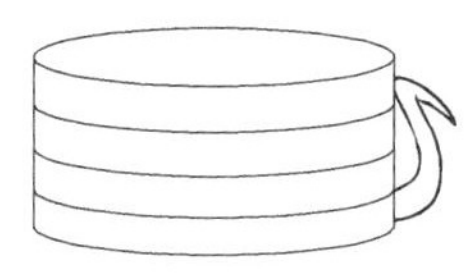

2. Number of faces plus the number of corners minus the number of edges.
   ______

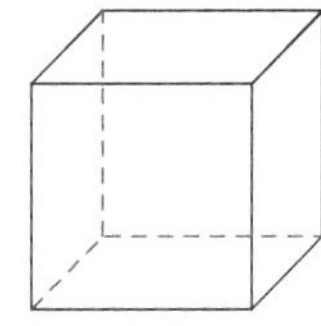

3. Circle the largest number.
   560 936,   560 963,   506 937

4. 30 + 600 + 900 000 + 70 000 = ______

5. I am making cubes with toothpicks and Blu tack. How many cubes could I make with 38 toothpicks if I don't break any? ______

6. a 85 − 25 − 25 − 27 ______
   b 125 − 15 − 15 − 28 ______

Challenge

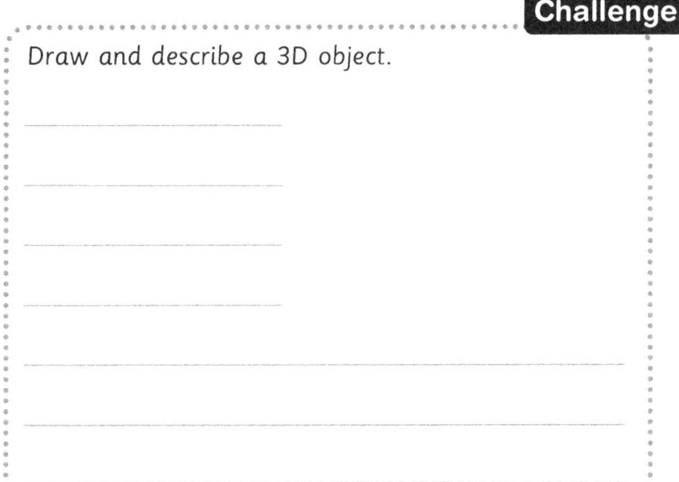

Draw and describe a 3D object.

Turn to ID card B on page 7.
Give the answers for these numbers.

(20) net of a ______   (24) ______
(25) ______   (26) ______
(28) ______   (29) ______
(30) ______

Fill out the table for this cube.

	Faces	Edges	Corners
Number			

36:1

out of 15

1. 13 + 7 ______
2. 23 + 7 ______
3. 33 + 7 ______
4. 43 + 7 ______
5. 91 − 24
6. 18 + ______ = 20
7. 17 + ______ = 20
8. 8 + ______ = 20
9. 7 + ______ = 20
10. 55 − 16
11. What two shapes are used to make this model?

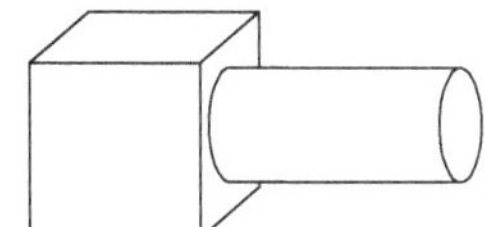

12. Favourite shape

Pentagon	⬠⬠⬠⬠
Hexagon	⬡⬡⬡
Rhombus	◊ ◊ ◊ ◊ ◊ ◊

a What was the most popular shape? ______

b What was the least popular shape? ______

c How many more rhombuses than hexagons? ______

d How many hexagons and pentagons altogether? ______

13. Circle the largest number.

991 399   901 657   991 567

14. How many digits in 546 790? ______
15. I had 46 buttons and used 24. How many do I have left? ______

36:2

out of 16

1. 36 + 9 ______
2. 136 + 9 ______
3. 43 − 19 ______
4. 57 − 19 ______
5. 755 − 7 ______
6. 462 − 4 ______
7. 65 + 19 ______
8. 45 + 19 ______

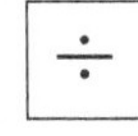

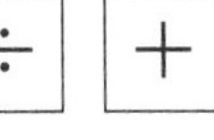

9. 4 × 5 = ______ so 20 ÷ 5 = ______
10. What is in position:

a 2C? ______

b 3B? ______

C	×	÷	+
B	wavy line	triangle	corner
A	circle	zigzag	square
	1	2	3

From the grid above, give the position of the:

c triangle. ______

d wavy line. ______

11. Do we measure length using litres, square centimetres or metres? ______
12. Use the jump strategy to find:

67 + 28 = ______

13. If 45 + 8 = 53 then 145 + 8 = ______
14. Is this a pyramid, a prism or neither? ______

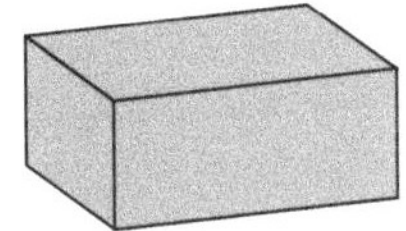

15. 1000 − 401 = ______
16. a 67 + 9 = 70 + ______

b 45 + 8 = 50 + ______

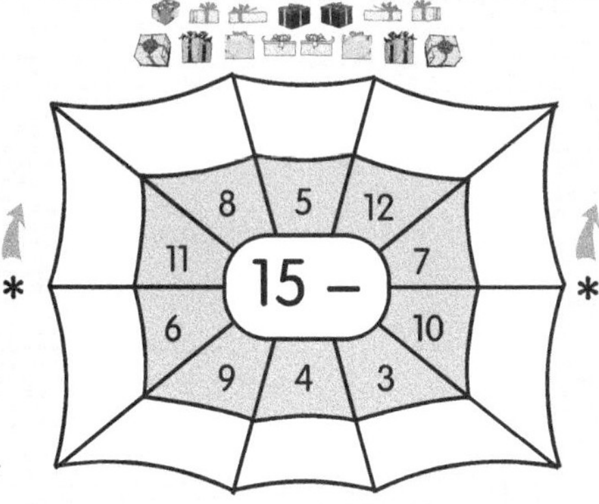

 • *AUSTRALIAN SIGNPOST MATHS NSW 3 MENTALS* • ISBN 978 0 6557 0910 7

36:3 ☐ out of 6

1. 700 000 + 50 000 + 3000 + 200 = ______

2. Bridge to the next ten to find:

   a 36 + 5 ____ b 28 + 5 ____

   c 57 + 6 ____ d 69 + 3 ____

3. 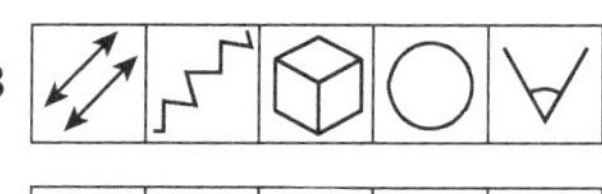

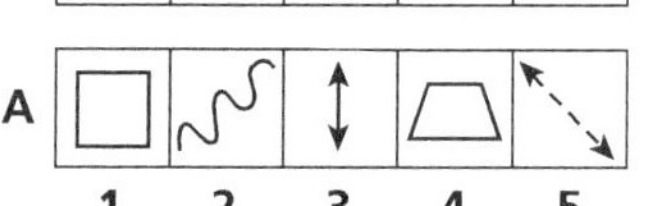

What shape has coordinates:

a 3B? ____ b 1A? ____

Write the coordinates for the:

c trapezium ______

d parallel lines ______

4. Do we measure capacity using centimetres, litres or square metres? ______

5. Use the jump strategy to find:

   a 49 + 36 = ____

   b 72 − 34 = ____

6. What is the cross-section of a:

   a cylinder? ______

   b cube? ______

   c sphere? ______

36:4 ☐ out of 4

Extension

1. 6 + 500 000 + 8 000 + 70 = ______

2. How many faces could be seen if I walk around this 3D object when it is placed on a table? ______

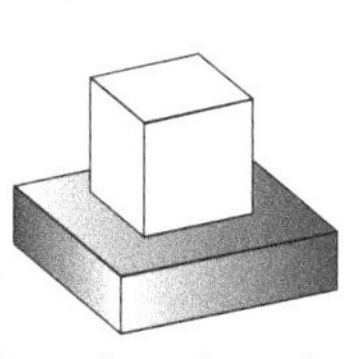

3. Three bricks were placed between each pair of poles.

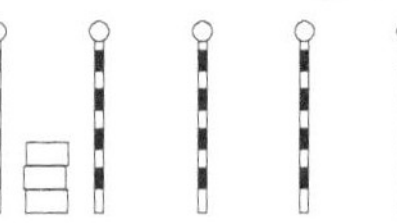

   a How many bricks were used? ______

   b How many would be used if there were 10 poles? ______

4. The bottom part is cut off.

   The part left would be:

   A half of the volume

   B more than half

   C less than half ______

Challenge

Draw a map of a room in your home.
Draw a key to show things in the room.

Complete each multiplication fact family.

a

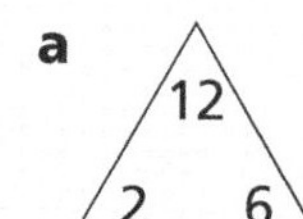

2 × 6 = ____
6 × 2 = ____
12 ÷ 2 = ____
12 ÷ 6 = ____

b

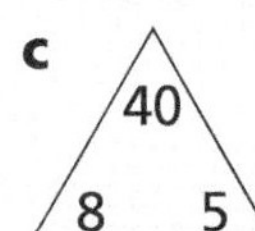

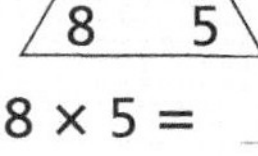

9 × 4 = ____
4 × 9 = ____
36 ÷ 9 = ____
36 ÷ 4 = ____

c

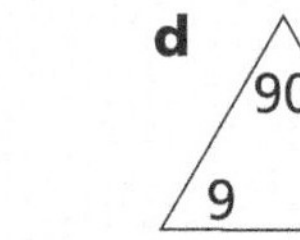

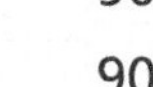

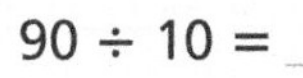

8 × 5 = ____
5 × 8 = ____
40 ÷ 8 = ____
40 ÷ 5 = ____

d

90
9 10

9 × 10 = ____
10 × 9 = ____
90 ÷ 9 = ____
90 ÷ 10 = ____

Multiplication and division are opposites.

37:1 — out of 17

1. 18 + 5 ______
2. 28 + 5 ______
3. 38 + 5 ______
4. 48 + 5 ______
5. 53 − 15 ______
6. 16 + ______ = 20
7. 6 + ______ = 20
8. 4 + ______ = 20
9. 14 + ______ = 20
10. 72 − 24 ______

11.

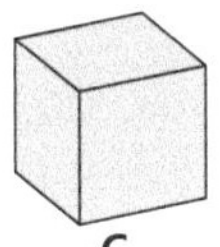
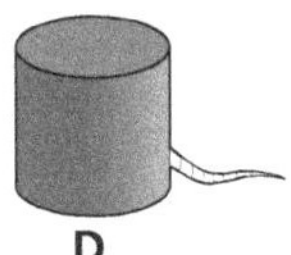

A B C D

a Which is a cylinder? ______

b Which is a cone? ______

12. Is this the net of a cube? ______

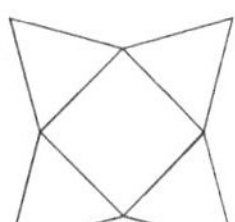

13. How many days in April? ______
14. 400 000 + 30 000 + 9000 + 10 + 7 ______
15. Order from smallest to largest:

    65 195   71 920   4320

    ______
16. How many digits in 920 817? ______
17. What date is the:

    a third Friday? ______

    b second Sunday? ______

DECEMBER						
Sun	Mon	Tue	Wed	Thu	Fri	Sat
		1	2	3	4	5
6	7	8	9	10	11	12
13	14	15	16	17	18	19
20	21	22	23	24	25	26
27	28	29	30	31		

37:2 — out of 16

1. 16 + 9 ______
2. 26 + 9 ______
3. 36 + 9 ______
4. 46 + 9 ______
5. 72 − 39 ______
6. 44 + ______ = 60
7. 47 + ______ = 60
8. 64 + ______ = 80
9. 35 + ______ = 70
10. 54 − 18 ______

11. How many days in:

    a one week? ______ b one fortnight? ______

    c January? ______ d November? ______
12. Is this the net of a cube? ______

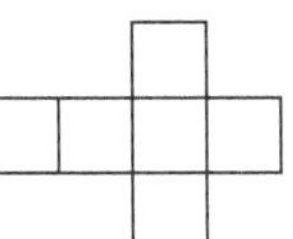

13. 560 000 + 2000 + 90 + 2 ______
14. **Number of flowers**

    Pansies

    Tulips

    Irises

    0 1 2 3 4 5 6 7 8 9

   a Which was the smallest group? ______

   b How many irises and tulips? ______

   c How many more tulips than pansies? ______

15. a 600 000 + 3000 + 70 + 9 = ______

    b 900 000 + 50 + 6000 + 1 = ______
16. a 67 − 38 = ______ − ______ = ______

    b 85 − 37 = ______ − ______ = ______

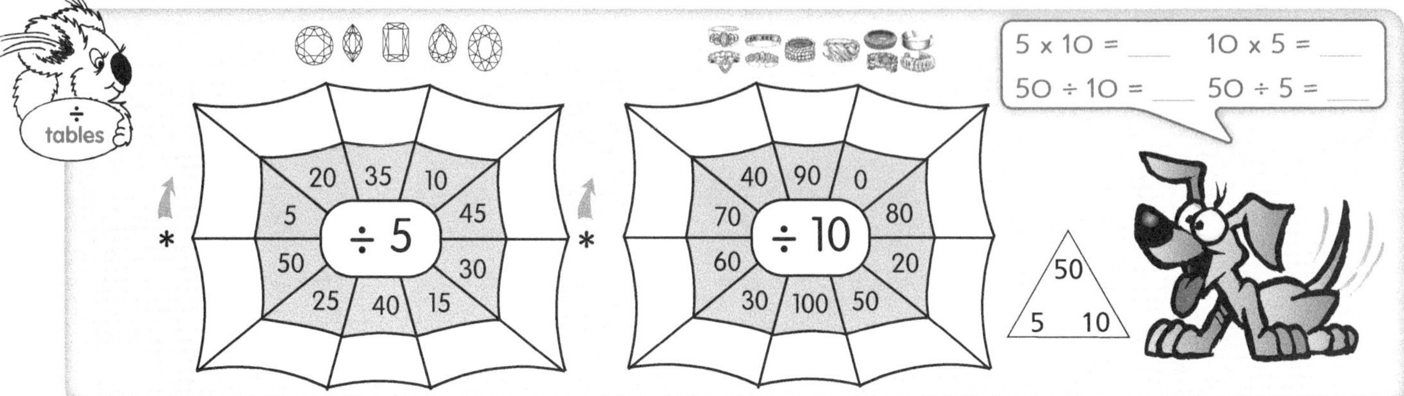

 • *AUSTRALIAN SIGNPOST MATHS NSW 3 MENTALS* • ISBN 978 0 6557 0910 7

37:3

out of 8

1.

tens	ones
4	5
+3	2

2.

tens	ones
6	2
−3	1

3. Write the short date for the 18th of February, 2026. ______

4. How many days in 2 fortnights? ______

5. What unit would you use to measure the:
   a length of your book? ______
   b capacity of a bin? ______

6. Circle the change I would get from $2 when I spend 65 cents.

7.

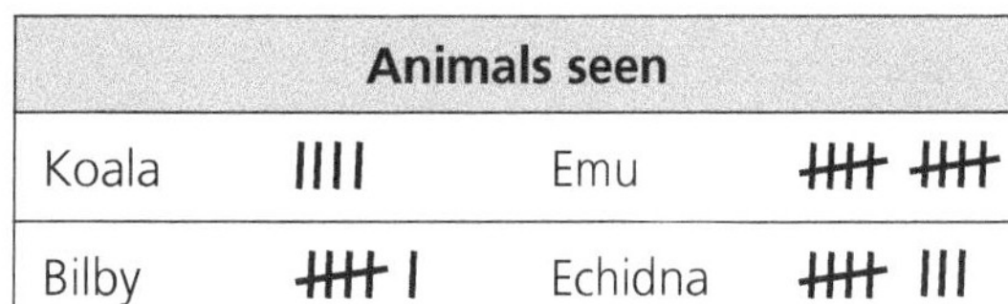

Animals seen			
Koala	IIII	Emu	~~IIII~~ ~~IIII~~
Bilby	~~IIII~~ I	Echidna	~~IIII~~ III

   a How many bilbies were seen? ______
   b Which animal was seen most often? ______
   c How many more echidnas than koalas were seen? ______

8. Jack caught 17 fish and Scott caught 6 more than Jack. How many did they catch altogether? ______

37:4

Extension

out of 9

1. How many 50c coins make $5? ______
2. How many 20c coins make $5? ______
3. How many 10c coins make $5? ______
4. How many 5c coins make $5? ______
5. We bought 67 apples and ate 34. We were then given 12 more. How many do we have now? ______
6. Circle three quarters of the boats.

7. Add 15 each time.

   30, ____, ____, ____, ____, ____

8. Ten toy soldiers were standing in a row. Between each pair there are two toy cars. How many toys are there altogether? ______

9. What is my change from $14 if I spend $5.60? ______

Challenge

Write down each set of 3 counting numbers that have a total of 7.
(Numbers can be used more than once.)

Fill out this table for the person measured in unit 1.

Name: ______ **Date:** ______

Age: ______	Mass: ______ kg	Shoe size: ______
Height: ______ cm	Waist: ______ cm	Neck size: ______ cm

How have these measurements changed since unit 1 was done?

How would you name the lizards?

Find two lizards hidden on each page of this book.

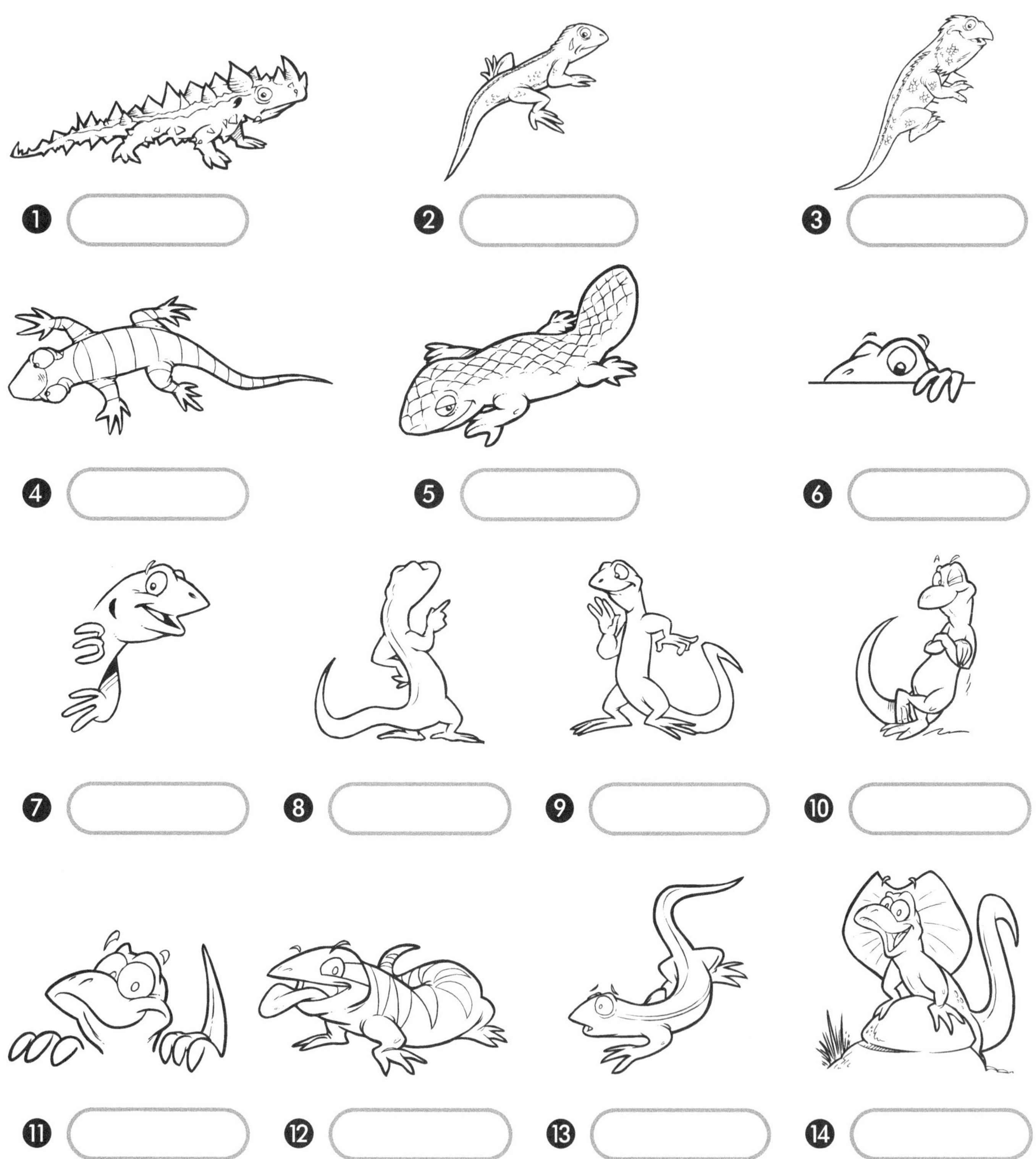

Real names:

1 Horned lizard **2–3** Bearded dragon **4** Gecko **5** Shingle-back lizard
6–11 Common garden lizard **12** Blue-tongue lizard **13** Skink **14** Frilled-neck lizard